# Improving Services for Transgender and Gender Variant Youth

*of related interest*

**Transgender Health**
A Practitioner's Guide to Binary and Non-Binary Trans Patient Care
*Ben Vincent, PhD*
ISBN 978 1 78592 201 5
eISBN 978 1 78450 475 5

**Transition Denied**
Confronting the Crisis in Trans Healthcare
*Jane Fae*
*Foreword by Amanda De Courcy*
ISBN 978 1 78592 415 6
eISBN 978 1 78450 778 7

**Counselling Skills for Working with Gender Diversity and Identity**
*Michael Beattie and Penny Lenihan with Robin Dundas*
ISBN 978 1 78592 741 6
eISBN 978 1 78450 481 6
*Part of the* Essential Skills for Counselling *series*

**Supporting Young Transgender Men**
A Guide for Professionals
*Matthew Waites*
ISBN 978 1 78592 294 7
eISBN 978 1 78450 601 8

**Counseling Transgender and Non-Binary Youth**
The Essential Guide
*Irwin Krieger*
ISBN 978 1 78592 743 0
eISBN 978 1 78450 482 3

# IMPROVING SERVICES FOR TRANSGENDER AND GENDER VARIANT YOUTH

Research, Policy and Practice for Health and Social Care Professionals

TIFFANY JONES

Jessica Kingsley *Publishers*
London and Philadelphia

First published in 2019
by Jessica Kingsley Publishers
73 Collier Street
London N1 9BE, UK
and
400 Market Street, Suite 400
Philadelphia, PA 19106, USA

*www.jkp.com*

Copyright © Tiffany Jones 2019

All rights reserved. No part of this publication may be reproduced in any material form (including photocopying, storing in any medium by electronic means or transmitting) without the written permission of the copyright owner except in accordance with the provisions of the law or under terms of a licence issued in the UK by the Copyright Licensing Agency Ltd. www.cla.co.uk or in overseas territories by the relevant reproduction rights organisation, for details see www.ifrro.org. Applications for the copyright owner's written permission to reproduce any part of this publication should be addressed to the publisher.

Warning: The doing of an unauthorised act in relation to a copyright work may result in both a civil claim for damages and criminal prosecution.

**Library of Congress Cataloging in Publication Data**
A CIP catalog record for this book is available from the Library of Congress

**British Library Cataloguing in Publication Data**
A CIP catalogue record for this book is available from the British Library

ISBN 9781785924255
eISBN 9781784507893

Printed and bound in the United States

# Contents

*Glossary* . . . . . . . . . . . . . . . . . . . . . . . . . . . . 7

*Disclaimer* . . . . . . . . . . . . . . . . . . . . . . . . . . . 11

Introduction . . . . . . . . . . . . . . . . . . . . . . . . . 13

1. Who Are Transgender Youth? . . . . . . . . . . . . . . . 21

2. Transgender Youth, Mental Health and Mental Health Services . . . . . . . . . . . . . . . . . . . . . . . 37

3. Transgender Youth, Physical Health and Physical Health Services . . . . . . . . . . . . . . . . . . . . . . . 75

4. Transgender Youth, Sexual Health and Sexual Health Services . . . . . . . . . . . . . . . . . . . . . . . 103

5. Transgender Youth and Education . . . . . . . . . . . . 135

6. Transgender Youth, Social Supports and Social Services . . 160

Conclusion . . . . . . . . . . . . . . . . . . . . . . . . . . 187

*References* . . . . . . . . . . . . . . . . . . . . . . . . . . . 193

*Subject Index* . . . . . . . . . . . . . . . . . . . . . . . . . 205

*Author Index* . . . . . . . . . . . . . . . . . . . . . . . . . 211

# Glossary

*Note:* This glossary was compiled to offer a starting point for discussing words with the transgender youth readers serve. Some definitions first featured in previous publications (Jones *et al.*, 2015).

**Androgynous:** Can mean having both masculine and feminine characteristics, or having neither specifically masculine nor feminine characteristics.

**Binder/Binding:** Binding involves flattening/de-emphasising one's chest tissues using a binder. Binders can range from a generic piece of loose cloth/rag, which is tied or wrapped around the chest and held in place with a clip or fastening, through to specially designed and commercially available materials, vests, compression tops or singlets. Binding should not involve Ace bandages or duct tape, and should not be engaged in for more than 8–12 hours at a time.

**Bisexual or Bi:** Refers to people whose sexual and romantic feelings are for both men and women, and who identify with these feelings.

**Blockers:** See Puberty blockers.

**Bottom surgery:** Can involve, for example, sterilisation, hysterectomy, bilateral salpingo-oophorectomy (BSO) and/or genital reconstructive procedures (GRP).

**Chest surgery:** Can involve reduction (the surgical reduction in size/amount of the chest tissue), mastectomy (surgical removal of one or both breasts/chest tissue, partially or completely), chest contouring/reconstruction (giving the chest a male aesthetic through implants, sculpturing of tissue, tattooing, etc.), breast implants or related surgeries.

**Chests:** Male, female and other people's chest areas or breasts. An inclusive term.

**Cisgender:** Describes gender identity where an individual's self-perception of their gender matches the sex they were assigned at birth. For example, a cisgender male was assigned male at birth, and this label fits his gender identity.

**Cisnormativity:** The expectation and assumption that people only have gender identities which align with their sex as allocated at birth, or that only these people are normal or worthy to be catered for in service provision.

**Cissexism:** Discrimination based on the assumption that transgender people are inferior to, or less authentic than, cisgender people.

**Depo-Provera/depot medroxyprogesterone acetate/DMPA:** Can be used to reduce or eliminate menses/menstruation, generally injected every three months.

**FtM/F-M/F2M:** See Transgender FtM.

**Gametes:** Reproductive cell material, e.g. ova and spermatoza. An inclusive term.

**Gay:** People whose sexual and romantic feelings are primarily for the same sex and who identify primarily with those feelings.

**Gender dysphoria:** A medical diagnosis related to transgender people in the DSM-V, which refers to extreme discontent with the assigned sex allocated to an individual at birth.

**Gender identity:** The gender-related identity, appearance or mannerisms or other gender-related characteristics of an individual (whether by way of medical intervention or not, socialisation or alternative expression), with or without regard to the individual's designated sex at birth, and includes transsexualism and transgenderism.

**Gender Identity Disorder/GID:** An old medical diagnosis for transgender people used in the DSM-IV and since replaced with gender dysphoria (which is seen as less stigmatising).

**Genderqueer:** People who do not comply with their traditional gender expectations through their dress, hair, mannerisms, appearance and values.

**Genital reconstructive procedures (GRP):** Various procedures which construct a vagina or a phallus (e.g. metoidioplasty, phalloplasty, vaginoplasty and other options).

**Genitals/genitalia:** Can include penises, vaginas, and other variations. An inclusive term.

**Gonads:** Can include ovaries, testes, ovo-testes and other variations. An inclusive term.

**Homophobia:** An individual's or society's misunderstanding, fear, ignorance of, or prejudice against gay, lesbian and/or bisexual people.

**Homosexual:** People whose sexual and romantic feelings are primarily for the same sex and who identify primarily with those feelings. People who feel this way often identify as gay or lesbian.

**Hysterectomy:** Surgical removal of the uterus.

**Intersex status:** The status of having physical, hormonal or genetic features that are:
- neither wholly female nor wholly male; or
- a combination of female and male; or
- neither female nor male.

**Lesbian:** Women whose sexual and romantic feelings are primarily for other women and who identify with those feelings.

**LGBTIQ:** Lesbian, gay, bisexual, transgender, intersex and otherwise questioning (people).

**Hormone Therapy/Hormone Replacement Therapy/HRT:** For transgender and transsexual people this form of treatment introduces hormones associated with the gender that the patient identifies with (e.g. testosterone for FtM transgender individuals). The treatment causes the development of secondary sex characteristics, although impacts vary. Hormones may be delivered via injections, transdermal applications (patches, creams, gels), subcutaneous pellets (inserted under the skin every few months), orally (as tablets), or sublingual/buccal form (absorbed through the mouth mucus rather than 'eaten' as such). Androgens, pro-hormones or supplements also might or might not be part of a treatment plan.

**Mastectomy:** The medical term for the surgical removal of one or both breasts, partially or completely.

**MtF/M-F/M2F:** See Transgender MtF.

**Packing/padding:** Wearing padding in a bra or pants, or a phallic object (can be a specially designed 'packer'/phallus), to create the desired body contour effect.

**Pansexual or Omnisexual:** Refers to people whose sexual and romantic feelings are for all genders; this rejects the gender binary of male/female and asserts that there are more than two genders or gender identities. These are terms that consider the gender diverse community.

**Prosthetic:** A medical term for an artificial device that replaces a body part that is missing.

**Puberty blockers:** Non-testosterone-based hormone treatment (GnRH agonists) used to suspend the advance of sex steroid induced and thus block pubertal changes (and secondary sex characteristics) from occurring/developing further for a period of time. No changes in terms of transition to the desired sex/gender identity occur; this measure is generally understood to be preparation for transitions/decisions around transitions, rather than a transition process itself.

**Queer:** Queer is an umbrella term used to refer to the LGBT community in pride, inclusivity and sometimes even a kind of political subversiveness (a resistance to 'normative' identity).

**Sex:** The physiological make-up of a person. It is commonly expressed as a binary and used to divide people into males and females. However, in reality, sex is a complex relationship of genetic, hormonal, morphological, biochemical and anatomical differences. These various differences impact both the physiology of the body and the sexual differentiation of the brain.

**Sexual orientation:** The direction of one's sexual and romantic attractions and interests towards members of the same, opposite or both sexes, or all genders.

**Strap on:** A dildo/external prosthesis strapped on to the outside of the body/worn with a harness, which may be used in sex, but is sometimes used for packing (to fill out clothing).

**Trans/Transgender:** A broad umbrella term, including people who identify as a gender different to the one assigned at birth and who may choose to undergo affirmation/surgery(ies). Describes a broad range of non-conforming gender identities and/or behaviours.

**Transgender FtM:** A person who was born as female or intersex (or otherwise not strictly male) who identifies as a sex different to the one assigned at birth (as male, a trans man or genderqueer, for example) and who may choose to undergo sex affirmation/reassignment surgery(ies). Describes a broad range of non-conforming gender identities and/or behaviours.

**Transgender MtF:** A person who was born as male or intersex (or otherwise not strictly female) who identifies as a sex different to the one assigned at birth (as female, a trans woman or genderqueer) and who may choose to undergo sex affirmation/reassignment surgery(ies). Describes a broad range of non-conforming gender identities and/or behaviours.

**Transition/Gender affirmation**: Refers to the process (either past, current or future) of personally, socially, physically and/or legally changing one's gender presentation/sex to some extent (whether slightly through to wholly). This process can involve changing how one refers to/sees themselves, changing the way one dresses or presents themselves (hairstyle and so forth), changing how one is referred to/seen by others (pronouns like his/her, he/she/they/ze), and/or changing one's social role or role in relationships if relevant. It might also involve changing one's body through hormonal therapies/cosmetic procedures/a range of surgeries, and/or changing the way one is identified by sex on legal or reporting documents (birth certificate, passport, license, and/or other records like academic records).

**Transphobia:** An individual's or society's misunderstanding, fear, ignorance of, or prejudice against transgender people.

# Disclaimer

Every effort has been made to ensure that the information contained in this book is correct, but it should not in any way be substituted for medical advice. Readers should always consult a qualified medical practitioner before adopting any complementary or alternative therapies. Neither the author nor the publisher takes responsibility for any consequences of any decision made as a result of the information contained in this book.

# Introduction

I'm very open about it. I feel if people are willing to learn about gender identity, I'm willing to share what I know. (Draconem, FtM transgender, 24 years)[1]

It just came to me as I went through puberty that I wasn't the same as other people. I had some hard times struggling but I eventually came to terms due to certain websites about people like me. (Nina, MtF transgender, 17 years)

My life right now is kinda rocky. I've just recently found out I'm transgender. I have found people like me through various websites. After outing myself to my mother, I started to notice that a lot of other people were like me too. I feel more comfortable in boy clothes and I mostly get along with boys. Though I still like cute things XD! My girlfriend lives three hours away from me, so I can't see her very often. She also won't let me be her first kiss. Then what's the point of going out with me if we barely see each other and not kiss when we do? I've told my mother and my grandmother about me. They accepted me straight away (my grandmother's brother is gay), I'm too afraid to tell my dad. I left school when I was in year 10, before I could do my school certificate, so I haven't really got much to hope for in the future. But at the moment, I want to do photography. (Ed, FtM transgender, 16 years)

---

1. The quotes used at the start of each chapter featured in survey, interview and discussion board data collected by the author's teams over the past decade from transgender youth or adults retrospectively discussing their youth (Hillier *et al.*, 2010; Jones & Hillier, 2013; Jones, Smith *et al.*, 2016; Smith *et al.*, 2014; UNESCO, 2016d). Pseudonyms were selected by participants, or else assigned by the author.

## Why does this book exist?

Years ago one of my favourite researchers was speaking at a cross-sector conference for professionals. This scholar was known for investigating transphobia and homophobia – let's call them DrvSuperstar. Dr Superstar delivered arguments using a voice with depth and gravitas I especially admired (I myself sound like Mickey Mouse: when I answer my own phone strangers say, 'Put Mummy on, dear'). Dr Superstar was telling the service professionals what was wrong with their industries. That their industries were transphobic, cisnormative, cissexist and other words we calmly pretended to understand (see the Glossary in this book).

Seated in the audience and listening with bated breath were social workers, nurses, politicians, sexual health clinicians, policy makers, medical doctors, teachers, psychologists…more professionals and practitioners of other kinds than I could count. Dr Superstar had them leaning forward, nodding their heads, exclaiming 'yes!' in agreement. The air was thick with a magical potential for widespread industry changes; we could all taste it. Dr Superstar reached the end of a thorough analysis of the problems of different industries (education, health, mental health and so on). Then, with hands wide spread, Dr Superstar asked, 'Any questions?' A sea of raised arms answered. Dr Superstar pointed at an education practitioner in the audience. The practitioner stood up and said, 'Thank you for telling us about the problems with these industries in such detail. We all feel awful. What is your solution?'

With a dismissive wave of the hand, my idol unfortunately responded with, 'As an academic it is not my responsibility to provide solutions! I'm just here to point out the problems.' You could hear the 'click' of an off-switch in the brain of every person in that room, as Dr Superstar's non-answer trailed on. The practitioner shook their head and sat back down. People leaned backwards into their chairs, crossed their arms and looked out of the windows. Some took books out of their bags and blatantly began to read. A few people simply walked right out of the lecture hall.

The very first professional issue I want to raise and try to address in this book is a problem for my own (academic) industry. We scholars of transgender issues can be too focused on pointing out problems, and not focused enough on providing solutions. My research work considers the negative experiences for transgender youth in areas like mental health, health, education and so forth – however, it is not enough for me to simply state that problems exist. So when my commissioning editor at Jessica Kingsley Publishers contacted me to create a book on practical solutions for professionals working with transgender youth, I gratefully accepted the challenge. I don't have all the answers, however, where research offers something useful to or about service provision, I have collated the key points together. I aim to outline vital information, problems and solution ideas for a range of professionals serving transgender youth. Research-based and literature-supported recommendations are made where possible, and some ideas come from transgender youth, scholars, provider leadership, practitioners and professionals around the world whom I have been honoured to survey or interview over the years. I call on my fellow researchers to join me in seeking to answer the difficult questions posed to us by and for professionals. Solutions must be co-constructed by all stakeholders including scholars, professionals and practitioners. Our work should show due respect for the ideas offered to us by transgender youth themselves, whose voices are foregrounded in this book.

## Who is this book for?

This book is specifically intended for service providers, professionals and practitioners working with transgender youth. It may also be of use to transgender youth, their families and guardians, academics and general readers who are stakeholders in transgender youth issues. The advice in this book is based on the author's many years of research into transgender youth themes across a range of fields, as well as studies and evaluative work in literature and reports from around the world. However, this book uses the research in a pragmatic manner to particularly focus on providing problem-solving strategies for those working with transgender youth – including, for example:

- educators in primary, high school and higher education contexts
- school administrators
- school counselling and nursing staff

- parents and family/guardians
- psychologists and general counsellors
- health service workers
- transgender youth advocates
- government organisations, international civil society bodies and other policy makers
- non-government organisations (in gender, bullying, social work or other areas).

It provides an in-depth, research-based and pragmatic exploration of the key issues in a variety of service provision fields.

## How is this book structured?

The book is divided into some logical service provision areas; however, due to the need to keep it a manageable size, it could not possibly cover all service provision areas or all topics. The chapters cover transgender youth demographics, mental health, physical health, sexual health and sex education, general education and social and religious services engagement. In addition, some decisions had to be made about where information went in the book; it is mostly placed under the professional field (e.g. education, social services, mental health) most relevant to that information. For example, gender dysphoria is described in the chapter for mental health professionals (who are most likely to make the diagnosis). However, sometimes this decision is subjective and material relevant to all service providers is sometimes contained within a particular chapter only. For example, legal gender affirmation information has been placed in the chapter on physical health, because it is part of a larger discussion of gender affirmation processes, but it could rightly sit in the social service chapter, as social workers may help youth seek out correct documentation. Therefore, whilst service providers, professionals and practitioners are especially directed to read the chapter most relevant to their own service area, all service providers (including those whose service areas may not be directly represented as a chapter heading, such as lawyers) will expand their knowledge of relevant information about transgender youth to their own work by reading all of the different chapters. The book includes a glossary and references.

## How are chapters structured?

Each chapter opens with quotations from transgender youth relevant to the topic theme. Each provides a list of key points. The service-specific chapters (from the third chapter onward) then contain an introduction, historic industry influences and practices, and some contemporary thinking and practices relevant to their work now. Informative subsections then follow in all chapters, which include research data, arguments and advice about different theme-specific matters for transgender youth which are important for service providers, professionals and practitioners in that area to understand. Deficiencies to be overcome, helpful professional characteristics and practices to emulate, and ideas for combatting cisnormativity (the pervasive assumption that clients are not transgender) are then described. Tips on training are supplied, and practical recommendations for services and professionals.

## What does each chapter cover?

There are six chapters in this book, as well as this introduction and a conclusion. Following is a summary of the remaining chapters.

### Chapter 1: Who Are Transgender Youth?

The first chapter describes transgender youth based on actual research data to help service providers, practitioners and professionals of all kinds have a better understanding of the group. It defines key terms common to transgender youth cultures, considers the age of transgender 'youth', and the years most covered in research data. It outlines some basic demographic data and common pathways seen in youth acknowledging their transgender status. It offers useful points for professionals from this demographic information.

### Chapter 2: Transgender Youth, Mental Health and Mental Health Services

The second chapter provides research-based and pragmatic exploration of mental health issues for transgender and gender diverse youth. It considers past historic treatment of mental health issues for transgender youth, and the development of a key contemporary diagnosis: gender dysphoria. It includes statistics on life satisfaction, mental health issues, negative wellbeing and contributing factors, as well as protective factors which reduce wellbeing risks. It details techniques for combatting cisnormativity, ethics and training issues, and key steps for professionals.

### Chapter 3: Transgender Youth, Physical Health and Physical Health Services

The third chapter supplies practically oriented data and consideration of physical health issues for transgender and gender diverse youth. It details historic treatment of physical health issues for transgender youth, and contemporary gender affirmation options. It explores transgender youth satisfaction with gender affirmations, potential to live physically healthy lives, substance use, cancer risk, and black market hormone use. It details negative and positive approaches in health services, and lists positive approaches for professionals.

### Chapter 4: Transgender Youth, Sexual Health and Sexual Health Services

Chapter 4 addresses past treatment of sexual health issues for transgender youth, and contemporary views of these young people as needing inclusion and agency. It includes information on transgender youth consideration of marriage and relationships, romantic and sexual attractions, sexual identity labels, and the impact that gender dysphoria and transitions can have on their sexual lives. It considers sexual protection, STIs and pregnancy, partner violence and sexual abuse. It outlines steps for developing services and professionals.

### Chapter 5: Transgender Youth and Education

This education-focused chapter considers the history of the treatment of gender in schools, and the development of international human rights legislation and policies in educaiton. It includes data on transgender students' education attendance and attainment levels, experience of structural supports, uniforms, bullying and violence. It considers key ideas on bathroom access and education policy protection. This chapter finally describes areas of need, training models and vital steps for improvement for both education services and professionals.

## Chapter 6: Transgender Youth, Social Supports and Social Services

Chapter 6 provides statistics and stories on the social issues and services for transgender youth. It compares the dominance of religious service provision in the past to more contemporary services providing equitable access. It includes information on social attitudes; identity disclosures; social rejection; homelessness, unemployment and poverty; engagement in underground economies and police mistreatment. Religious rejections and activism are explored. Recommendations are listed for social service organisations and professionals.

## Conclusion

The conclusion distinguishes the roles of different service providers, practitioners and professionals in the lives of transgender youth. It emphasises repeated themes for improvement across all service provision. It finally offers areas for future research to develop service provision.

# Chapter 1

# Who Are Transgender Youth?

When I read an article at 12 or 13 on transsexualism I googled a lot to try and work out more about it and better understand what I was feeling. I had a pretty good understanding of sexual identity, but none of gender identity, so that was where (the internet) was the biggest help. (Tenson, FtM transgender, 17 years)

I'm female, or rather, I'm a woman (or girl, I guess, depending how you perceive age). It's the label that I find fits me best. More than any of the alternatives, anyway. And I guess I feel it fits me because how I (like to) express myself aligns with what women in society do. I think that's it, really. If I got to decide to be anything, whatever it meant, and I was given a blank space and could write whatever I want, I'd write female. And I don't really see my gender identity as different from a ciswoman's in that respect. They identify as female, as do I. (Siobhan, girl/woman, 22 years)

I identify as 'Genderqueer' I like being visually ambiguous, but to friends who don't understand that concept I let them know I prefer masculine pronouns. 'She' definitely makes me feel dysphoric. (Hansel, genderqueer, 22 years)

## KEY POINTS

- Transgender youth are defined as people with a range of potential gender identities different to those allocated to them at birth, aged under 25 years. They may use different identities to the ones service providers have previously heard of, or may use their identities inconsistently depending on their development, changing preferences or feelings of safety or support.

- Researchers can more easily gather large-scale data on transgender youth in their teens and twenties than younger transgender groups or older transgender groups.

- Transgender status can be measured in young people by consideration of their own perspectives on their gender expression incongruence (with their sex assigned at birth), their own perspectives on their gender identity incongruence and their self-identified or declared transgender status.

- Transgender status should not be allocated to a young person without their own involvement, however, a young person may be aware of their transgender status from infancy and is usually aware by puberty.

- Transgender youth come from a variety of locations, family backgrounds (including ethnicities and religious backgrounds) and lifestyles.

- There are many different gender identities and many different pathways to realising a transgender status; not every child's identity, expression or experience follows the one pattern.

- Professionals across all service sectors relevant to transgender youth are encouraged to respond to members of this group as individuals with their own particular personalities, histories, experiences, preferences and ideas on their gender.

Service professionals can hear a lot of myths and misconceptions about transgender youth: that they are all from Western countries, all want surgical changes, or could not possibly know their gender identity at a young age. This chapter describes transgender youth based on actual research data, not myths, to help service providers, practitioners and professionals of all kinds have a better understanding of the group. It defines key terms including transgender, gender diverse, pangender and other terms common to transgender youth cultures. It considers the age of transgender 'youth', and how research data is skewed towards those in their teenage years and early twenties in particular. It outlines some basic demographic data showing who belongs to this group and in what ways. It covers transgender youth experiences of disabilities. It considers the group's sex as assigned at birth, compared to their gender expressions and identity now, and their gender pronouns used now. It then outlines a range of common pathways seen in youth realising and acknowledging their transgender status. Finally, the conclusion reflects on some useful points for professionals in general taken from this demographic information.

## Defining 'transgender youth'

The way transgender and gender diverse youth define themselves is not how they were defined twenty or even ten years ago. The word 'transsexual' – which use to be used distinctly for people who had medically transitioned – is now less popular, and the concept of being 'transgendered' in some kind of past-tense verb is now offensive. Across the data from large Western democratic nations especially, whilst transgender youth do still largely think of themselves as 'transgender' (not transgender*ed*), around half identify as a sex fitting into 'binary' models of male–female gender; whereas around half identify in a 'non-binary' manner as more than one gender, pangender or as no gender (James *et al.*, 2016; Jones, Smith *et al.*, 2016; Smith *et al.*, 2014). A glossary has been provided at the start of this book to help service providers familiarise themselves with the new terminology young people are using and the current thinking behind it. However, I note that over time terminologies can shift (in any identity category, not just for transgender youth) so what matters is that you remain open to the idea of talking to a young person in the language they prefer, and accept their corrections. Affirming discussions about a young person's gender identity and expression should reflect their self-image, rather than enforce an external one upon them. For this reason, the book uses the phrase 'transgender' in inclusive, complex and unstable ways as a large encompassing 'umbrella term'. Underneath this umbrella sits a diverse group, including:

- youth whose gender identities differ from their allocated sex at birth, including those questioning their gender or who are non-conforming to the gender norms associated with their gender
- youth with both female-to-male/FtM and male-to-female/MtF transgender identities who feel they have a distinctly different gender identity to the one they were allocated at birth
- youth who are genderqueer (pangender – identifying with multiple genders, gender-fluid – identifying with shifting genders, non-binary – identifying in ways not exclusively described by masculinity or femininity or otherwise) and go beyond binary male–female sex models
- youth who like to fit in and be an active part of a 'transgender youth' culture or community, and youth who do not.

The book also includes those transgender youth identities fulfilling culturally specific gender roles, including (but not limited to):

- Malaysia's *mak nyahs* (including femininised young males doing 'female work' and MtF trans persons)
- Thailand's *kathoey* (young MtF trans and feminised gay men)
- India's *hijra* (young people seen as a third sex)
- Iran's *tara-jinsi* (youth who have undergone state-sanctioned gender transition)
- Pacific Islands' *fa'afafines* (those youths allocated a male sex at birth who later embody elements of both male and female social roles)
- others (UNESCO, 2016d).

Transgender youth – both in service provision scenarios and beyond them – can also engage with such identities inconsistently across their development, or in response to the legal protections and social prohibitions surrounding them, or in responses to the level of support in the treatment and reactions of service providers towards them (Jones, 2017c). So, in thinking about what it means to be 'transgender' – especially for youth – we have to open our minds and throw away the more rigid definitions we may have heard years ago.

Some specialists say one in 500 children are significantly gender variant, others have lower or higher estimates, and it is generally agreed that the proportion who declare themselves as transgender is growing (Brill & Pepper, 2008; Carroll, 2005a; James *et al.*, 2016; Jones, 2017a). Many transgender people say that people can only rarely or sometimes tell that they are transgender if they don't formally tell them so, regardless of their stage of transition (James *et al.*, 2016; Jones, 2016a; Smith *et al.*, 2014), and this can mean that service providers are already dealing with transgender youth in their work – whether they realise it or not. So it is important for service providers in a range of fields to assume that they are already serving transgender youth and may not be able to tell who they are.

## The age of transgender youth

For the purposes of this book, youth is defined as people who are aged 25 years and under. However, I note that in transgender youth research, there is more literature about adolescent transgender and gender diverse youth (those in their teens and twenties) than younger groups (infants and children). The limited research considering prepubescent transgender childrens' experiences mainly relied on adult recollections of childhood experiences and feelings, which may be distorted (Carver, Yunger & Perry, 2003; Grossman & D'Augelli, 2006; Savin-Williams, 1996; Stieglitz, 2010). Only a few studies directly on transgender children and infants were found (Brill & Pepper, 2008; Herdt & McClintock, 2000; Martin & Ruble, 2013; Olson, Key & Eaton, 2015). On the other hand, from their late teens adolescents are usually understood as being able to give their own informed consent to participation in research, and transgender adolescents (from generations x, y and millennials) can be particularly willing to share about their gender identity with researchers. They grew up in a culture of openness and disclosure impacting both trans cultures and youth cultures more broadly (with the advent of social media sharing), unlike those in older generations who may value privacy more.

For example, around half of the 273 female-to-male (FtM) transgender people in an Australian study open to people aged 16+ were in their teens or 20s (Jones *et al.*, 2015), and all of the participants in several Australian transgender and gender diverse youth studies (Jones, 2017a; Jones & Hillier, 2013; Jones, Smith *et al.*, 2016;

Smith et al., 2014). Similarly, around half of the 27,715 participants in the 2015 US Transgender Survey open to people aged 18+ were in their teens or 20s (James et al., 2016), and large-scale studies on youth populations alone in the Canadian-American, European and Asia-Pacific region were also able to garner strong representation. A nationally representative Australian study of 189 transgender youth survey participants and 16 interviewees (Smith et al., 2014), targeted youth from 14–25 years with a spread of ages represented. The average age was 19 years and the middle 50 per cent were aged between 16 and 22 years. Therefore, sometimes the discussion of research data may concentrate more on transgender youth in their teens and twenties, or retrospective accounts of their experiences during their earlier years.

Researchers and professionals of any kind should not try to officially allocate a child a transgender status against their will (even if it occurs to the professional that evidence about the child suggests they might be transgender in some way); the point is to acknowledge, reflect back or ask whether the individual child perceives an incongruence in their gender or perceives themselves as transgender, rather than for the professional to decide to declare a transgender status on behalf of someone who may not wish to be considered 'transgender'. Best-practice guidelines offer three transgender status dimensions:

1. *Gender Expression Incongruence* (with assigned sex)
2. *Gender Identity Incongruence* (with assigned sex)
3. *Self-identified Transgender Status* (Bauer et al., 2017; Brown, Herman & Park, 2017; National LGBTI Health Alliance, 2016; The GenIUSS Group, 2014).

The first measure for transgender status in youth is 'Gender Expression Incongruence (with assigned sex)': an incongruence in a child or young person's assigned sex (such as their sex/sex marker on their birth certificate as allocated by a doctor) and their current expression of gendered behaviours (e.g. their use of pronouns/clothing/preferred play style and toys/behaviours). Non-conforming or incongruent gender expression (in play, toys, style) starts in infancy; and infants with non-conforming or incongruent expressions of gender can often experience reprimands from their peers and parents, due to the emphasis on teaching of gender norms during the first five years of life (Martin & Ruble, 2013; Olson et al., 2015). The second measure for transgender status in youth is 'Gender Identity Incongruence (with assigned sex)': an incongruence in a child or young person's assigned sex and their current alignment to a gendered identity (e.g. their sense of fitting a male, female or other social role). Studies have repeatedly shown that transgender youth may know their gender identities do not match their assigned sex by five years of age or even earlier (Jones *et al.*, 2015; Jones & Hillier, 2013; Olson *et al.*, 2015). The third measure for transgender status in youth is 'Self-identified Transgender Status': the child or young person's sense of alignment to a transgender self-description or identity (e.g. their sense of self as fitting the definition of transgender, genderqueer, non-binary or gender non-conforming or another status under the transgender umbrella).

These three dimensions may not align due to non-binary or fluid identity, developmental change, stigma, socio-cultural values, legal, or economic issues (Bauer *et al.*, 2017; Brown *et al.*, 2017; Haas *et al.*, 2011; Smith *et al.*, 2014; The GenIUSS Group, 2014). Transgender youth in democratic Western countries like Australia more frequently have social gender affirmations than medical affirmations (Jones, Smith *et al.*, 2016; Smith *et al.*, 2014) – whereas in Iran, medical affirmations have been strongly promoted, so the three dimensions may end up more strongly aligned. Each dimension provides relevant information for how transgender youth may have needs which stand out from other clients' needs in service provision (such as complexities in documentation histories) and may be relevant for understanding how the youth may become victims of discrimination or violence. Researchers consider gender expression incongruence the most important element to consider for transgender youth due to its potential visibility from the youngest age, and due to how gender non-conforming children may not have a clear transgender status (depending on their exposure to such terms) or may not have an oppositional gender identity to the one assigned to them at birth if they are non-conforming or not yet able to resist the adults defining them in that way (The GenIUSS Group, 2014).

Across several studies, one third or more of the young people declared that they had questioned their gender identity for *as long as they could remember* whilst around two thirds nominated a specific age (Herdt & McClintock, 2000; Jones *et al.*, 2015; Jones, Smith *et al.*, 2016; Smith *et al.*, 2014). The youngest age directly nominated (other than 'always') was generally three years of age, and most young people knew their gender identity at the onset of puberty (Herdt & McClintock, 2000; Hillier *et al.*, 2010; Jones *et al.*, 2015; Jones, Smith *et al.*, 2016; Smith *et al.*, 2014). Within this range, the average age that the young people began questioning their gender identity was between 10 and 14 years. However, questioning one's gender identity can be a complex process that does not necessarily begin and end at a specific time.

## Location and background

Transgender and gender diverse youth come from all global regions and all countries (UNESCO, 2012a, 2015, 2016b). Transgender youth are distributed in a pattern reflective of the general population in their nations, and the family background should not be seen as a key predictive factor around whether or not one is transgender; except in cultural contexts where transgender roles exist as allocations by parents for economic purposes – such as in societies where a son or daughter role might be allocated to one child or another by parents to help with gendered housework or wage accumulation (including in some Pacific Islands cultures). However, notably, transgender adolescents and adults can become disproportionately concentrated in urban settings; moving away from rural areas and towards locations where gender services are available (Jones *et al.*, 2015).

Most transgender youth are currently engaged in education and/or employment. However, risks to their disengagement in education and employment are high and in some countries such as Argentina around 46 per cent report early school dropout (UNESCO, 2016b). A 2010 survey of Australian youth showed transgender youth were around 8 per cent less likely to be at school, and were slightly more likely to be unemployed (at 16.4%) than same sex attracted youth (Jones & Hillier, 2013). An online survey of 189 young transgender and gender diverse people aged 14–25 years, which included 16 interviewees, showed that whilst 55 per cent were either studying or studying and working, 16.5 per cent were unemployed (Smith *et al.*, 2014). Studies of older populations showed that transgender youth, whilst more likely to drop out of high school, had also been more likely to remain in higher education facilities for longer in order to avoid the stressors and documentation issues they would potentially face in employment and industry (Jones, 2016a).

## Disability

The large majority of transgender youth in research (usually more than four fifths) have not identified themselves as having a disability – an important point to emphasise given the fact that transgender people have historically been construed by some psychological and psychiatric bodies as disordered on the basis of their gender identity alone, and have had to use disability/disorder framings to access services (Garofalo *et al.*, 2006; Haas *et al.*, 2011; Jones, 2016a; Jones, Smith *et al.*, 2016; Smith *et al.*, 2014). Where disabilities were cited in studies, in the main these disabilities related to mental health (such as anxiety, depression and stress; Jones, Smith *et al.*, 2016). However, there were also individuals with cognitive and social disabilities and learning/processing disorders (such as ADHD, autism, social phobia and others), and people with physical issues (asthma, chronic pain and so on).

There have been some more recent efforts in the research literature to make links between autism and transgender status (van Schalkwyk, Klingensmith & Volkmarb, 2015). Part of the difficulty in this is that masculine behaviours in autistic non-conforming females or FtM transgender youth can be written off as 'a characteristic of autism itself' rather than gender incongruence. Sometimes a focus on either autism or transgender identity can get in the way of or be used to incorrectly avoid the management of the other by service providers. More rarely, individuals framed their gender dysphoria as a birth defect and therefore a disability (Smith *et al.*, 2014). The overall resistance of transgender youth to doing so perhaps explains the tensions around classifications of gender identity diagnoses as disorders (Drescher, 2013).

## Sex assigned at birth

Early studies, and indeed earlier media representations, focused on MtF transgender people – those assigned a male sex at birth with a female or non-conforming gender identity now (Edwards, Fisher & Reynolds, 2007; Gooren, Sungkaew & Giltay, 2013; Hare *et al.*, 2009). Even studies that were only on transgender people broadly seemed to mainly focus on MtF transgender people (Couch *et al.*, 2007). Perhaps the decorative nature of femininity made feminine transgender people more visible in our societies, or perhaps the dominance of historic patriarchal rule around the world made those who gave up male privileges and clothing stand out more. Over time, more studies have been done on FtM transender people – those assigned a female sex at birth with male or non-conforming gender identity now (Jones *et al.*, 2015; Newfield *et al.*, 2006).

The majority of transgender youth in general transgender studies from Western democratic nations now, however, have indicated that they were assigned a female sex or sex marker on their birth certificate at birth as opposed to an alternate sex marker or none at all (James *et al.*, 2016; Jones *et al.*, 2015; Jones & Hillier, 2013; Smith *et al.*, 2014; UNESCO, 2016b). A US survey of almost 30,000 transgender people (James *et al.*, 2016) found most had been assigned a female sex or sex marker at birth (57%), the remainder were assigned male. An Australian study of youth aged 14–25 years even found 72.5% of participants were allocated a female sex at birth (Smith *et al.*, 2014). A quarter (26.5%) were assigned male at birth and two young people chose 'other'. A small percentage of most studies on transgender people include a portion of people who had an intersex variation; however, the portion is aligned with the 2 to 4 per cent of people generally receiving an intersex diagnosis in the broader cisgender population (Carroll, 2005b; Fausto-Sterling, 1993; Jones *et al.*, 2015; OII Australia, 2012; Smith *et al.*, 2014). Having an intersex variation (atypicality in sex-related chromosomes, hormones and/or anatomy) does not automatically make an individual transgender, or vice versa.

## Gender expression and identity now

Despite the growing diversity of gender identities, research on transgender youth does not often explore the way in which people relate to and/or use these terms (Kuper, Nussbaum & Mustanski, 2012). However, allowing young people to describe their own gender identities and expression has been found to increase young people's resilience (Singh, Meng & Hansen, 2014). A 2010 Australian survey considered 101 young people who were transgender – specifically, 43 were genderqueer, 21 transgender FtM, 18 transgender MtF, and nine were 'other' (Jones & Hillier, 2013). The remainder identified solely as their gender identity (male or female) and did not regularly use 'transgender-related' terminology. Many survey participants from the 'other' group were of indigenous descent. Of this group, those who expanded on their gender identity gave the following descriptions:

- androgynous (Addison, 17 years)
- hermaphrodite (Alex, 17 years)
- FtM transsexual, and genderqueer (Payton, 19 years)
- no gender (Drew, 17 years)
- not 100% male, but not female either, somewhere in between (Reese, 17 years)
- gender fluid, biologically male, taking estrogen, generally a girl (Kendall, 18 years)
- born biologically male, but extremely androgenous (possibly intersex? probably not) but I somewhat identify as a transguy because I don't like being mistaken for a woman (Sage, 20 years)
- not really sure yet, physically female but not sure mentally. I feel most comfortable in guys' clothes and when I am treated like a guy but I still wouldnt define myself as transgender, not yet anyway (Ashley, 17 years).

A later survey on 189 transgender Australian youth has shown that even more young people are resisting the idea of fixed gender-identity categories over time (Smith *et al.*, 2014); around half the participants identified with the 'opposite' gender to the sex they were assigned at birth, half identified with terms that rejected the binary notion of gender. Figure 1.1 shows the identities transgender youth declared (Jones, Smith *et al.*, 2016).

Transgender youth who have been interviewed or surveyed increasingly tell researchers that they understand their own gender in highly personal ways which are not necessarily attached to a fixed category (Jones, Smith *et al.*, 2016; Smith *et al.*, 2014). For example, Alex (15 years), who also participated in an interview, explained: 'I don't feel like I have a gender at all.' The majority of young people in a 2014 Australian survey who chose either 'man' or 'woman' gender identity categories were assigned an 'opposite' 'female' or 'male' sex at birth (Smith *et al.*, 2014). A few individuals (n=20), chose a gender identity that 'matched' their sex assigned at birth. It was interesting to find that these young people also indicated that they had, or wanted to, socially transition (as well as other indicators of diverse gender). One young person who identified as a woman and who was assigned female at birth said, 'transitioning entails changing my appearance and mannerisms based on my whims of the day.' Sean, a 22-year-old who participated in an interview, also described this ambiguity:

> I identify as a feminine young male. For me this means I fit into identities and subcultures associated with the queer community, but I personally don't embrace or identify with trans* identities. Identity, to me, is my self-concept. I think it can be fluid, but haven't found it particularly so in my case.

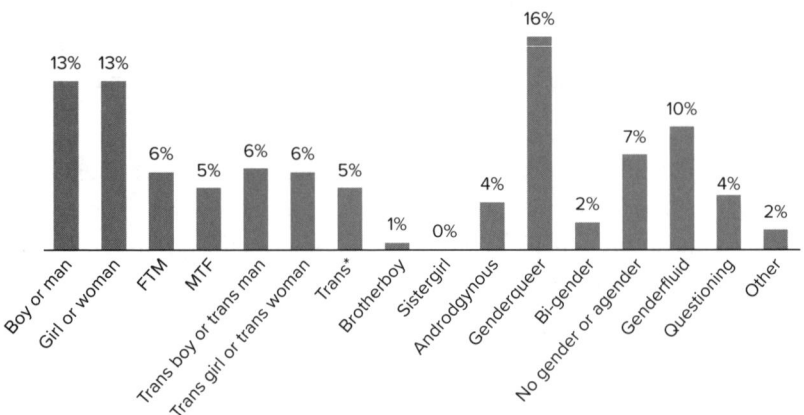

Figure 1.1: Current gender identities held by 189 transgender youth

Eli (genderqueer, 20 years) explained how the notion of gender felt irrelevant, 'I am most comfortable within myself and as a member of society as a person defined through character.' Theo (non-binary, 14 years) said, 'I identify as non-binary, which is kind of a vague term but I don't really feel like any of the specific words fit me right'. Charlotte (trans woman, 24 years) explained how being transgender was not necessarily as straightforward as being assigned a sex at birth but identifying with a different gender: 'I identify as female but there are times where I identify as male.' Stan (genderqueer, 22 years) spoke about gender identity as an individual journey: 'Just go your own pace and if your identity changes, it's not the end of the world. People change.'

## Gender pronouns used now

Pronouns are the (usually gendered) article by which we are referred to in third-person discussions: often they, he or she. For transgender youth, pronouns can be highly loaded, even a battleground once declared if people insist on 'mis-gendering' them. Part of having one's gender affirmed, is having it affirmed by others, in language use. Acknowledging a transgender young person's pronouns can make them feel deeply affirmed and supported in ways that are difficult for a cisgender person (who is more often discussed with 'correct' pronouns) to fathom (Jones, 2017a). An Australian study found transgender youth especially used 'she' (46%, n=88) and 'he' (42%, n=49) and 'they' 35% (n=67) (Jones, Smith *et al.*, 2016; Smith *et al.*, 2014). Furthermore, 20 per cent indicated that they 'don't care' what pronoun is used to describe them.

## Pathways to realising transgender status

One study of transgender people aged 16+, however, did retrospectively explore the age and means by which participants came to discover their transgender identities in great detail (Jones *et al.*, 2015). Three broad developmental trajectories emerged in the participants' first awareness of gender incongruence:

1. Participants who had an early and ongoing awareness of gender expression and identity incongruence from infancy.

2. Participants who had a series of fluctuating periods of awareness of gender expression and identity incongruence throughout infancy/childhood/adolescence/adulthood.

3. Participants who had an early lack of awareness about their transgender status accompanied by an inexplicably strong sense of discomfort (which they did not understand as directly tied to gender) until late adolescence/early adulthood.

Most participants fell in the first category. They had an early, clear and ongoing awareness of gender expression and gender identity incongruence. As children they had a strong sense of wrong embodiment for as long as they could remember. This manifested in refusals to wear certain clothes, non-conforming playmate and toy preference, and adopting play characters and behaviours of the gender they aligned with. In addition, they felt a strong desire to develop the associated genitalia. They dreamed and hoped that one day they would wake up changed. For example, Lance (male/transsexual male, 40 years) recalled that at four years old he would start each morning by checking to see if he was a boy. He was 'really upset' by the daily discovery that he was not. These early feelings of difference, magical thinking and daydreaming, and early attempts at 'making the change' reflected the themes in the international research (Pazos, 2000). The emergence of unwanted secondary sexual characteristics during puberty was traumatic. It brought disgust, embarrassment, withdrawal, isolation and depression. Nikozilar recalled:

> When I was really little, I thought I was a boy. I didn't realize that I wasn't. I was really weirded out by my genitalia and I deliberately hurt it. The day I got my period, depression hit like a brick. Suddenly I knew there was something seriously wrong. (Nikozilar, male, 20 years)

Whilst some people went to extreme measures to deal with these issues, others withdrew into a world of books, reading or video games to distract or comfort themselves. This reflected international clinicians' accounts of the trend to dissociation as a coping mechanism (Brown and Rownsley, 1996; Pazos, 2000).

However, a second and different trajectory was followed by some participants, who during their childhood and teenage years experienced fluctuating periods of awareness that they did not satisfy or fit the traditional gender expectations. This group actively suppressed this painful awareness, because they thought there was no solution. Sometimes this effort to ignore thoughts and feelings about their gender was related to their parents' negative reactions (dismissal or rejection) upon the disclosure of their gender identities:

> I had moments as a teen where I knew. But I suppressed it all. It all came crashing down around me when I was about 20. It happened when I saw the results of one guy's transition. I guess I didn't know that transitioning was possible until then. (Harry, FtM transgender, 24 years)

Sam (male/trans guy, 22 years) said, 'I spent a little while trying to deny/ignore it, but also did a lot of research into transitioning.'

GladlyGiddy (male, 55 years) had always considered himself as a boy as far back as he could remember, but had to repress this due to his family's responses. At age two he tried to pee like a boy but always wet his pants trying. His mother thought he was regressing in his toilet training. He was rejected by the boys he wanted to play with in his teens and realised he would not be one of them, and was pressured by family and friends to 'become a lady'. He was often called a lesbian or a butch, and had many straight women become attracted to him, but tried to integrate into life as a woman. He got married to try to fit in. At 55 he is now 'taking the bullet by the teeth'.

The remaining participants followed a third trajectory; they described a sense of inexplicable discomfort and dysphoria throughout childhood and adolescence, but claimed that a clearer understanding and awareness of 'why' they felt this way only came later in life. They reported always feeling different, 'ugly', 'ill-fitting' and depressed; but not knowing that this discomfort was actually about their gender. Ramir (transgender, 25 years) felt 'different my whole life', without a strong sense of why. Anthony (male, FtM transgender, 19 years) experienced additional complications coming from a culture 'which is very separatist when it comes to gender', so he mainly had to be around girls and felt like 'an alien around others'. The confusion often brought people to sexual experimentation to find out who they were during late adolescence or young adulthood. Many participants had gay relationships and identified as such for a time, but continued experiencing dysphoria until they had the realisation they were transgender. This generally occurred as a result of having access to relevant information on gender diversity or meeting a transgender person. On many occasions this newly acquired self-knowledge brought a deep sense of relief, depression vanished or significantly improved and the individuals then started the gradual journey of transitioning. Ramir reflected that, 'looking back, knowing that I was transgender makes my whole life make sense.' For the genderqueer participants, moments of discovery had more to do with exposure to queer and post-modernist feminist theory. They also mentioned particular books covering gender concepts, or periods of their life where they engaged in formal study that helped inform their perspectives.

## Conclusion

The data shows that service providers, professionals and practitioners can only sometimes tell if someone is transgender or not without being told (simply by looking or observing), and should never ever force their opinion of a young person's transgender status on to that individual. They should rather respond to the individual's self-perception and self-declaration of their transgender status or gender identity and expression, or simply ask the individual how they like to be treated in terms of gender or socially. Research has shown some more common pathways and ages for realisation patterns. However, what research has shown most of all, is that there are *no set rules for who transgender youth are*. Therefore, all services and professionals need to, above all else, respond to members of this group as individuals with their own particular personalities, histories, experiences and preferences. These individuals (and youth in general) contribute exciting and constantly evolving creative ideas on gender to our world.

# Chapter 2

# Transgender Youth, Mental Health and Mental Health Services

I would have been about four? I used to get really upset when in the mornings I'd check to see if I was a boy and wasn't. I'd then start my day upset and not understand why I wasn't a boy. (Lance, male/transsexual male, 40 years)

I couldn't find any info when I was beginning my journey. The trans therapy/surgery circle is hard to discover without knowing someone who is in it. Even knowing whom the right therapists/surgeons are, you still can't discover any info about their work specific to the transsexual field. (Harry, FtM transgender, 24 years)

I'm really happy with how my life is going, especially since coming out as trans. I still struggle with my mental health, I've always had very low downs that can feel debilitating, so I am continuing therapy and considering medication. I am often lacking in sex drive for long periods of time, but that could be due to depression and being busy. Otherwise my life is really great. I have wonderful friends and care for rescue dogs, I have a kind and understanding partner, a great and satisfying job and enough money to get by (most of the time anyway). I wish I could feel a bit more stable and enjoy more drive (whether it be for work, creativity or sex) but I am working on that and am lucky to have great support. … Looking back, I'm just proud to still be here today! (Sam, transgender, 25 years)

# KEY POINTS

- Transgender youth and their families may be wary of mental health professionals due to historic mistreatment.

- The diagnosis of 'gender dysphoria' should not be considered a pathologising mental illness. It is intended to be used as a non-pathologising way of facilitating mental health services for transgender youth, whilst allowing an 'exit clause' from the diagnoses later in life.

- Most transgender adults feel satisfied with their lives in general. This should be emphasised to youth and their parents/guardians, as it is often overlooked.

- Transgender people have high rates of depression and anxiety and these diagnoses can interact with other gender dysphoria in subtle ways or can be wrongly interpreted as in a direct relationship to it – the nuanced nature of the inter-relationship of mental health diagnoses should not be presumed or pre-emptively asserted, but observed.

- Transgender youth have significantly increased rates of self-harm, suicidal ideation and suicide attempts compared to cisgender populations. Younger, FtM transgender and non-binary/genderqueer transgender youth are particularly at increased risk. These increased negative wellbeing outcomes relate to their personal issues in regards to gender, experiences of transphobia and other issues.

- Improvements in mental health issues tied to gender dysphoria are related to the process of coming out about gender identity, parental support, gender affirmations, activism and finding support and information.

- Mental health professionals are encouraged to become educated on transgender issues, avoid mis-gendering transgender youth, confront their own cissexism and consider a holistic tiered approach to combatting transphobia rather than just treating individuals.

The changes in mental health services for transgender youth have impacted their treatment in every other service area, especially the shift away from the old pathologising ideas and towards the view that mental health diagnoses should 'serve' this population rather than hinder it. This chapter provides an in-depth, research-based and pragmatic exploration of mental health issues for transgender and gender diverse youth. It considers past historic treatment of mental health issues for transgender youth, and the development of a key contemporary diagnosis in the field: gender dysphoria. It includes statistics on the positive life satisfaction of transgender people as well as mental health issues besides dysphoria sometimes seen in the population, such as stress, anxiety and depression. The chapter addresses issues of self-harm, suicidality and their contributing factors, as well as discussing five key groups of protective factors which have been seen to significantly reduce these wellbeing risks and how these can be fostered. It details issues with transgender youth missing or avoiding mental health services or having negative experiences, and what makes mental health professionals helpful. It details in light of this information some important techniques for combatting cisnormativity and cissexism in mental health services, providing mental health services in schools and understanding ethics and training for professionals. Important actions are listed for services, practitioners and professionals in mental health.

## Historic mental health services: Inversion, GID and conversion therapies

Variance in sexual partner desire and cross-dressing before the 19th century was read in relation to violation of social roles and marital ritual in European theory, rather than any specific 'identity' (Foucault, 1980; Garber, 1992). By the end of the 19th century both same sex desire and non-normative gender expression was associated in a Freudian psycho-analytic frame with the psychological disorder of 'inversion' – which combined early concepts of homosexuality and role confusion, or lesbianism and penis envy (Chauncey, 1989; Freud, 1905). Whilst Freud proposed varying talking cures and other treatments to overcome what he understood as a pathological fear of the opposite sex caused by traumatic parent–child relationships, it is notable that he identified how many inverts did not want 'treatment' or believe their inversion was curable, despite religious or family pressure to change (Freud, 1910). Inverts generally became associated in psychoanalysis and sexology with aberrant sexual desire emanating from severe cross-gender identification, and were cast by conservatives and traditionalists as a sign of the 'ills of modern life' – a weakening of males and coarsening of females, loss of separation of gender spheres and family structures, and degeneration of the species (Halberstam, 2012). During World War I these anxieties were furthered as women took over 'male' factory jobs and domestic tasks. In schools (particularly in the US, Australia and UK) there developed alongside fears over the disruption of normative gender roles a parallel concern for the seduction of students by 'deviant' teachers (Sears, 2005).

Inversion became understood as in fact containing separate conditions that could exist distinct from each other: homosexuality and transgenderism. In the 1950s the widely influential American Psychological Association's *Diagnostic and Statistical Manual of Mental Disorders (DSM)* – listed homosexuality as a sociopathic personality disturbance (Sears, 2005), despite evidence from researchers like Kinsey that homosexuality was indeed a common and healthy occurrence (Kinsey, Pomeroy & Martin, 1948). Similarly, as recently as in the first few years of the 2000s the (now outdated) *DSM-IV* still labelled transgender youth with a diagnoses of 'Gender Identity Disorder (GID)' (Drescher & Byne, 2012), which described the misfit between their allocated sex and gender identity as a form of personal dysfunction within the 'Paraphilias and Sexual Dysfunction' section of the book. Through the widespread dominance of these pathologising conceptualisations many transgender people – including youth – have been subjected to harmful but *ultimately useless* treatments to change their identification ranging from shock therapies, institutionalised living, right through to more modern ex-gay/ex-trans conversion therapies involving public shaming or invasive changes to their dress/mannerisms and lifestyles (APA Task Force on Appropriate Therapeutic Responses to Sexual Orientation, 2009). The American Psychological Association and many other bodies have publicly declared that these conversion therapies *do not work* and *do more harm than good* to transgender youth. Similarly, historic studies on whether or not parents 'were at fault' through doing something to make their children become transgender or gender non-conforming (child abuse, divorce, being over-bearing or being lenient, being absent, etc.) are now widely disputed and disparaged (Brill & Pepper, 2008). Mental health service practitioners and professionals, like parents and guardians, cannot make transgender youth align or misalign their internal gender identities or internal choices in gender expressions with the practitioners' own external ideas of what these 'should' be. Making transgender youth conform to expectations for their sex marker as allocated at birth through sheer force could break anti-discrimination laws in many countries, makes no 'authentic' change, is retrogressive and outdated, is repressive and cruel, and is ultimately bad mental health practice.

## Contemporary mental health services: Gender dysphoria and anti-discrimination

In 2011 the United Nations Educational, Scientific and Cultural Organisation (UNESCO) held the First International Consultation on LGBTIQ issues in Educational Institutions in Rio de Janeiro, Brazil (December 6–9th). The event was attended by government and non-government representatives and education research experts on the topic from all continents (including the author), and they created the *Rio Statement* on the tenth International Human Rights Day (UNESCO, 2011). The statement asserted that the right to education must not be 'curtailed by discrimination on the basis of sexual orientation or gender identity'. During the same period, 200 UN Member States attended the New York convening: 'Stop Bullying – Ending Violence and Discrimination Based on Sexual Orientation and Gender Identity.' The UN Secretary, General Ban Ki-moon, contended that bullying on these bases was 'a grave violation to human rights and a public health crisis'. This framing of human rights has subsequently been supported by the United Nations as a body, with the release of the United Nation's transgender-affirming *Born Free and Equal* policy (United Nations, 2012). This document outlined the UN's position in interpreting transgender rights as inherent in 'human rights' for the first time, and asserted the protection of all people against discrimination (including in schools) on the basis of sexual orientation, gender identity and intersex status in international human rights law. It pushed for legislative protections and violence prevention measures in all nations, and for schools to make active efforts towards inclusion to support transgender students' psychological wellbeing.

The key contemporary mental health research on transgender youth shifted from stigmatising perspectives, using a combination of psychological and sociological analyses to give an account of how internal and external factors impact youth wellbeing (Jones & Lasser, 2017). Most international mental health research on gender diverse and transgender youth is primarily focused on psychological interventions, risk determinants, negative pathways, suffering and social victimisation (Carrera, DePalma & Lameiras, 2012; Donatone & Rachlin, 2013; Menvielle, 2012). Whilst this focus can reinforce a different type of negative stereotype of transgender people as living risky lives with poor mental health outcomes, the 'problem' envisioned now is more social responses to transgender youth than transgender youth themselves. It may still be important, however, to emphasise transgender youth − and transgender adults' − great capacity to live satisfied lives or engage in activist responses to social backlash and resilient self-care (Jones *et al.*, 2015; Smith *et al.*, 2014). The research mainly focuses on adults due to difficulties in access to transgender youth, however, there are more and more studies on youth mental health as governments and mental health organisations (like beyondblue, an independent Australian non-profit organisation working to address issues associated with depression and anxiety) have started to proactively fund them (Couch *et al.*, 2007; Jones *et al.*, 2015; Jones, Gray & Harris, 2014).

Overall, contemporary psychology perspectives show a significant shift in their treatment of transgender people. The standard focus for mental health professionals therefore is now more about being supportive of clients to achieve their own (varying) personal goals within a broader context of social reform and affirmation, rather than forcing transgender youth into outmoded and exclusionary frames of traditional male or female roles and identities. Modern psychology is influenced by post-structuralist feminisms from the 1980s, and Queer theory popularised in the 1990s by Judith Butler, which were much more affirming of transgender and genderqueer people. These frames instead attack essentialist notions of identity, and cast gender as culturally constructed. In these perspectives, a transgender person's gender identity is seen as no more a 'performance' than anyone else's (Butler, 1990). Transgender studies and particularly the work of Sandy Stone (Stone, 1991), also influenced modern psychology by affirming transgender people's right to self-definition and positive representation. There are also currently theories of transgender identities based on brain sex which understand transgender people as having had brain areas develop chemically as a sex other than the one allocated to them at birth through hormonal exposure in the womb (Pease & Pease, 2003). During the last few years there have been heated international debates between academics and activists informed by various old and new perspectives.

Drescher recounted many gender diagnosis controversies during his tenure at the DSM-5 Workgroup on Sexual and Gender Identity Disorders and the ICD-11 Working Group on the Classification of Sexual Disorders and Sexual Health (Drescher & Byne, 2012). At the time, many activists pointed to how the previous removal of homosexuality from the manual had been a positive step against homophobia in the past, and were of the opinion that retaining notions of transgender issues as a psychological problem was pathologising. Others were concerned that – unlike gay, lesbian and bisexual people – transgender people needed 'a diagnosis' to facilitate their access to medical aids if they choose to pursue transition processes. Drescher explained that ultimately the decision was made to enable transgender people to maintain access to care through maintaining the construction of gender identity as a psychological/medical issue requiring diagnosis.

However, in the DSM-5 the diagnosis was changed from gender identity disorder to *gender dysphoria* – a marked and verbalised difference between the individual adult or child's experienced gender and the gender others assign them, for at least six months, that causes clinically significant distress or impairment in social or other functioning (Drescher & Byne 2012). This diagnosis was no longer bundled with the paraphilias and sexual dysfunction section but given its own chapter within the manual to reduce stigma. The addition of a post-transition specifier was to be used in the context of continuing treatment procedures that serve to support the new gender assignment (a kind of 'exit clause' from the diagnosis, which reduces stigma, when the post-transition individual is no longer gender dysphoric but still requires access to ongoing hormone treatment). Currently under this dominant 'diagnostic model' of care, a written gender dysphoria diagnosis is required for transgender people to access medical treatment; mental health professionals write the letters of diagnosis. New Zealand and US advocates are pushing for future 'informed consent' models which will skip the diagnostic stepping stone, allowing transgender people to access hormone treatments and surgical interventions without undergoing mental health evaluation or referral from a mental health specialist to further break away from pathologisation – such proposed 'informed consent' models will likely be debated and advocated for in future years.

Young people in an Australian study were more likely to report that they experienced gender dysphoria (46%) or its earlier counterpart, gender identity disorder (33%), than they were to report that they had a diagnosis from a health professional (27% and 30% respectively) (Smith *et al.*, 2014). The young people described what gender dysphoria felt like to them in various open-ended survey responses. One young FtM transgender person (17 years), who, when asked what they thought might improve their mental health, said, 'I get really bad gender dysphoria, especially given that my body is so curvaceous yet I still have good muscle mass. Hopefully surgery and hormones can change that.' Fifteen-year-old Alex, who participated in an interview and described their gender identity as agender, explained the measures that they took to reduce feelings of dysphoria including, 'It's awful, I've started just labelling things with my last name to avoid first name-related dysphoria but even that seems kind of weird, people only see me as female.' When asked what transitioning meant to them, another young boy/man (21 years) described what gender dysphoria felt like to him:

> Pre medical transition, dysphoria was hell; not just insecurity, but panic attacks, deep depression, and what I can only describe as a physical feeling that I was not meant to exist in that form.

In some contexts minors seeking bodily interventions (puberty blockers/surgeries) with or without parental support have historically been able to access these through the family court system by age 16 (rarer cases have been won for those as young as 11/12), but there have been other contexts where no such transition aid is available (Bannerman, 2014; UNESCO, 2016b). The emphasis on contemporary mental health provisions for transgender youth should therefore be around:

- supporting the individual to access experts in the field of gender dysphoria

- seeking out an appropriate diagnosis as and if relevant whilst acknowledging the issues of cisnormativity and transphobia in the given context

- identifying and understanding any relationships or lacks of relationships between gender dysphoria and other mental health issues so these can be treated appropriately as relevant

- working towards creating a network of support for the youth which would ideally (but does not always) include some family members supportive of their process of self-discovery, a future that includes bodily autonomy, and institutional and social environments affirming of the youth's needs.

## The positive life satisfaction of transgender people

Transgender people are capable of fulfilling, joyful lives. It is so easy to lose sight of this, especially when faced with the mental health statistics that mental health professionals working with this population need to be aware of in order to do their work to prevent or manage crisis situations. Overall, Table 2.1 summarises data from a study that showed a majority (63%) of transgender people aged 16+ were *satisfied with their lives in general* (10% felt neutral about their lives and 26% were dissatisfied) (Jones *et al.*, 2015). This wonderful finding about the positive life satisfaction of transgender people should be proactively emphasised by mental health professionals to transgender youth and their parents/guardians where appropriate, as it is often completely overlooked in the mental health literature. Knowing about this research finding, in itself, may be a point of deep affirmation for transgender youth broadly, and also for their parents and guardians who will naturally worry for any child's future happiness potential. Of those transgender people who were satisfied with their lives in the study, the comments tended to focus on the sense that *their own self-acceptance of their gender or transgender status had greatly improved their life*. For example, one participant said that their life was a, '10 out of 10. I feel I have been true to myself regardless of fear and challenges.' In addition, several other transgender people reflected on how things were steadily improving and how they had much to look forward to now that they knew who they were.

Table 2.1: Life satisfaction of 220 transgender people aged 16+

| Level of satisfaction with | Dissatisfied | Neutral | Satisfied |
| --- | --- | --- | --- |
| Life in general (n=220) | 26% | 10% | 63% |
| Social life (n=220) | 31% | 14% | 55% |
| Romantic life (n=219) | 32% | 14% | 54% |
| Sexual life (n=218) | 45% | 18% | 37% |
| Physical health (n=219) | 32% | 14% | 53% |
| Job/studies (n=220) | 35% | 9% | 56% |

When it came to specific areas of their lives, the results were not as strong as they were for general life satisfaction. For example, regarding their jobs/studies, 56 per cent of the respondents were satisfied (9% felt neutral about their jobs/studies and 35% were dissatisfied). The qualitative data suggested that satisfaction was closely tied to having a supportive work/study environment, enough money to live comfortably and a focus on an area of interest – this could be hindered by transphobia. Regarding relationships, the results similarly showed only a slight trend towards satisfaction. In regards to their social life generally, a majority of 55 per cent of the respondents were satisfied (14% felt neutral about their social lives and 31% were dissatisfied). Dissatisfaction could relate to issues around transphobia or the need for transition. Most of the participants responding positively spoke of having one or more good friends. Several of those who were dissatisfied expressed feeling 'behind' in terms of socialisation for their current gender identity. Regarding their romantic life, a majority of 54 per cent of the respondents were satisfied (14% felt neutral about their romantic lives and 32% were dissatisfied). Those who were satisfied discussed having loving partners or enjoyable dates, for example. The respondents were less satisfied with their sexual lives: only 37 per cent of the respondents were satisfied, 18 per cent felt neutral and 45 per cent were dissatisfied. There were mainly comments on the need for 'More sex!', but also comments by people who did not enjoy sex generally and for whom frequency of sex would not be an improvement. For some the issue was with the quality of what could be achieved in their experience; given their current bodies and desired abilities to perform sexually. Therefore, mental health service professionals need to think of transgender youth both as having particular needs for self-acceptance and for aid in dealing with the stresses of waiting to live out their lives in the gender they know themselves to be, and also as having similar needs to other clients around aid in other areas of life satisfaction (that simply undergoing a gender affirmation of some kind may not resolve).

## Stress, anxiety and depression

Transgender individuals are more likely to experience mental health conditions (besides gender dysphoria) than the general population (Lenning & Buist, 2013; McNeil *et al.*, 2012). Studies of transgender and LGBTI youth populations also found increased anxiety and depression rates (Clark *et al.*, 2014; Couch *et al.*, 2007; del Pozo de Bolger *et al.*, 2014; Jones *et al.*, 2015; Jones & Hillier, 2013). Figure 2.1 illustrates Australian research which found 69 per cent of FtM transgender survey participants aged 16+ reported being diagnosed with depression and anxiety in the previous 12 months (Jones *et al.*, 2015), which was higher than in previous Australian studies of transgender populations (Couch *et al.*, 2007). In addition, some respondents had received other mental health diagnoses as shown (post-traumatic stress disorder (PTSD), obsessive compulsive disorder, body dysmorphia and others).

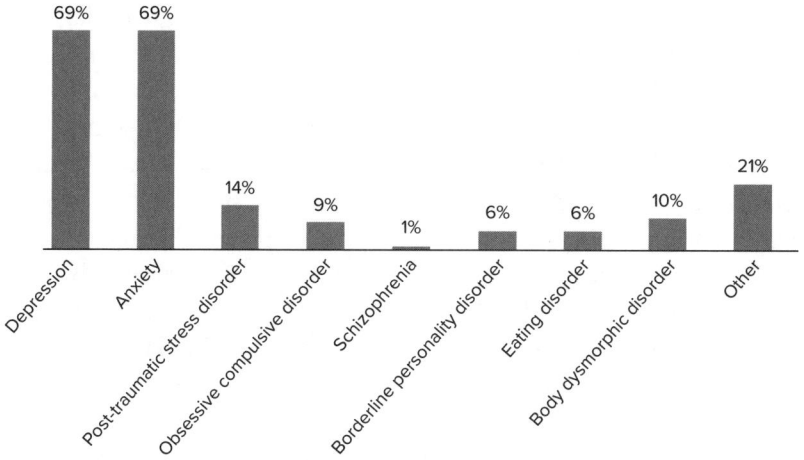

*Figure 2.1: Mental health disorders of 127 transgender people aged 16+ in the last 12 months*

Gender identity – particularly when it could not be expressed fully – was understood by participants as a contributing factor for depression and anxiety. Draconem (FtM transgender, 24 years) said he got depressed occasionally, usually at night, and had been diagnosed with depression and social anxiety. 'These issues have arisen due to family problems (abuse), and self-ostracising, and in part gender identity,' he explained. Many participants said that being able to express their gender to a greater extent – whether through transition or other affirmations of self – was associated with improvements to their mental health. Harry (FtM transgender, 24 years) commented that although he had previously been diagnosed with social anxiety and depression he was 'doing pretty well, basically since I started passing (as a man) full time'. He had been off his medication for two years, and whilst he still occasionally got depressed it was related not to his own feelings about his gender anymore, but to his lack of a social life (due to a high study load and the fact he lived in a rural area with no LGBTIQ community). He said, 'I'm happier than I ever remember being in my life (since passing as male)'. Maddox (male/FtM/trans man, 21 years) had been diagnosed with anxiety and depression, but was careful not to make his pursuit of happiness dependent on gender milestones. 'I try not to allow myself to focus on the belief that I will be happier when… (Insert next stage of medical transition),' he explained. 'This can cause negative thinking that clouds the positive forward movement'. He pointed out that medical transition could be a long process, whilst 'life happens every day'.

For a few participants, it was possible that the original diagnoses they had received pre-transition were not a long-term mental illness, but only related to their gender identity issues. For example, Aid (socially male, 18 years) said that a doctor had tried to diagnose him with depression and anxiety, which Aid instead 'took as symptoms of gender dysphoria'. Four psychologists had subsequently worked with him and said he had no presenting mental illnesses since he had started to express his gender. 'I feel happy and settled now, and very rarely feel upset for long periods of time,' he said. However, for other people, diagnoses such as depression and anxiety remained after transition, arising instead in relation to other catalysts. For Gavin (male/FtM transgender, 23 years), who preferred not to be medicated, his depression was particularly bad before he came out, and he was constantly fatigued and would sleep for days. After seeing a psychologist regularly, and coming out as male to his family and girlfriend, he got better. But sometimes other factors caused him to be depressed such as being overworked, or stress about study. He found when that occurred 'the dysphoria hits me and then I go over the same pattern of my body just shutting down and needing to sleep 24/7 from depression'. Junk000 (male, 22 years) had been diagnosed with anxiety and mood dysregulation (which was possibly chemical), but said that 'neither have to do with my gender identity'. He was frustrated because his doctors 'only ever want to talk about that instead of the problems I want fixed', slowing his access to gender-related treatments. Several participants on the discussion board forum openly engaged with topics of mental health diagnoses, telling their stories and making gentle jokes about their own situations.

Transgender youth face particular risks compared even to transgender adults, and in part this relates to the way youth can be held back from being able to express their gender. Research in New Zealand (Clark *et al.*, 2014) found that gender diverse and transgender young people were almost four times as likely as cisgender young people to experience significant depressive symptoms (41% compared to 12%). Another study, funded by mental health organisation beyondblue, explored if this was also the case for transgender youth in Australia (Jones, Smith *et al.*, 2016; Smith *et al.*, 2014). Figure 2.2 brings together the data on the mental health conditions the youth felt they had, and those they had been diagnosed with. Stress was the most common mental health condition nominated by participants (48%) and the majority of these young people had spoken to a health professional about this (40%). Stress is a broad term that is used to describe mental or emotional strain and can be related to particular circumstances. The concept of minority stress is useful for examining the effects that socio-economic stressors, linked to social bias (such as difficulty finding work or housing), can have on individuals' levels of stress (Levitt & Ippolito, 2014). Participants were asked to explain what they thought would improve their mental health and some mentioned external circumstances such as 'to not be struggling to find housing and work at the very least' (Delta, girl/woman, 20 years). The study also showed 45 per cent of the group had been diagnosed with anxiety; this was significantly higher than the quarter of the general population who experience anxiety at some point in their lifetime (Smith *et al.*, 2014). The youth in this research were also more likely to report that they had depression.

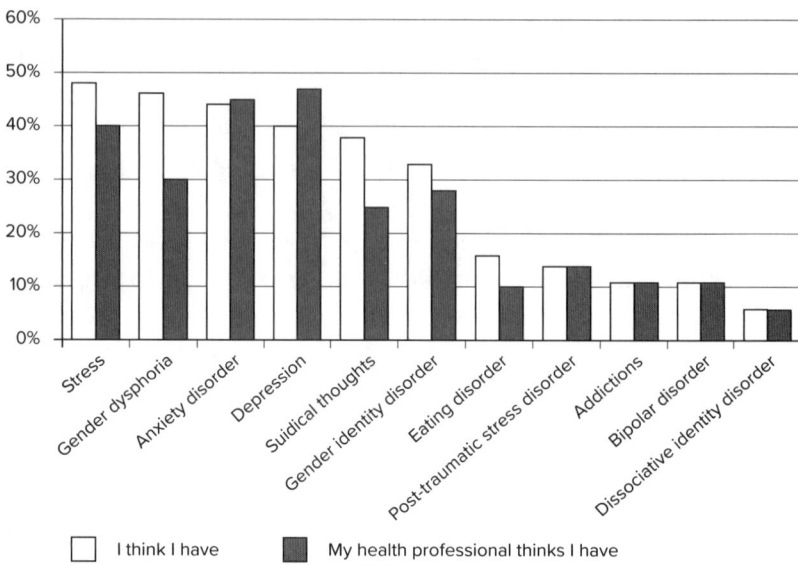

*Figure 2.2: Mental health conditions which transgender youth had according to their own perspective vs. mental health professionals' perspectives (n=189)*

There is a need for mental health workers to probe more deeply into the relationships between stress, anxiety, depression, substance use and gender dysphoria for transgender youth. Whilst we cannot pre-empt or presume the nature of these relationships – or even the existence of these relationships – for any single individual, mental health professionals need to understand that there may be a relationship and try to work with the young person to understand what (if anything) that is. Sometimes transgender youth have clinical depression and they are experiencing issues which are more readily mediated through medication than consideration of their needs around gender; sometimes transgender youth are experimenting with drugs because they are young and it is a local trend rather than because they are transgender, and sometimes several mental health issues (of stress, anxiety and depression) can be very directly related to the young person's gender dysphoria and only really mediated by its resolution. There is a danger in presuming the relationship between these factors, or a lack of one, incorrectly. This can lead to one or more of any of these issues going untreated for those transgender youth for whom they are relevant (and they are not relevant to all transgender youth). Mental health service professionals must treat each transgender young person as an individual who may or may not be impacted by these broader trends and mental health issues, and try to understand the particular nuances at play for the individual, so as best to treat or aid them.

## Self-harm, suicidality and contributing factors

Many studies reveal the alarming rates of suicide and self-harm risks that these populations face, and point to the need for positive strategies in mental health interventions and social/institutional provisions (Clark *et al.*, 2014; del Pozo de Bolger *et al.*, 2014; Grant *et al.*, 2011; Jones *et al.*, 2015; Veale *et al.*, 2017). A Canadian study found that transgender youth experienced increased reports of psychological distress, self-harm, major depressive episode, suicidal ideation, and suicide attempts compared to cisgender populations (Veale *et al.*, 2017). The study reflected broader international research highlighting that FtM transgender boys and non-binary youth were most likely to report self-harm and non-binary youth also reported lower overall mental health (Holt, Skagerberg & Dunsford, 2016; Veale *et al.*, 2017). The Canadian study also found that younger adolescents (those aged 14–18 years) were more likely to have considered or attempted self-harm and suicide than older adolescents (aged 19–25 years). A New Zealand study of over 8000 high school students found that two fifths of the transgender students had significant depressive symptoms and had harmed themselves, and one in five had attempted suicide in the previous 12 months (Clark *et al.*, 2014).

In order to understand the ways to approach mental health interventions, we must first understand the contributing factors to self-harm and suicide for transgender youth. Data has shown that there are several factors particular to transgender youth which may contribute:

- personal issues in regards to being transgender/their gender identity
- transphobia, harassment, discrimination and/or abuse in key environments (home, school, public transport, the street)
- efforts to feel better about or 'correct' gender identity or body issues
- increased mental health issues which may or may not have a relationship to transgender status or experiences of transphobia (depression, anxiety, trauma, PTSD, etc.).

Other life events (grief over a loss, financial problems and so on) which may be contributors for other groups too can be an issue, but it is particularly important here to understand first the issues transgender youth may uniquely face. Most transgender people aged 16+ in an Australian study (81%) had thought about self-harm and for approximately 70 per cent, their personal issues in regards to their trans* identity were a catalyst (Jones, 2016a). More than half (58%) referred to other reasons including depression or specific incidents like poor surgery outcomes. One third (33%) cited transphobia as a contributing factor. A large portion (68%) had engaged in self-harm, and this was mostly attributed (70%) to their personal issues in regards to their trans* identity, followed by other issues in 60 per cent of the cases, such as body loathing. Finally, a quarter (26%) referred to experiences of transphobia as a contributing factor. Darkneko (FtM transgender, 21 years), for example, reflected that several factors contributed to his self-harm, ranging from depression and social anxiety, to childhood trauma. Most of the group (81%) had experienced suicidal ideation and in 68 per cent of the cases these thoughts were linked to their personal issues in regards to their trans* identity. More than half of the group (56%) referred to other life events as a catalyst, and one third (33%) related their suicidal ideation to transphobia. Finally, more than one third of the participants (35%) had attempted suicide and for 76 per cent these attempts were related to their personal issues in regards to their trans* identity. Half (53%) cited other life events and one third (32%) referred to transphobia experiences as a contributing factor.

Another Australian study of transgender youth aged 14–25 years asked participants if they had experienced any of four negative health outcomes (thoughts about self-harm, self-harm, suicidal thoughts and suicide attempts) specifically due to harassment, discrimination and/or abuse (Jones, Smith *et al.*, 2016; Smith *et al.*, 2014). One hundred and twenty-eight participants (68%) answered these questions, all of whom had experienced abuse, or harassment, of some kind. Figure 2.3 collates the data, which shows that in total 81 per cent of transgender youth who had experienced abuse and/or discrimination due to their gender expression had thought about suicide and 37 per cent had made suicide attempts (Jones, Smith *et al.*, 2016; Smith *et al.*, 2014). Further, 80 per cent of this same cohort had thought about self-harm and 70 per cent had harmed themselves. In a separate question, the young people were asked if they self-harmed in order to feel better: 36 per cent of transgender youth told the researchers that they felt at least somewhat better to completely better for having engaged in self-harm. Around 4 per cent felt about the same and 11 per cent felt worse.

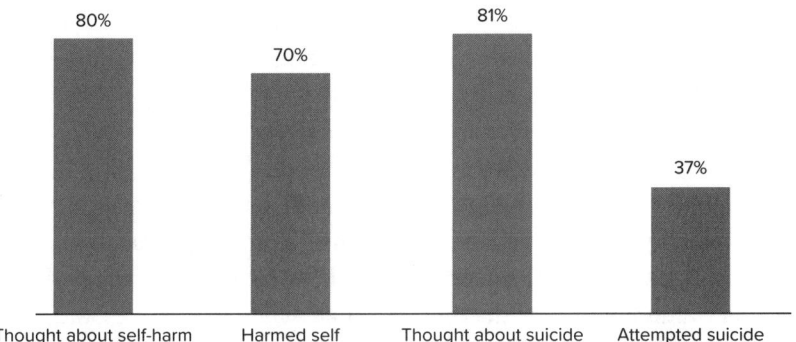

*Figure 2.3: Transgender youth (n=128) self-harm and suicide ideation and attempts on the basis of abuse, harassment or discrimination*

Over fifty young people provided qualitative text about their suicidal thoughts and attempts, and experiences of self-harm thoughts and behaviours. For some of the young people, these were related to their struggles with gender identity. For example, one boy/man (19 years), responded, 'What's to tell, if I could have cut off the offending parts I would have'; and another boy/man (21 years) told us, 'At 13, I tried to stop the feminisation of my chest by burning it with a lighter. I don't actually classify this as self-harm, because the aim wasn't to hurt myself; it was to fix what I perceived as a legitimate physical defect.' Other young people explained that they did not think that their suicidality and self-harm thoughts and behaviours were linked to their gender identity; a gender-fluid young person (24 years), attributed this to 'anxiety and PTSD [rather] than distress over my gender identity and expression'.

Resilience or mediating factors around suicide also emerged in some of the responses. One girl/woman (21 years) described how family support had made a difference to her suicidality: 'I used to think a lot about suicide, but since my mother and father started supporting me I've not thought of suicide in a long time.' Whilst support from family and friends made a positive impact on the young people, non-supportive and, sometimes, abusive parental behaviour increased self-harm thoughts and behaviours, such as one genderqueer young person (23 years) who explained the emotional and verbal abuse that they experienced from their family:

> I experienced very severe emotional abuse at home, including my father suggesting I should kill myself if things got too hard. During these times I was very suicidal, and often had the urge to self-harm, especially to cut myself, although another part of me didn't want to and I didn't. I used to hit myself though.

For other young people, suicidality and self-harm thoughts and behaviours were lessened by social and/or medical transition such as one young FtM transgender teen (16 years) who explained that he had 'attempted suicide the first time when I was 12, and have felt suicidal on and off for the years since. I have been a bit better recently, since I have fully transitioned socially.' Another young trans man who participated in an interview, Kenny (22 years), explained how thoughts about society and broader political trends affected how he felt about the future:

> More so during high school days, I've done a lot in the past few years that has developed me into a resilient adult and it takes a lot more to bring me down to feel suicidal but sometimes it happens when I see no options about how society is going to improve when we have capitalist governments, fascists and religious bigots in the world.

Bohdi (boy/man, 22 years) explained that engaging in self-harm or suicide attempts in some moments did not mean he felt suicidal in other moments, and cutting was not only a communication to both himself and others about his variable feelings, but a coping mechanism:

> I liked cutting myself because it fulfilled a lot of needs I have. ... It was a social badge to communicate the situation I was in. It made me feel like I had control over my will, and that I was powerful. Finally, in the initial painful cut and bolt of brain chemicals in

response, it cleared my head of muggy upset feelings (which were often clouding my ability to think even further than 'I want to die' and lying on the ground) and allowed me to reconnect with reality, recover, and get on with my life. I have stopped self-harming, though, in order to move my transition on easier. Since I always made the decision to do it, and made sure I had good reason to, it wasn't a problem to simply make the decision not to do it – it's just a bit harder to get through things, and I miss it.

## Protective factors, activism and knowledge

Whilst some transgender youth have seen self-harm as a way of coping with gender issues or expressing themselves, there are many other ways of coping with gender issues and expressing themselves that they can adopt which are less dangerous. These methods need to be promoted to transgender youth and their guardians by mental health professionals. Research-supported options for transgender youth to protect themselves around gender dysphoria and to express themselves include:

- engaging with supportive parents/families/guardians
- building support information and networks
- engaging in creative self-comforting
- engaging in gender affirmations of varying kinds
- engaging in activism against transphobia, cissexism or cis-normativity.

These options are discussed in the following subsections.

### Protecting and expressing self with parents/families/guardians

Parents and families play a vital role in fostering the wellbeing of gender diverse and transgender young people (Lindner, 2014). Social affirmation of the child's gender from a loved one can be a deeply therapeutic and life-changing experience. It will not make the child more likely to be or to stay transgender – mental health practitioners can reassure parents that nothing they have done (divorce, being absent, being strong or weak, supportive or cruel) has indirectly contributed to their child being transgender (Brill & Pepper, 2008). Conversely, family rejection does increase the risk of suicide and poor mental health of these young people (Grossman *et al.*, 2005).

Parental support was a clear protective factor for transgender youth in the beyondblue-funded study (Smith *et al.*, 2014). Transgender youth whose parents or carers were supportive (63%) fared better on a number of indicators than those whose parents or carers were not supportive (33%). For example, young people who had parental/guardian support were:

- less likely to have experienced harassment or abuse in the home (15% compared to 40%)

- half as likely to feel that they had depression (30% compared to 60%)

- half as likely to have had suicidal thoughts (30% compared to 58%)

- twice as likely to see a health professional if they did have suicidal thoughts (32% compared to 16%).

One young boy/man (18 years) explained that, 'my parents are not supportive… I'm no longer part of the family' and a trans girl (14 years) explained that her father, 'tries to say my feelings don't exist'. One genderqueer youth (22 years) discussed the support that they receive from their father:

> There's a forest right near my house where I walk and I like to go with my dad to vent. Being able to talk to him and being in such a nice place always helps.

This young person had the support and protection of a parent, and a special and private place to express themselves to that parent, that made them feel better. Mental health professionals should try to offer this space to young people as well, and should try to understand whether other adults in the lives of transgender youth can similarly offer some kind of support or safety (especially where parental support is absent), or some opportunities for expression, not only as mediating factors against negative wellbeing outcomes, but because all youth deserve the chance to feel affirmed and heard.

## Protecting and expressing self via building support information and networks

Transgender youth can feel disconnected from peer support and education relating to their particular needs in ways which limit their ability to protect themselves and enjoy self-expression. Building support information and networks can be a way to both protect oneself as a transgender youth, and to express oneself or one's gender identity. The Internet has helped to correct the invisibility transgender youth can feel, for example, 98 per cent of transgender youth found websites to be an important source of information (Smith *et al.*, 2014). More than just a virtual space, the Internet is also a conduit for real-time and face-to-face support and connection in a world that can be hostile to those who do not fit societal gender-norms. Transgender youth also cited the importance of blogs (88%), YouTube (87%) and social media (83%) as specific sources for information and support. Research, as a source of information and knowledge, was nominated by 91 per cent of transgender youth and this could be due to their desire to find out about medical transition and medical technologies. One young man (21 years) explained, 'Research – I keep an eye on for technological medical advances in the field of surgery.' Furthermore, social research may be used for activist efforts with schools and governments, and provides access to the youth voices and stories and experiences they can learn from.

Casey (transgender girl/woman, 18 years) explained that she came to accept herself as a transgender girl through viewing websites, blogs and YouTube videos on the subject: 'This is where the majority of my education on the overall issues and theory of transgender people's existence came from.' The practical aspects of transition were explained to her mostly by the Internet, and some support groups and individuals helped. One androgynous young person (17 years) explained how Tumblr provided inspiration for learning more: 'I joined Tumblr and due to many of the members' acceptance and knowledge of sexuality and gender I was inspired to begin researching and understanding.'

Over half (57%, n=95) of transgender youth found support services to be important sources of information and support. Many reiterated the need for face-to-face contact and the role that these support services and online communities can play in fostering community that spreads into friendship and families-of-choice. One androgynous young person (17 years) explained, 'Minus18 events give me a sense of community, so do the friends I have made on tumblr (and often meet irl [in real life]).' Crisis-lines, community-building events, inclusive health services, and supportive individual psychologists were all nominated as particularly good supports. For young people who lived in rural geographies, community centres and support groups in their towns were important, along with the anonymity of online communities. One interview participant, Charlotte (trans woman, 21 years) explained a support service was the first 'to address me as "her" and "she". It was a surprise and initially the warmth, love and openness definitely had a profoundly euphoric effect on me'.

### Protecting and expressing self via creative self-comforting

The beyondblue study asked transgender youth to indicate which activities made them feel better, and what made them feel worse (Jones, Smith et al., 2016). Transgender youth showed they protect and express themselves through many creative strategies to self-comfort (see Figure 2.4). Finding ways to deal with emotions as they were happening was important for many participants and, as one example, music was nominated as a useful way to shift thoughts/feelings or express them; 98 per cent of transgender youth reported that they felt at least a bit better after listening to music. One trans* young person (25 years) explained, 'listening to music helps me let out my emotions, so first I might be more down, but then I am more up' and a transgender woman (21 years) explained, 'fast quick happy music also helps cheer me up'. Spending time with friends helped 77 per cent of the participants to feel better. One young boy/man (17 years) said 'supportive friends who know everything' about him, help him to see that he 'shouldn't be feeling down about something because it's just a little bit silly'.

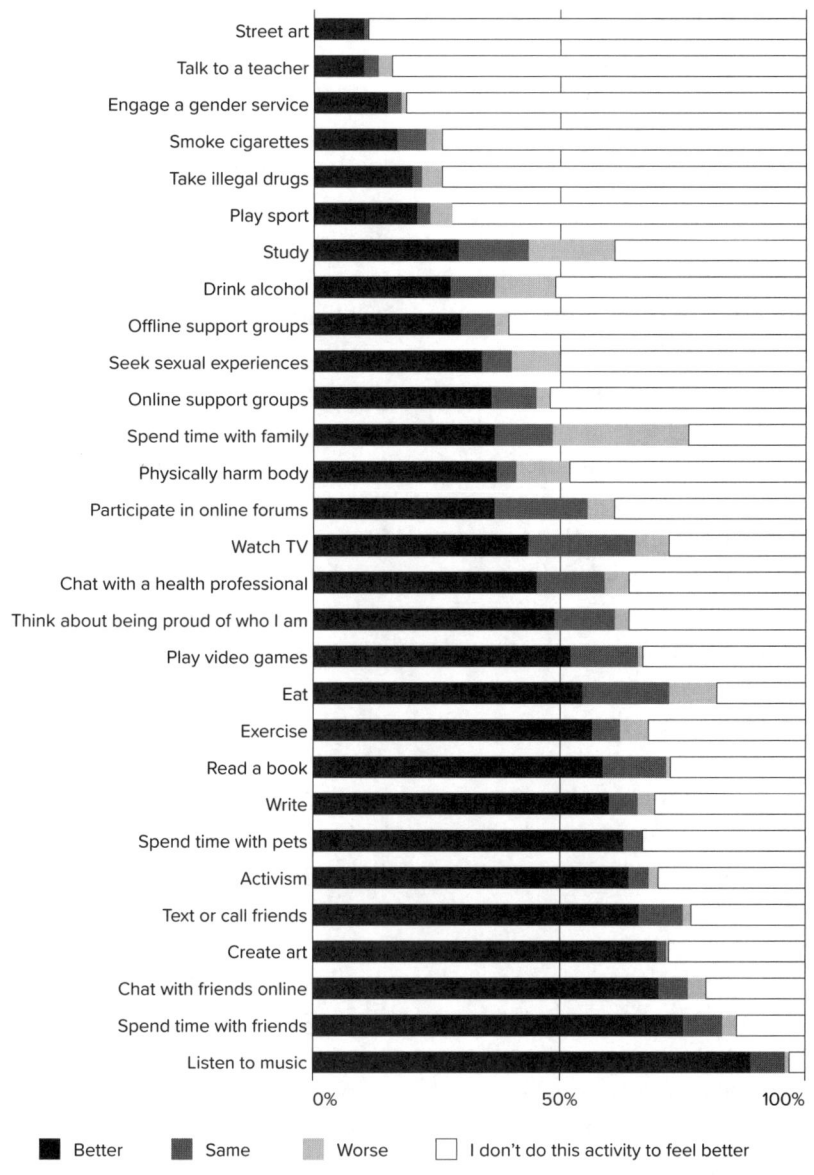

*Figure 2.4: Transgender youth's use of activities to self-comfort when they feel sad*

## Protecting and expressing self via gender affirmation

A recent UK study explored the process of transitioning (social or medical) and how this impacts mental health (McNeil *et al.*, 2012). Using 889 participants across England, Scotland, Wales and Ireland aged over 18 years, their findings demonstrated that 90 per cent of participants had been told that transgender people were not normal and 84 per cent had thought of suicide, with at least 35 per cent attempting it. Yet once someone had medically transitioned, there were significant increases in social and mental satisfaction; findings echoed in other research discussed already in this chapter (Jones *et al.*, 2015; Smith *et al.*, 2014). Part of a gender affirmation involves the individual coming to accept their gender expression incongruence with the sex allocated to them at birth, their gender identity incongruence with the sex allocated to them at birth or outright transgender status of some kind – therapy may support youth as they move further along the paths they have taken in self-acceptance. The individual feeling this self-acceptance is in itself a protective factor in relation to self-harm and suicidality; sometimes even without anything happening external to their acceptance (Jones *et al.*, 2015).

However, gender affirmations can also involve changes to clothing, hairstyles, play or activities. They can have social elements, involving other people being told about or witnessing the gender of the youth in some way or perhaps being directed to use the young person's pronouns (he, she, they) and include them in gendered groupings/ events. The affirmations can be legal or institutional, involving updates to recognition of the transgender youth's gender in paperwork or documentation at school, for example. Or gender affirmations may be medical, involving a range of potential hormonal or surgical options (which not all transgender youth necessarily desire, or desire in the same combinations). Gender affirmations – even medical ones such as taking 'puberty blockers' – do not need to initially involve permanent changes for young people trying to cope with negative emotions or express themselves in an urgent way. It can be as simple as trying certain shoes, hair options and so on. Gender affirmations are discussed in more detail in the chapter on health, but need to be seriously considered here for their protective impact on mental health and the opportunities they provide for self-expression. Mental health professionals should keep the young person's goals and concerns about matters such as privacy at the centre of any gender affirmation plans they discuss together, and should be willing to advocate for the young persons' needs in institutional or medical contexts when necessary or relevant to their level of expertise/role.

## Protecting and expressing self via activism

Finally, transgender youth can contribute to their own protection and self-expression through activism. Previous research has found that transgender youth are more likely to be involved in activism (27%) than their cisgender same sex attracted peers (12%) (Hillier *et al.*, 2010). One reason for this increased engagement in activism may be the higher levels of marginalisation these young people face (Jones & Hillier, 2013). Figure 2.5 shows the ways in which the majority (91%, n=172) of participants in the beyondblue study had taken part in at least one activism activity (Jones, Smith *et al.*, 2016). Further, 62 per cent reported that they became involved in activism as a place they could be heard and feel better. One transgender young person (23 years) described how, 'I feel proactive, and that my voice is valued and worthwhile.' A 17-year-old explained that activism 'lifts my spirits greatly and allows me to feel like a stronger and a better person'.

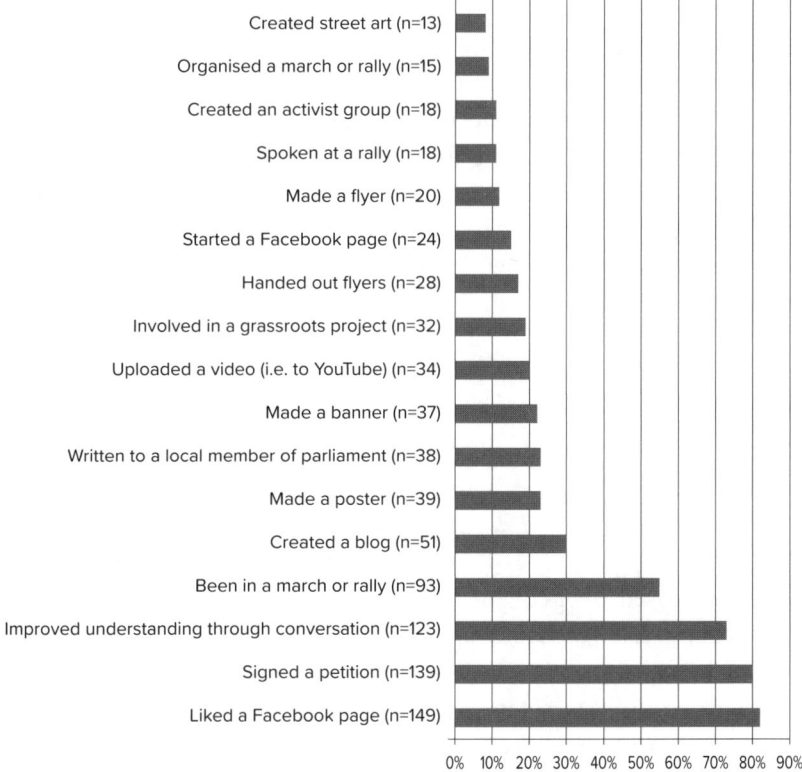

*Figure 2.5: Transgender youth's activism on gender diverse, trans\*, intersex or LGBTIQ issues*

Over half (60%) of transgender youth felt better about their gender identity, had fun (57%) and felt part of a community (55%) when they participated in activism. Around a third reported that it eased depression, and that it prevented a suicide attempt. Activism did not have to be arduous or require elaborate skills sets – some was easily done online without leaving one's own room. The participants were most likely to have 'liked' a Facebook page or other social media site, for example, (83%), signed a petition (80%), improved understanding through conversation (73%), or been part of a march or rally (55%). Significant numbers had even spoken at a march/rally (11%), or contributed to the organisation of a march/rally (9%). Additionally 30 per cent had created a blog and 20 per cent had uploaded a video to the Internet. Further, 22 per cent had written to a local member of parliament. Youth could engage in anonymous online activism under the gendered identities of their choice in safe ways which were not reflected in real lives before (or in place of) committing to more exposing types of activities. These options still gave many transgender youth a way to feel they had protected themselves from the gender dysphoria or negative feelings or discrimination they can be subject to, and had given them a positive form of self-expression, that stood in sharp contrast to engaging in methods like self-harm. Mental health professionals can discuss the full range of options of engaging with family support, building other support and information, using creative self-comfort, exploring gender affirmation and trying activism with transgender youth when planning to help build resilience.

## Missing or avoiding mental health services

Despite high levels of depression, research has also found that transgender people have a reluctance to seek mental health advice and assistance (Clark *et al.*, 2017; Jones *et al.*, 2015; McNeil *et al.*, 2012; Smith *et al.*, 2014). A Canadian study of 923 youth, ages 14–25, showed 68 per cent of transgender youth aged 14–18 years and around half of those aged 19–25 years had forgone needed mental health in the last year (Clark *et al.*, 2017). However, this is a complicated finding, since an Australian study of transgender people aged 16+ investigated the value of gender clinics and related services in assisting in understanding one's gender identity, and the ways visits to such services can be mandated in some countries (Jones *et al.*, 2015).

There was a strong message from the data that there was *a distinct lack of gender identity clinics, or related experts and services, by comparison to need.* Many participants had never had access to gender clinics through which to discuss or understand gender identity issues. These participants often reported a lack of readily available information at the beginning of their transition journey; so whether transgender youth actively avoided mental health services or could not seek them, access to mental health support was an issue even in countries like Australia where access was required for gender affirmations. For instance, Conor (male, queer, trans*, person of colour, 24 years) said he had no engagement whatsoever with services of any kind. Darkneko (FtM transgender, 21 years) said, 'There are no gender identity clinics operating in my area'; and Junk000 (male, 22 years) even asked the researchers, 'What is a gender identity clinic? I got my information through a queer youth group which included gender questioning support.' There was a strong sense that unless one lived in the right area (particularly inner-city areas in supportive countries), one's access to gender identity clinics would be problematic.

Overall 77 per cent of transgender youth in the beyondblue study nominated at least one reason why they have not consulted mental health professionals at one time or another (Smith *et al.*, 2014). Many young people felt that a professional wouldn't be able to do anything for them (34%) and that they wouldn't be understood (33%). A few participants thought that they could 'fix' themselves, such as one participant (22 years) who explained, 'I will fix it myself because they can't understand exactly.' Parents were also an obstruction to professional mental health care for 28 per cent of the participants, who had avoided seeking professional help for mental health issues due to concern that their parents would find out. In the case of one 16-year-old, their parent denied them the money to seek professional help because they did not think that they were in need of it. Bad past experiences with health professionals had prevented some (30%) from seeking mental health care. The young people described negative experiences that they had had with mental health professionals which included the language that they used, not feeling validated or listened to, and deliberately and consistently being mis-gendered (i.e. the use of the wrong pronoun or name).

Transgender people aged 16+ were asked about the types of mental health services they had accessed alone or with parents and guardians, and why, and their experiences using them (Jones *et al.*, 2015). The types of mental health services the participants had used included psychologists, psychiatrists, counselling through sexual health organisations or mental health organisations, gender identity experts, special queer youth counsellors and emergency hotlines. Their motivations for using these services ranged from being 'purely for the purposes of paperwork' and diagnosis steps towards starting their transition or specific surgeries, through to dealing with long-term issues in depth. Some sought help in understanding their gender, learning coping skills, or strategising around how to come out to people and how to best deal with their reactions. There were also specific times of crisis, when a participant would seek assistance because they were severely depressed, and in such cases the hotlines were mentioned as the most immediately accessible and helpful service. For many, using mental health services for their gender issues or their mental health needs many times over was not optional, but a necessary requirement for a transition they wished to pursue. This put them in a vulnerable position, as regardless of the quality of services they might need to use them several times over if access to alternatives was limited in their area.

Most (66%) transgender youth in the beyondblue study had seen a mental health professional in the previous 12 months (Smith *et al.*, 2014). Of those transgender youth 60 per cent were mostly or very satisfied with their experiences, 17 per cent were neither satisfied nor unsatisfied, and 15 per cent were mostly or very dissatisfied. However, a satisfactory experience for one individual may be unsatisfactory for another. For example, an individual may feel that the experience was satisfactory because they received what they went to the mental health professional for (i.e. medication, or approval for hormones), whereas another individual may feel dissatisfied with the experience due to the way that the mental health professional responded to them. The participants across the studies reported mixed experiences in their contact with mental health services (Jones *et al.*, 2015; Smith *et al.*, 2014). Generally, the services which specialised in gender identity were more useful than the mainstream services. A recurrent topic was the cost of psychiatrist services, and this was prohibitive for almost a third of the young people (32%). Turbogroove (genderqueer, 25 years) had been seeing a psychiatrist for some years, and said, 'He hasn't helped me at all and I can barely afford him.' As one young boy/man (24 years) described, 'It feels like a slap in the face when you see their BMWs parked out the front.' Fang (FtM transgender, 29 years) reflected that disclosing personal gender issues to a stranger 'is a HUGE deal', and that when his professional called him too pretty to transition, to 'be brushed off like that is just fucking bullshit'.

## Helpful mental health professionals

Experienced, affirming gender-focused providers with *streamlined processes, high knowledge and ongoing support* were the most valued (Jones *et al.*, 2015). Those who focused specifically on youth issues, coping skills and advice around the social realities of gender diversity were particularly saluted. Transgender youth have discussed other factors common to best-practice mental health professionals (Smith *et al.*, 2014):

- *Knowledgeable about transgender issues.* Transgender youth had better mental health care experiences when the professional was knowledgeable about gender diverse and transgender health care. One genderqueer young person (20 years) explained that they felt lucky because they had found a 'wonderful psychologist who is a passionate feminist and is very empathetic and also extremely knowledgeable on gender and/or sexuality issues'. Another genderqueer young person (23 years) said their university provided access to a 'queer counsellor' and that, 'it is the first time I have ever had queer-specific mental health services accessible to me, and I am finding them very helpful'. For another young person (18 years), having a therapist who is 'understanding, accepting, competent and helpful' stood out from other mental health professionals, who may only focus on the mental condition, instead of the whole person.

- *Comprehends gender diverse identities.* For young people who identify as gender diverse, finding health professionals who are knowledgeable about the dynamic spectrum of gender identities may be even more difficult. However, given the rise in rates of young people who are identifying with these diverse genders, it is important that professionals are equipped to provide care that takes these identities into account.

The lack of understanding about this diversity is illustrated in the experience of one survey participant (Smith *et al.*, 2014) who said that 'with surprise and a sense of intrigue' their mental health practitioner declared, 'You don't seem really like you have GID (i.e. you don't 100% strongly and consistently identify with the gender opposite to your sex at birth), it's sort of like you're gender-bisexual!' An androgynous young person (16 years) described an experience where the mental health professional 'didn't seem to know what they were doing, had never heard of non-binary sex, and kept doubting what I said'.

- *Does not make transgender youth 'the educator'.* Transgender youth often find themselves in the position of educating the mental health professional and this was raised by many of the young people in this research. One transgender youth (20 years) said, 'for the most part I felt as if I were educating them on the issue.' Chloe (transgender girl/woman, 18 years) commented that her psychiatrist asked 'intrusive, pointed questions in irrelevant areas (mostly about crossdressing; I've never done it)'. Harry (FtM transgender, 24 years) had worked with a psychiatrist who specialised in gender identity: 'They have been great. The process has been very simple and they are very knowledgeable *and welcoming.*' Seeking training and doing self-learning (reading), and having a specialist service for transgender mental health care may help to fill this gap.

- *Does not link being transgender to being abused.* Transgender youth negated those mental health professionals who linked past childhood experiences of sexual abuse with being transgender now. One trans girl/woman (21 years) described an experience where a mental health professional was insisting on fitting this young woman's experiences into a framework of past childhood trauma: 'He said he didn't believe in trans problems and that they most likely stemmed from childhood trauma. (…) I never went back.'

- *Asks for and follows stated gender.* Transgender youth much preferred mental health professionals who asked their pronouns or gender identity and then simply used that information to refer to them from then on. One young man/boy (15 years) struggled not to speak out when people did *not* use his pronouns, 'I bit my tongue, because it's the frigging coordinator of my medical transition.' He said that next time he would try to say something 'because messing up my pronouns and gender, and just failing to grasp any of the problems a transgender teenager might experience is pretty bad when it's what I'm there to see her for.'

## Combatting cisnormativity and cissexism in mental health services

Despite the many issues which can prevent transgender youth from seeking help from mental health professionals, they were around twice as likely as same sex attracted students to have disclosed their diverse identity to their mental health professionals/counsellors once contact was made (Jones & Hillier, 2013). Transgender youth are reaching out to the mental health practitioners they do see, and as individuals they need to be met with appropriately affirming responses. However, an individualistic approach to evidence-based practice within mental health services – including clinical psychology, counselling and other types – primarily relies upon a positivist interpretation of the world which fails to recognise the impact of social contexts (Riggs, 2011). Yet research has repeatedly shown how social contexts play a significant role in producing negative mental health outcomes for transgender youth (Haas *et al.*, 2011; Jones, 2017a; Jones *et al.*, 2015; Jones & Hillier, 2013; Smith *et al.*, 2014). Mental health services can fail to take into account the contexts in which evidence is produced about transgender youth lives and the broader social context in which the discipline sits – even its foundation upon particular neo-liberal forms of white heteropatriarchy (Jones & Lasser, 2017; Riggs, 2011). A wider range of methodologies and clinical approaches are needed, alongside an approach treating as evidence the fact of social marginalisation (Baum, 2007).

Thus, evidence-based practice requires as its starting place recognition of the fact that the evidence we have about, for example, transphobic hate crimes, constitutes an evidence base upon which to develop practice responses. Cisnormativity – the set of social norms based upon the assumption one's gender identity and expression will be congruent with one's sex marker as allocated at birth; and cissexism – the bias against those who are transgender and/or not cisgender, are significant, if not the key variables for engaging with transgender youth in mental health service settings (Jones & Lasser, 2017; Riggs, 2011). Riggs argues for an alternate 'Queering' account of evidence, where the fact of social norms is taken as the evidence base and where practitioners actively strive to examine power in the clinical or counselling setting and in the lives of clients (Riggs, 2011). It is important to acknowledge, thus, the evidence of:

- how gender norms are so structurally and repetitively ingrained into society – and to children from their infancy – that any individual will struggle to recognise the ways they do not fit or actively disrupt them because it means they may be treated as 'different' or 'less than' (Butler, 1990; Grossman & D'Augelli, 2006)

- how hate crimes against young transgender youth like Larry/Latecia King and media denigration against transgender people make it difficult not only to declare a transgender status but to even work with transgender youth and support them to continue declaring that status in many settings (Jones, 2016b, 2017b)

- how cisnormativity and transphobia formed part of the original bedrock of psychology and other disciplines feeding into mental health services such that even today where it is recognised more broadly that the field has much to learn, this must be proactively challenged by professionals in mental health fields and settings through professionals creating and following new practice ideals for which there are few pre-existing models (Drescher & Byne, 2012; Jones & Lasser, 2017).

Building on work in the field of narrative therapy in productive ways, Riggs (2011) argues for an approach to mental health service provision and counselling in relation to issues of gender and identity that:

1. recognises the operations of top-down power both within the counselling space and in the world more broadly.
2. understands individuals as a 'fold' of the social.
3. holds practitioners to account for the evidentiary claims that we make.

Damien Riggs (2011, pp.92–93) discussed how he held himself accountable in a case study of his counselling practice with one young transgender girl, Amy, and her mother Kathleen:

> Kathleen was clear throughout that she accepted her daughter's gender identity, but reported that she had considerable fears about Amy's future. We spoke at length over ongoing sessions about gender identity and expression, and worked on an understanding of gender that uncoupled it from bodies. This of course did not mean that we ignored the pragmatics of possible future sex reassignment surgery or the soon-to-come effects of puberty upon her child. Rather, we spoke about an understanding of her daughter as being a 'girl with a penis', and that this was a valid gender identity that was experienced as a core belief by her child. This was an instance where it was important for me as a practitioner to speak from a position of relative knowledge in a top-down fashion. To do otherwise would have been to fail to potentially meet the needs of the child to be supported, and to work with her mother to meet these needs. At the same time, however, there were often times when I was called upon as a fiand of authority to legitimate Kathleen's thoughts or to provide witness to the 'realness' of her child as a daughter. In these instances, I was critical of the 'expert practitioner' position, and instead encouraged Kathleen to reflect upon Amy's clear claims to a gender identity as a girl. ... We also spoke at length about my role as an 'expert witness' in the future, and that playing such a role would be undertaken pragmatically to meet the needs of Amy as they arise, rather than perpetuating the idea that my knowledge as a practitioner should automatically be privileged above those of Amy and her family. ...my intent was to recognise that such top-down authority must always be accountable – that my ability to speak for Amy and her family in the future (i.e. to other professionals) must always be contingent upon recognition of the reasons why this may be necessary (i.e. existing social norms that perpetuate topdown authority through the privileging of 'professional' over 'lay' knowledges).

## Providing mental health services in schools

An Australian survey found that more younger transgender respondents (14–17 years) were provided with trans-inclusive counselling at school (67%; compared with 37% for 18–21 years, and 22% for 22–25 years) (Jones, Smith *et al.*, 2016) – possibly a result of improved psychology guidelines (Drescher & Byne, 2012). Mental health support provision in school or institutional settings for transgender youth has three 'tiers' (Jones & Lasser, 2017): the universal, targeted and individual levels.

### Tier I – Universal level

Prior to developing universal-level (Tier I) supports, school psychologists may begin with an assessment of a school's climate for transgender youth (Jones & Lasser, 2017; Lasser & Tharinger, 2003). A climate assessment involves the collection of data, both qualitative and quantitative, to determine the degree to which the school environment promotes and/or inhibits the positive development of transgender youth. Such an assessment may provide valuable information about student and staff attitudes towards transgender youth, levels of acceptance, recent history of harassment and current support systems in place. This climate assessment will provide school psychologists with a baseline and help identify areas that need improvement. For example, assessment data may indicate that school events and policies are generally heterocentric (i.e. assuming that all students are heterosexual), an observation that can lead to changes at the universal level by implementing more inclusive language and practices. Other school psychologist roles at Tier I include promoting the use of inclusive language and activities, implementing programmes to prevent bullying and harassment of transgender youth, and designating student resource offices as 'safe spaces' for transgender youth (Alvarez *et al.*, 2013; Fisher, 2014).

### Tier II – Targeted level

At the targeted level (Tier II), the role of the school psychologist serving transgender youth turns from prevention to intervention, assisting students and their families with supports that facilitate positive and healthy adjustments and transitions (Jones & Lasser, 2017). School psychologists recognise that services provided at Tier I will not meet the needs of all students and develop targeted interventions to support those with mild to moderate needs through Tier II activities such as group counselling, psycho-educational interventions and collaborative problem solving. School psychologists may need to establish and articulate clear criteria to differentiate those students whose needs are met with Tier I supports from those who have needs that will be addressed by Tier II interventions. The focus at this level may be the promotion of wellbeing through support groups, consultation with parents and teachers, family–school partnering activity and the bridging of community and school resources.

### Tier III – Individual level

Tier III services are reserved for those students who continue to need support after Tier II interventions. The role of the school psychologist at this level is to provide services and supports that are tailored to the unique presenting challenges of the student in need (Jones & Lasser, 2017). Fisher (2014) notes that, at Tier III, the school psychologist may provide individual counselling to address concerns related to a student's transgender youth, or perhaps other issues that may be impacted by one's transgender youth, but should not assume that a student's transgender youth is central to the counselling referral. When working individually with students, the school psychologist's role should be affirmative and supportive of sexual minority youth. When appropriate, the school psychologist will often address the need to support healthy identity development and coming out, or visibility management (Lasser & Tharinger, 2003). Moreover, school psychologists are sensitive to the well-documented risk of suicide for transgender youth and should work to reduce risk through prevention and intervention.

## Ethics and training

The International School Psychology Association (ISPA) states in its code of ethics that mental health professionals should acknowledge differences 'associated with age, gender, gender identity, race, ethnicity, culture, national origin, religion, sexual orientation, disability, language, or socioeconomic status' (2011, p.2). Moreover, ISPA states that mental health service professionals 'do not engage in discriminatory procedures or practices based on "the categories listed above"' (p.2). With such a strong ethical imperative to acknowledge, support and promote fairness for transgender youth, it follows that mental health professionals and especially school psychologists have an obligation to provide training that addresses professional relationships, responsibilities, competencies and practices; training in school psychology often falls short (Hillier et al., 2010). This may be addressed by integrating content in graduate coursework and by working to provide graduate students with field-based experiences (e.g. practicum internship) working with transgender youth. Failure to do so may be damaging, wrongly suggesting these issues are marginal to mental health or are too controversial to address. Mental health professionals can contribute to their own personal and professional development by exploring their personal values and ideas around working with transgender youth. What would stop you, and how would you ensure that you personally are supported and empowered if faced with organisational barriers? You may look into opportunities for peer supervision or create a toolkit of evidence over time to understand your development needs.

## Conclusions and recommendations

The histories, data and case information presented in this chapter have offered insight into many approaches to psychology for transgender youth – ranging from those well past their use-by date, such as conversion therapies, through to those illustrating innovative world standard techniques, such as a tiered approach. The shifts in thinking about the psychology behind transgender identities, even quite recently in terms of new work on understanding gender dysphoria, offer dramatic and exciting potentials to develop mental health service provision. It is likely the future will bring further change as researchers begin to study best-practice approaches based on these new theoretical frames. However, given what we currently know, this chapter has emphasised the value of an awareness of social justice struggles, structural supports in schools and a multi-faceted approach to supporting transgender youth.

Many transgender youth explained what they would like to happen to improve their mental health, and detailed steps that they are taking to do so, for example, through searching for mental health professionals, using the Internet and affirming their genders socially or medically. Too many had experienced depression and other conditions or suicidal ideation and self-harm. However, youth were also agents of change within themselves and other people. They had much to give both themselves and others through their work promoting positive mental health to other transgender youth online or in-person, alone or in groups. Mental health professionals and services need:

- to train both pre-service and in-service mental health professionals about transgender youth

- to provide professional development training for mental health support staff (i.e. administration staff) on inclusive practice for transgender youth

- to access information about specialist services for transgender mental health care in order to make appropriate referrals when issues beyond their expertise arise

- to promote transgender youth-friendly health and social services as needed for gender affirmations or other services

- to address complaints about inappropriate behaviour towards transgender youth in an appropriate and timely manner

- to provide parents of transgender children with information about where they can seek information and support

- to discuss the full range of options for making transgender youth who are experiencing difficulties feel better with the young person and their guardians/other supporters – such as engaging with family support, building other support and information, using creative self-comfort, exploring gender affirmation and trying activism to help build their resilience and make them feel better

- to provide easily accessible support for these young people on multiple platforms including face-to-face and online

- to provide education and peer-led support for parents of transgender youth

- to create spaces where young people can bring their voices to the community in a safe manner

- to recognise the unique challenges experienced by transgender youth and that these needs and challenges are separate to those of cisgender lesbian, gay and bisexual individuals
- to facilitate opportunities for transgender youth to improve their resilience-building skills through sessions on researching access to support and information online, creative ways to self-comfort, and various forms of activism (including less personally exposing forms) which can help them to feel more empowered or connected.

# Chapter 3

# Transgender Youth, Physical Health and Physical Health Services

I woke up from an overdose attempt at 10 years old to see a nurse was taking a selfie with me in my hospital bed, without permission. She sent it to her friend and called them to discuss 'the suicidal tranny kid with long hair'. I was too young to understand that I had a right to complain about mistreatment. I just knew that she made me feel like my suicide attempt over really being a girl (the biggest crisis in my life) was a joke. (Betty, MtF transgender, 14 years)

I went to four GPs (doctors) until I found one that would listen to me . ... One GP said to me, 'Why would you want to change your gender, you're such a pretty girl'! Disclosing something so personal to a stranger is a HUGE deal, and to be brushed off like that is just fucking bullshit. (Fang, FtM transgender, 20 years)

Doctors in my area (censored) have little to no knowledge of trans healthcare. I am educating them and I am not comfortable with this. ... Good experiences has been welcoming doctors, one of which allows me to communicate via email so that I don't have to travel over two hours to see them. They are also assisting me to find a good local GP. Bad experiences have been doctors who just don't care, have no idea about trans healthcare and ask me to basically tell them what my medical plan should be. (Harry, FtM transgender, 24 years)

## KEY POINTS

- Transgender youth and their families may be wary of health professionals or alternately may mystify health professionals' abilities to 'fix' the transgender young person's problems in ways that can make health service fraught for all parties.

- The physical hormonal and surgical treatments available for transgender youth, and their availability to younger age groups, have increased and improved over time. Sterilisation practices which still exist in some countries are linked to a history of eugenics in Swedish policies, and stand in contrast to modern human rights stances.

- For many transgender youth a social transition is more affordable and manageable than a medical one, and those who do have medical transitions may privilege chest surgeries (especially FtM transgender youth) above other options. Most transgender youth expressed that these interventions had benefits to their wellbeing, even when surgical results were not optimal.

- A transgender body is not automatically an unhealthy one; transgender people can be Olympians, world class athletes and admired models. In the main, transgender people considered their physical health to have been good or very good in the past year.

- Some issues to consider for transgender youth include multiple fertility pathways, substance abuse, the mixed information on cancer risk around hormone therapies, and the temptations of black market treatments when gender affirmations are delayed.

- Health service providers had a lack of knowledge about transgender issues and need to understand that their ignorance or prejudice can lead transgender youth to avoid or delay necessary general health care, and avoid disclosing their transgender status.

- Health professionals are encouraged to seek self-education and professional training on transgender issues, communicate support for transgender youth through the general display of materials/symbols and a warm approach to any individuals, treat transgender youth as their gender identity and react to their bodies in a professional manner, and flexibly negotiate language use around anatomy with individuals.

Some of the most admired and fit bodies in the world – including those of athletes, models and glamorous actresses – belong to transgender people. This chapter provides detailed, research-focused and practically oriented consideration of physical health issues for transgender and gender diverse youth. It details historic treatment of physical health issues for transgender youth, and contemporary interventions and practices in the field – including social, legal and medical gender affirmation options. The satisfaction of transgender youth with their gender affirmations is considered, alongside their potential to live physically healthy lives based on statistical evidence. The chapter addresses issues of alcohol use, drug use and complications to cancer risk, and black market hormone use seen in transgender populations. It details issues with transgender youth having mixed or bad experiences with health services, and goes into detail about what constitutes helpful health professionals for transgender youth. It outlines the most important techniques for combatting cisnormativity and cissexism in health services and issues of ethics and training for professionals. Key approaches are listed for services and professionals in health.

## Historic physical health services: Dangerous experiments and Swedish sterilisations

Historically, many transgender youth lived in a chronic state of conflict between self-understanding and physical being, one in which there was a continual misalignment between others' perceptions of them and their internal self-perception of gender (Tishelman *et al.*, 2015). However, it is important to note that some lived their lives openly as their own internal gender identity in clothing, social role and employment; including in Native American, Indian and Polynesian societies for where there were various historic recognitions of gender diverse social or spiritual roles (Brill & Pepper, 2008). Other times, transgender people lived their lives in secret and it was not known that somebody who had integrated into the role of their gender identity and affirmed their gender socially, was indeed transgender (or other less savoury terms from the past), until after their death.

Early physical sex transition or reassignment procedures were pioneered in Europe for transgender people dealing with the 'sexual problem' of having to hide their bodies whilst living out their gender identities in Western societies where diversity was less embraced (Hirschfield, 1908). The early surgical efforts were incredibly dangerous for the patients, and were experimental in nature, however willingly the patients underwent the procedures. Patients had to accept not only being sterilised by the procedures (which originally were focused on removing or transplanting whole organs) but risks of excruciating pain and death. Magnus Hirschfield reportedly conducted a vaginoplasty for the first known transgender woman to undergo it (Dora Richter) in 1931 in Berlin, and a uterine transplant for his unnamed housekeeper (Hirschfield, 1908). He also supervised the removal of Lili Elbe's sex organs in Dresden during 1930–1931, although after four more subsequent operations that included an unsuccessful uterine transplant, her body rejected the uterus and these early experimental efforts resulted in her death.

In the early 1970s, Sweden became the first country in the world to allow transgender people to reassign their sex legally (H, 2017). However, as part of this change the country enforced a strict sterilisation policy on the grounds that such people were mentally ill and unfit to care for a child, within the nationwide eugenics programme which sought to ban mentally ill people from reproducing. The Swedish eugenics programme ended in 1976 after 42 years, but sterilisation remained a condition for sex reassignment until 2013, by which time it had already spread to many other countries across Europe, Asia-Pacific and other regions when they started tackling the recognition of transgender individuals in law. There are still many countries (Switzerland, Greece, and over a dozen mainly European countries) where sterilisation is enforced to this day, stemming from the old Swedish eugenics laws. The practice of forcing sterilisation contrasts against modern human rights perspectives (United Nations, 2012). International human rights laws support non-discrimination on the basis of gender identity and expression, and this means that views casting transgender people as less capable of rearing a child or deserving of medical sterilisation merely because of their diversity are now retrogressive, cruel and inappropriate for health professionals to promote.

## Contemporary physical health services: Hormonal, surgical and other options

The physical hormonal and surgical treatments available for transgender youth, and their availability to younger age groups, have increased and improved over time. Transgender people may now engage in gender affirmation (self-affirmation/transition) processes with any or all of internal, social, legal and institutional, and/or multiple medical elements. Transition is, however, still a *conditional* possibility for transgender youth around the world. To even socially transition in terms of pronoun use, a young person must have a level of tolerance, compliance or support from those around them. Legal transitions (on identity documents such as school records, passports and so on) can only occur in line with the laws of their country context. Further, with regard to buying clothing or accessing medical interventions, young people generally do not have their own money or access to transition services, health care or health insurance more broadly without government or parent/guardian aid. There can be age limits on access to hormone therapies or surgical interventions, puberty blockers and other aids (Jones, Smith *et al.*, 2016).

In some countries, costs for some or all medical transition interventions are covered by the government, including Canada (McHardie, 2016), Spain (Esteva de Antonio & Gómez-Gil, 2013) and the United Kingdom (Davies *et al.*, 2013). However, there are some countries where current coverage is uncertain or under threat due to issues of accessibility, changes in policy or administration or other complications. In South Africa transition care access is limited due to a lack of expertise, a lack of comprehensive transgender health care clinics and strong gatekeeping processes by psychiatrists and psychologists (Wilson *et al.*, 2014). In Thailand three quarters of *kathoeys* (trans women) may have access to hormones through non-prescription sources due to the low availability and expense of transgender health care clinics; only a third of *toms* (trans men) access testosterone due to a low supply in the country (Gooren *et al.*, 2015). Many American transgender youth continue to remain uninsured or are underinsured because of payers' refusal to cover medically necessary gender-affirming health care services such as hormone therapy and reconstructive surgeries (William & Kellan, 2017). The Affordable Care Act explicitly protecting health insurance for transgender youth is under threat under the Trump Administration, despite the fact that coverage refusal results in higher costs and poor health outcomes amongst transgender people (William & Kellan, 2017); changes reducing insurance in the US could also undermine transgender youths' health broadly. Research suggests health benefits of insurance coverage for gender-affirming care for transgender individuals actually far outweigh the costs; nevertheless many countries still do not provide coverage or access to medical transition interventions (Schaefer *et al.*, 2016; William & Kellan, 2017).

Physical health providers and professionals need to understand that physical or medical gender affirmations take many forms. Not all transgender youth will want to transition, indeed not all adults transition. A study of 273 transgender Australians aged 16+ showed non-surgical measures (such as binding one's chest or wearing prosthetics) for gender affirmation were the most common, and a strong majority of participants had used hormones (87%; Jones *et al.*, 2015). Most (73%) have had physical interventions and 70 per cent intend to have additional modifications – chest surgeries were the most popular type. Almost half of the participants spent between $1000 and $10,000AUD on this process, some who engaged in multiple surgeries, including complex bottom surgeries, spent over $100,000. The great majority (97%) expressed that these interventions have made a difference to their life and wellbeing, even when results were not optimal. In future, some New Zealand and US transgender health care advocates (Kondou, 2016; Schulz, 2018) wish to replace 'Diagnostic Models' using a diagnosis of 'gender dysphoria' as a pre-requisite to medical affirmation procedures with an 'Informed Consent Model'. If the latter model emerged; hormones would be prescribed in primary care after a GP assessment and basic laboratory tests, a consultation about the effects of treatment, and the young person signing a consent form stating they understand potential treatment risks and benefits:

> The basic premise is that the client – not the health professional – is the expert on their gender identity, and that the person's own goals regarding their transition should guide their care. It is a trans-affirmative, person-centred approach, where the practitioner recognises the client's basic right to self-determination and bodily autonomy. (Kondou, 2016, p.25)

## Social gender affirmation

Social transitioning involves affirming how one wishes to be perceived and treated, one's ideal social role (e.g. declaring one's gender identity and preferred pronouns, changing or affirming one's presentation and role, etc.). Physical health providers' options for supporting social affirmations and changes in gender expression include aiding transgender youth in:

- offline and online peer support resources, groups, or community organisations that provide avenues for social support and advocacy
- offline and online support resources for families and friends
- voice and communication therapy to help individuals develop verbal and non-verbal communication skills that facilitate comfort with their gender identity
- hair removal through electrolysis, laser treatment, or waxing
- healthier practices (such as at-home breaks) when breast binding or padding, genital tucking or penile prostheses, padding of hips or buttocks at ages of developmental readiness (World Professional Association for Transgender Health, 2011).

Most (77%) of the participants in an Australian study of transgender youth aged 14–25 years had been or were involved in this process, 7 per cent wanted to do so in the future, and 15 per cent did not want to (Jones, Smith *et al.*, 2016). For some survey participants, social transitioning mainly involved not conforming to gender norms: 'I don't wear make-up, I don't shave, I don't wear heels, I don't wear bras very often…and I feel I have a male persona, at least sometimes' (Spencer, gender questioning young person, 18 years). Draconem (FtM transgender, 24 years) wore a binder that cost about $60, and said, 'that's all I can afford right now'. He also had some new jeans from his dad for his birthday and clothes donated by other people and a $30 haircut. He was not completely satisfied with all elements of his social gender affirmation, but even this relatively small amount spent had made him more positive. Financial issues prevented him from getting a packer, hormone therapy or surgery.

## Legal gender affirmation

Legal transitioning involves having one's desired gender identity affirmed on official documents (e.g. birth certificate, licence or passport, etc.). Physical health providers' options for supporting legal affirmations will depend on context and requirements for sterilisation or surgical transition in some countries; where these are not requirements, options include aiding transgender youth in:

- changes in name on identity documents

- changes in gender marker on identity documents (World Professional Association for Transgender Health, 2011, p.10).

Only 11 per cent of 27,715 American transgender adults surveyed had all of their identity documents in the name and gender they preferred, whilst more than two thirds (68%) reported that none of their identity documents had the name and gender they preferred (James *et al.*, 2016). Of 169 Australian transgender youth (aged 14–25 years) surveyed who had key identity documents, 17 per cent had changed their birth certificate and driver's licence, only 13 per cent had changed their proof of age card and only 10 per cent had changed their passport (Jones, Smith *et al.*, 2016). Participants' stories suggested that their age and perceived inexperience impacted on opportunities to proceed with legal transitions such as changing their passport, despite over half (54%) of the survey participants wanting to do so. In another study of transgender youth aged 16+, most had changed some kind of document to reflect their identity. Many other participants intended to change one or more documents to reflect their name, a male sex or a neutral identity in the future. Aid (socially male, 18 years), found changing his documentation 'a hard and long process' and his efforts were often met with resistance – some government staff refused to do it.

## Medical gender affirmation

Medically transitioning contrastingly involves accessing medical, hormonal and/or surgical aids (e.g. using puberty blockers or hormone injections/pills/creams, getting 'top' or 'bottom' surgeries, etc.) to transform one's body and affirm one's gender. Treatment options include the following (adapted from World Professional Association for Transgender Health, 2011, p.10):

- Ensuring liaison with mental health professionals and teams to supply psychotherapy (individual, couple, family, or group) for purposes such as exploring gender identity, role and expression; addressing the negative impact of gender dysphoria and stigma on mental health; alleviating internalised transphobia; enhancing social and peer support; improving body image; or promoting resilience – this can occur immediately from the age of first presentation.

- Acknowledging and supporting changes in gender expression and role (which may involve living part time or full time in another gender role, consistent with one's gender identity) – in young children treatment is generally restricted to such social and psychological treatment.

- Hormone therapy to prevent puberty's impacts whilst awaiting further gender affirmation – the use of puberty blockers as a treatment is generally restricted to prepubescent transgender youth and may not be required by all youth.

- Hormone therapy to feminise the body (creates body fat redistribution; facial/body hair growth; decreased muscle mass/strength; softening of skin/decreased oiliness; decreased libido and decreased male sexual function; thinning of facial and body hair) or masculinise the body (creates skin oiliness/acne; facial/body hair growth; muscle mass/strength; body fat redistribution; cessation of menses; clitoral enlargement; vaginal atrophy; deepened voice) – this type of hormone therapy is generally restricted to adolescents from puberty onwards depending on the legal context, and may not be required by all youth.

- Surgery to change primary and/or secondary sex characteristics (e.g. breasts/chest, external and/or internal genitalia, facial features, body contouring) – there may be age limits depending on local context for different surgery types, and any of these surgeries may not be required.

The criteria for hormone therapy are: persistent, well-documented gender dysphoria; capacity to make a fully informed decision and to consent for treatment; age of majority in a given country and control of any significant medical or mental health concerns (World Professional Association for Transgender Health, 2011, p.34). The criteria for surgeries (genital and breast/chest surgical treatments) acknowledge that these are for some not elective but medically necessary treatments for gender dysphoria which should not be denied on the basis of HIV, Hepatitis C or B, for example; however, they are to be undertaken only after assessment of the patient by qualified mental health professionals, once there is written documentation that this assessment has occurred and that the person has met the criteria (World Professional Association for Transgender Health, 2011, pp.55–56). This is to ensure that mental health professionals, surgeons and patients share responsibility for the decision to make irreversible changes to the body. Patients should be made aware of all possible options, and all possible impacts and maintenance issues for their treatments. This includes discussing the potentially varied impacts of hormones on osteoporosis, energy levels and sex drive; the need for dilation treatments for vaginas for MtF transgender people and the need to watch for infections; the need to take care of chest scars for FtM transgender people and to consider how genital surgery for FtM transgender people has variable outcomes in terms of genitalia size and functionality.

It is now best practice to consider the future reproductive possibilities for transgender youth before prescribing or starting hormonal or surgical treatments for gender dysphoria (World Professional Association for Transgender Health, 2011). This is especially important for puberty blockers, which can prevent the possibility of fertility. This involves the patient and team considering young people's potential to freeze eggs or sperm, to carry children using their owsn uterus and a host of other options when talking through the options for medical transitions. Health professionals should ensure transgender youth consider how these options relate to any sterilisation requirements for legal documentation depending on the country or area in which they live; and balance out their most important goals if these options are in conflict with each other. However, in considering issues of fertility, health professionals should be careful to note that for medical interventions the only case at stake is a genetically related child; it is potentially possible in some countries to adopt or to foster children, and there should not be a slippage between 'wanting a child' and 'fertility', which are two separate things (Riggs, 2018). It is vital that alongside advocating for transgender youth to access assisted reproductive technologies, health providers and professionals should also consider alternate pathways to parenting children; and acknowledge that many transgender people may not want children (Riggs, 2018). A study of transgender people aged 16+ showed that transgender people sometimes became parents through giving birth prior to, or through collecting gametes for use after, initial gender affirmations, through adoption, through fostering children, through having partners who already had children, through having their partners carry their babies, through donation of sperm to other couples and many other options (Jones *et al.*, 2015). Some transgender people were 'childless' but not childfree, getting involved in the rearing of nephews, nieces and friends' children. Some were contentedly childless *and* childfree.

Just over one quarter (26%) of Australian transgender youth aged 14–25 years had or were currently medically transitioning; 33 per cent wished to do so in the future (Jones, Smith *et al.*, 2016). For some survey participants, medical transitioning was linked to feelings of mental wellbeing; Sarah (MtF, 21 years) desired to have, 'a FULL transition i.e. name, clothes, sex reassignment surgery' to gain social acceptance and feel 'better'. However, 40 per cent of survey participants did not want to have a medical transition. This matched to some degree the relatively large numbers of non-binary gender identities in the survey sample compared to in other studies (Couch *et al.*, 2007; Jones *et al.*, 2015). Survey participant Shannon (trans*, 25 years), for example, explained that transitioning medically was unnecessary for their[1] particular gender affirmation: 'I doubt I will ever go "all the way" to "male" from "female"… I still wear the same clothes, do the same things, my life just makes more sense now.' For FtM transgender youth, chest surgery is far more likely to be privileged than bottom surgery. Over half the group in an Australian FtM transgender study (51%) had undergone chest surgery (reconstruction or reduction), 40 per cent had had a full mastectomy, and many discussed a desire to get such procedures done in the future (Jones *et al.*, 2015). A significantly smaller portion (6%) had had genital surgery, and only a few had gotten testicular implants. Harry best captured the fears of participants about genital surgery:

---

1 The gendered or non-gendered personal pronouns identified as preferred by individual participants (such as he, she, their, etc.) were used in writing this 2015 article.

I want phallo or meta but there is so little info out there and the idea really scares me. So many surgeries to make it work, chances of failure, no sensation. Absolutely terrifying. (Harry, FtM transgender, 24 years)

## Satisfaction with gender affirmation

Australian survey data showed that the overwhelming majority of participants (97%) said that the physical modifications they engaged in made a difference to their lives and 78 per cent were satisfied with the results (ranging from very to somewhat satisfied; Jones et al., 2015). This satisfaction often related to hormones and chest surgery. For example, thewaywesee (trans* male or queer male, 22 years) said he was very satisfied since starting hormones; calling the treatment 'One of the best decisions I've ever made.' A smaller 8 per cent were neutral on the outcome, 8 per cent were somewhat dissatisfied, 3 per cent were dissatisfied, and only 1 per cent were very dissatisfied. Many asserted that there was, in their experience, a direct relationship between transitioning and a reduction in mental health disorders and an increased general sense of wellbeing (Jones et al., 2015). For example, Harry (FtM transgender, 24 years) had suffered from anxiety prior to transition; he said that his social and medical transition made a 'massive difference', and commented, 'I now pass and I'm off my anxiety meds.' For Conor (male, queer, trans*, person of colour, 24 years), the major goal of transitioning was about becoming at peace with the look of his body, and did not require bottom surgery to achieve the overall masculine aesthetic he aimed at. The changes from both testosterone and top surgery have 'helped me to deal with my ED (eating disorder)'. Aid (socially male, 18 years), was suicidal as a young person, after transitioning: 'I feel at peace with my body,' he explained, 'and I am no longer suicidal.'

## The positive physical health of transgender people

Transgender people can have incredibly fit bodies and can also experience the full range of physical health variations the broader population experience. Some transgender people have been celebrated for achieving amazing athletic feats at the Olympic and international levels including Olympian and 'greatest athlete in the world' Caitlyn

Jenner, Olympic pole vaulter Balian Buschbaum, Olympic skier Erik Schinegger, golfer and physician Dr Bobbi Lancaster, martial artist Fallon Fox and many others (Brown, 2015). There are also transgender people with bodies widely admired in international modelling campaigns and television shows such as the young model Andreja Pejić who achieved success in male, androgynous and female modelling campaigns; Laith Ashley a New York male model; Carmen Carrera from *The Bold and the Beautiful*; Isis King from *America's Next Top Model* and many others. When thinking about the focus of physical health research for transgender people, we have to understand that research (especially clinical research) often focuses on health 'problems', body issues and how they can be fixed or prevented. The physical health statistics and stories that must necessarily be shared in this chapter with the physical health professionals reading along are aimed at helping them to do their work to prevent or treat health issues; however, this does not suggest transgender youth are unfit and unhealthy.

A majority of 62 per cent of transgender people aged 16+ described their physical health in the past 12 months positively – 45 per cent said it was good and 17 per cent said it was very good (Jones *et al.,* 2015). This was similar to the findings for adults (Couch *et al.,* 2007). A further 23 per cent answered that it was neither good nor bad. A smaller group of 14 per cent said that it was bad, and less than 1 per cent said it was very bad. For many of the participants, going to the gym, exercising or paying particular attention to their bodies had been a key part of affirming their gender identity or their chosen transition path in the last year. Several participants attributed becoming more involved in weight-lifting programmes (formal or informal), doing sports or exercise, and paying extra attention to their bodies as improving their physical fitness and health. Regarding improving their physical health, 53 per cent of the respondents were satisfied (14% felt neutral about their physical health and 32% were dissatisfied). To improve physical health, most comments were on the desire to lose weight, gain muscle, drink less or cut back on cigarettes.

## Alcohol and drug use
The transgender community's health can be adversely affected by relatively high rates of homelessness, familial rejection, social isolation, alcohol or substance abuse, low socioe-conomic status, anxiety,

depression, self-harm, and suicide risk (Couch *et al.*, 2007; Riggs & Due, 2013; Smith *et al.*, 2014). Broadly, these experiences should be seen as a result of stigma and discrimination, cisgenderism (the delegitimisation of genders and bodies that do not fit cultural norms of gender/sex), and the lack of access to gender-affirming treatments (Riggs, Ansara & Treharne, 2015).

Most of the participants in an Australian study mentioned that they consumed alcohol at least occasionally (33%), monthly (8%), fortnightly (12%), weekly (21%) or daily (8%) (Jones *et al.*, 2015). Almost one fifth never drank. Over half of the respondents never smoked, whilst around one fifth of the group smoked daily. The majority never used any other drugs, and no participant used heroin. About one fifth of the group smoked marijuana on occasion, 5 per cent used it daily, 3 per cent weekly. A group of 15 per cent occasionally used sedatives such as sleeping pills, and a few individuals used them more often. There was almost negligible regular use of all other drugs, with some participants using them only on occasion (11% used ecstasy occasionally, 7% used amphetamines occasionally, 5% used cocaine occasionally, and 2% used inhalants occasionally). Of the few participants who discussed having addiction issues, one explained how these issues were intertwined with his difficulty in accepting his gender identity and other complications:

> The same substance I was addicted to is now my prescribed medication and I have never functioned better! A number of people have commented that I was a self-medicator. A lot was tied up also with transgender issues. (Anonymous)

Other individuals related their addiction issues to childhood trauma, or a combination of mental health issues that they believed heightened their susceptibility to substance abuse.

Further, 11 per cent of transgender youth reported that they had addictions and 7 per cent indicated that they had spoken to a health professional about this; 23 per cent took illegal drugs to help them 'feel better' (Smith *et al.*, 2014). Further, 26 per cent of transgender youth smoked cigarettes and almost half of the young people (48%) drank alcohol to help themselves feel better. This underlines the need for physical health workers to collaborate with mental health workers on wellbeing strategies and to probe more deeply into the relationships between stress, anxiety, depression, substance use and gender dysphoria.

## Cancer risk, care and screening

Transgender youth are largely invisible in cancer literature, research and registries; however the medical and/or surgical technologies of gender affirmations can influence cancer risk and screening (Gooren & Lips, 2014; Kerr & Jones, 2017). Some predict that as more people present at younger ages for gender-affirming hormone treatment there may be an increase in cancer over time (Gooren & Lips, 2014; Jones & Hillier, 2013; Kerr & Jones, 2017; Smith *et al.*, 2014). However, as there have been few studies that address the effects that medical and/or surgical transition have on cancer, the extent to which transgender youth will be at risk remains unknown (Taylor & Bryson, 2016). The word 'cancer' may also seem to suggest one phenomena; however, hundreds of different malignant tumours can originate from vastly different cells in the human body – producing distinct and unique types (Kumar, Abbas & Aster, 2015). In thinking about cancer care for transgender communities, we must therefore throw away over-generalisations and see this topic as complex, requiring a broader research base which will help health care professionals to provide appropriate, sensitive and timely services, and inform outreach to transgender youth (Kerr & Jones, 2017).

Most cancer screening options related to sensitive organs for transgender people are relevant only as they become older; however, it is useful to explain these screening processes to transgender youth, and to do so in terms of body parts ('if you have chest/breast tissue you should…') not gender ('if you are female you should…). It is important to explain the expectation that they will later engage in:

- *cancer screening for chest/breast tissue*: Between the ages of 50 and 74 transgender people should have a mammogram (an x-ray of the breast) once every two years (Cancer Australia, 2016) – using the term chest tissue may be less intimidating to the patient (Kerr & Jones, 2017). For transgender people who have had a mastectomy (removal of chest/breast tissue), then as there is not enough tissue, an x-ray (mammogram) cannot be performed. Other imaging may be used such as ultrasound or magnetic resonance imaging (MRI); however, unless they are deemed high risk because of a family or personal history of cancer, it is unlikely that this is necessary. If they do not have a high risk of chest/breast cancer, visual inspection and touching their own chest (including up to the armpits) to monitor for abnormalities regularly is advised (Phillips *et al.*, 2014; Pivo *et al.*, 2016). Breast cancer screening in trans women is advised for those aged over 50, who have been on gender-affirming hormonal treatment for more than five years, in the form of a mammogram (x-ray of the breast) every two years (Phillips *et al.*, 2014; Pivo *et al.*, 2016). Breast implants may lower the sensitivity of mammograms, but have not been linked to an increased risk of breast cancer.

- *cancer screening for individuals with a cervix*: If transgender youth have a cervix and have been sexually active in any way, they should have their cervix checked every two to five years and should do especially from 25 years old (Cancer Council, 2017). The test is no longer a Pap smear, however, it is performed in a similar way; the health care professional needs to take a sample from the cervix, accessing the cervix through the frontal opening/vagina – using the term frontal opening may be less intimidating to the patient (Kerr & Jones, 2017). Transgender youth (especially trans boys/men) can find this a traumatising test, and can engage in inadequate tests due to the anxiety such processes cause and should thus be told they can:

    - say 'stop' at any time
    - bring a partner or a friend for support
    - try relaxation strategies (e.g. music, deep-breathing)
    - talk to their doctor about taking anti-anxiety medication beforehand
    - agree that it is either better to get it over and done with as quickly as possible or do it slowly
    - discuss any problems they may have had in the past with such tests
    - ask for a smaller speculum, more lubricant, or a numbing agent (Potter *et al.*, 2015).

- *cancer screening for individuals with a prostate*: Most genital surgeries for trans girls and women do not include removal of the prostate, and transgender youth should be taught that screening prostate cancer risk for people with a prostate who are at average risk may occur from age 50 years in the form of a prostate-specific antigen (PSA) test (Kerr & Jones, 2017). It is important that health care professionals are aware that for transgender people on gender-affirming hormone treatment and/or after surgical removal of the gonads/testicles, the PSA level may be lowered (Kerr & Jones, 2017). Alternatively, a digital rectal or frontal opening exam may be performed to feel if there are any irregularities (Weyers *et al.*, 2009).

- *cancer screening for individuals with ovaries*: There is currently no test that is sensitive enough to be able to diagnose this disease at an early stage. Ovarian cancer has a high mortality rate when diagnosed at a later stage, so it is very important for people noticing symptoms associated with ovarian cancer to see a doctor (Cancer Council, 2017). Signs and symptoms may include abdominal pain and bloating, and changes in bowel habits. For youth who have a family history or genetic susceptibility to ovarian cancer, it may be advisable to have regular pelvic examinations and/or ultrasounds.

## Black market temptations

Sometimes transgender youth might be tempted to access hormone therapy treatments through the black market due to the delays or blocks they experience in getting treated through regular health providers. Many young people have a phone or Internet access, and can order hormones online. Despite the anonymity of surveys, transgender youth survey participants rarely report having broken the law through using black market channels, unapproved treatments or someone else's prescriptions. However, a few said that they were tempted (Jones *et al.*, 2015). They cited financial and legal issues and accessibility (particularly denial of, or delays in, access to hormones) as the main motivator. For example, when Aid was a young teen of 15 years, he had experienced difficulties in seeking to get hormone therapy; he was not allowed to start the treatment before seeing a psychologist 'who put me on a six-month waiting list'. Despite his youth, he had actually already been waiting for years to start his transition. So in that period he said, 'I considered accessing black market T.' Other younger participants facing legal and financial obstacles to their transitions, and those who were otherwise in lower socio-economic demographics, mentioned that they had considered taking black market hormone options out of sheer desperation.

There were also reports of particular difficulties for genderqueer people, who wished to actualise a sense of themselves as neither female nor male by manifesting this more directly in their embodiment, around accessing transition-related treatments. Hansel (genderqueer, 22 years) explained that he had certainly been approached by other genderqueer people wishing to share his testosterone prescription. He said they approached him because, 'the whole process is pretty daunting and some psychologists are reluctant to give T to people who identify as genderqueer'. He explained that there were many stories online on genderqueer discussion boards and groups about bad treatment, 'so some people are afraid to go through the process for themselves'. It was clear there was a need for health professionals to show that they were 'genderqueer friendly' and willing to support younger people over time, so that people could feel safe to access hormones and help correctly, rather than seeking treatment through a friend or online source for fear they would be left in the lurch. If 'Informed Consent' models of health care emerged, genderqueer youth would have enhanced access to medical affirmation treatments without dysphoria diagnoses (Schulz, 2018).

## Mixed and bad experiences with health services

Factors such as transphobia, lack of knowledge about transgender youth, and a lack of institutional policies about appropriateness in health care settings, are barriers for transgender youth accessing health care even in relatively advanced transgender-friendly regions of Europe and the Americas (Corliss *et al.*, 2007; Gardner & Safer, 2013). Transgender people often experience stigma and discrimination when accessing health services even in these regions (Sperber, Landers & Lawrence, 2005), as health care providers are often uncomfortable during encounters with transgender patients (Lurie, 2005; Safer & Pearce, 2013). Transgender people have reported experiencing inconsistency in services and an invisibility of gender diversity

(McLean, 2011; Riggs & Due, 2013), and a lack of access to gender-affirming treatments for transgender youth broadly (Clark *et al.*, 2014; Riggs, Ansara *et al.*, 2015). Those who live rurally or remotely have even less access to key services, whilst many transgender people report professionals showing persistent misconceptions and prejudices (Riggs & Due, 2013; Winter *et al.*, 2016). Many individuals therefore delay or avoid accessing services or disclosing their gender identity (Clark *et al.*, 2017; Corliss *et al.*, 2007; Jones *et al.*, 2015).

A New Zealand study of over 8000 high school students found that 40 per cent of transgender students had been unable to access health care when they needed it (Clark *et al.*, 2014). Similarly, a Canadian study of 923 youth aged 14–25 showed 34 per cent of transgender youth aged 14–18 years and around half of those aged 19–25 years had not sought professional care for physical health problems in the last year, even when it was urgently needed (Clark *et al.*, 2017). A UK survey of 889 transgender participants aged over 18 years found that 65 per cent were discriminated against in general health services (McNeil *et al.*, 2012). Transgender people aged 16+ have reported that health service providers had a lack of knowledge about transgender issues; some even found that health professionals thought transgender was a type of sexual orientation (Jones *et al.*, 2015). 'Most have never heard of trans* or gender dysphoria,' said Aid (socially male, 18 years), who had experienced only two good doctors out of eight he had been to. Aid had actually had a doctor say to him that she 'hated treating trans people', and he suspected another treated him purely out of curiosity to 'get a look at my body'. He recalled times he had tried to explain his identity to a doctor for over 40 minutes and had then been asked if he was a 'hermaphrodite'. He had even had a doctor who was 'so shocked he was unable to type "testosterone" into his computer for a script' – to the point where the session had to end and he had to go back to a different doctor in the clinic that same day.

Bad experiences with health service providers also involved 'having to educate them and having to deal with being mis-gendered' (Conor, male, queer, trans*, person of colour, 24 years). It appeared that this also occurred in specialised services: 'I called the receptionist/nurse out on why she used my birth name and she was really rude about it' (Maddox, male/FtM/trans man, 21 years).

There were several reasons transgender youth aged 14–25 years might not have seen a health professional when they needed to (Smith *et al.*, 2014). Sometimes parents blocked their transgender children from seeing health professionals, for fear the meeting would start their transition or gender affirmation processes. For one 16-year-old, their parents 'have blocked me from seeing a HP [health professional] at all for the past few years'. This could lead to serious health complications if the child had faced a health crisis in that time, and means vaccines and check-ups are missed. Sometimes transgender youth were concerned or embarrassed about coming out to, or being physically examined by, a doctor or health professional. Almost a quarter indicated that the language that health professionals used to describe them made them feel uncomfortable or angry. For example, a 14-year-old genderqueer young person felt uncomfortable when health professionals would reduce their concerns by saying things like, 'it's probably just "girly" problems you [will] grow out of it'. Another genderqueer youth (23 years) said their consent, confidentiality, and autonomy were abused:

> The first doctor I made mention of my gender identity to, locked me in her office alone and left to consult with every other doctor in the surgery about what to do without my consent, my GP brought up my gender identity in front of my mother without having ever spoken to me about it (and not knowing if I had ever spoken to her about it) and a psychologist told me that there was no such thing as a non-binary identity.

Just over half (53%) the transgender youth surveyed had a negative experience with a health professional during their lifetime and the flow-on effects of these experiences included 22 per cent avoiding health professionals for a while, and another 11 per cent choosing not to see health professionals altogether. Only 6 per cent of all participants made a complaint. The outcome was not always desirable, such as one young boy/man (20 years) who explained that, 'they raised their voice at me and blamed it on me'. An MtF transgender young person said complaining was 'extremely disempowering and disturbing' and that they 'deeply regret' trying. Only half of the young people stopped seeing that particular health professional after a negative experience. Chloe (girl/woman, 18 years) said she didn't complain or leave because of the difficulty of even getting medical appointments and the power of the health professionals:

> If I complained, or said anything he didn't like really, he had the power to deny me treatment and then I would have had to find another way to get treatment. It would have been possible, but difficult. So I stayed quiet... The fact that it has been this difficult to get to the point of even being able to get HRT is ridiculous.

## Helpful health professionals

In describing good experiences with health service providers, transgender people aged 16+ mentioned their contact with 'friendly' health professionals who facilitated multiple avenues of communication and ensured their access to other care professionals (Jones et al., 2015). Transgender youth most praised health professionals who were:

- *clearly identified as trans-friendly through the display of supportive symbols/materials*: Transgender youth in the survey explained that health providers and professionals displaying supportive posters or symbols (even a subtle rainbow flag or transgender flag sticker), or who had information available on gender identity in the treatment space, were favoured. This was because in doing so, they communicated that the patient was safe to discuss their gender identity with service workers in a non-intimidating way. Conor suggested health care services should have 'preferred name and pronouns' on all their admission sheets; a way of declaring the location transgender-friendly and also getting some practical information on patients.

- *sensitive to their bodies and transgender status*: Some of the patients in the survey of transgender people aged 16+ years were out as transgender or as having a transgender past to their health practitioners, but not all were (Jones et al., 2015). For these transgender people, being able to reveal their bodies without the health professional gasping, being titillated, asking overly curious questions or reacting in any way that made them feel abnormal, was greatly appreciated. For example, Darkneko (FtM transgender, 21 years) said, 'I never informed any of my doctors of my trans status. One time I was wearing my binder and the doctor saw but didn't say anything'.

- *willing to treat the patient as their gender identity*: For Jake (male, 21 years) and others, being treated in a way that was consistent with their gender identity was of paramount importance. He said that when he had his hysterectomy as a public patient in a public hospital, there was 'not one slip up of male pronouns or being treated as male'. He appreciated that he was even 'offered a urinal bottle (for men obviously) but I simply just stated I would prefer to get up and walk to the bathroom'. Several others spoke about being shown to the bathroom area consistent with their gender identities or other appreciated social treatment at health services.

- *especially warm and helpful*: Harley (FtM transgender, 21 years) said his best experiences were with welcoming doctors, including one who 'allows me to communicate via email so that I don't have to travel over two hours to see them' and who was assisting him to find a good local GP. Doc79 fondly recalled one doctor who was particularly friendly and helpful in the early stages of transition:

> He used to arm wrestle me after he gave me my T shot, to see if I had any hormone induced strength... He used to let me win I think, but it was good because he was one of my first docs and it was at the start of my transition, so it was good for a laugh at a rough time.

There were other descriptions of doctors who called 20 psychologists until they found the one that would help their patient towards getting hormone therapy or gestures of warmth and acceptance greatly appreciated by the participants.

- *experienced in treating other transgender patients*: Other participants reported that being treated by doctors who had previously treated other transgender people was a positive factor. Nikozilar (male, 20 years) was very satisfied with his 'extremely open minded and friendly' GP, and particularly noted that she had 'treated trans* men and trans women before'. He recounted that she referred him to other services and practitioners, performed regular Pap smears on him to check his health, taught his partner 'very patiently' how to give him hormone shots, and 'always referred to me as he'. Maddox (male/FtM/trans man, 21 years) argued that younger healthcare professionals who had lived, worked and studied in cities had a fairly strong basis of what transgender is compared to those who were older or were mainly based in rural areas. He also felt it impacted their knowledge of terms like 'gender dysphoria and gender-neutral'.

## Combatting cisnormativity and cissexism in health services

Transgender youth were significantly more likely than same sex attracted students to have disclosed their diverse identity to a range of physical health professionals; approximately twice as many had told their doctors and school nurses (Jones & Hillier, 2013). Physical health practitioners and professionals need to respond to the gender identities of their patients, or ask about these in a professional way (without over-reacting or asking unnecessary questions) if unsure. They should think about patients' sensitivities around their bodies, and realise that for transgender youth these sensitivities may be greatly increased to the point where certain interactions, discussions or medical tests and procedures that are part of regular life may feel overwhelming (Jones *et al.*, 2015; Kerr & Jones, 2017). It is important to recognise that transgender youth think about their bodies, and especially particular organs, in different ways to physical health and medical experts. Doctors and specialists with expertise in certain areas in particular may have formed a habit of using really precise medical terms for anatomy when talking to their peers, but these terms will not always be understood or preferred by younger patients even in general. Sometimes transgender youth may especially be more comfortable with non-gendered ways of discussing their body parts. Indeed, all people are in the first seven weeks of life in possession of a genital tubercle and gonads, which have the potential to develop as a penis or clitoris, a set of ovaries or testes, or some other variation (Ainsworth, 2015; Jones, Hart *et al.*, 2016). It is human language and the influence of hormones that differentiates these body parts after all, and these influences can be reversed or changed. There is no need to be insistent about language when it creates stress for a young patient. An important way that physical health professionals can establish trust and make their transgender youth patients feel comfortable is to ask the patient's individual preferred words for body parts or to offer some examples and let them choose your shared language for your sessions together. For example, when it is relevant to an examination or procedure you might try: genitals, between the thighs, chest and so on.

Transgender youth may need extra time and understanding from their physical health service providers around tests which could make them feel awkward, upset or traumatised depending on their feeling of safety and comfort. They may feel uncomfortable removing their clothes, being inspected and so on. They need to be told:

- when they can avoid or defer tests until they are ready for them

- any different options for tests, procedures or health care treatments which could be less triggering to gender dysphoria/ discomfort around gender

- that they can say 'stop' at any time during tests or procedures where this is so, or plan with the health service provider how the procedure is administered (quickly, slowly, with a towel over a body part, etc.)

- be a directing party in elements of their health care, not just the recipient (Kerr & Jones, 2017; Potter *et al.*, 2015).

Alternately some transgender youth may be especially confident or unconcerned about receiving physical health care. Another key point was that transgender youth needed early and consistent support and affirmation for any disclosure of their identity, even if it was still being determined. Saying 'it would be ok if you felt you were transgender' is not foreclosing on the patient's identity.

In the event transgender youth are diagnosed with gender dysphoria, a clinician's letter may be requested from physical or mental health practitioners depending on the context. Brill and Pepper (Brill & Pepper, 2008, p.247) provide a general sample letter, updated here with the modern diagnosis terminology and for professionals to adapt:

To Whom It May Concern,

I am a (medical/mental health/gender identity/other clinician) licensed to practise (medicine and surgery/psychology and counselling including in the field of gender identity) in the state of (X).

John (/Jane) is a transgender boy (/girl/person). He has been diagnosed with (insert locally specific diagnosis e.g. Gender Dysphoria). Part of the treatment of youth with (this condition), as John has, involves allowing them to live in the gender role appropriate to their true psychological gender, which in John's case is male. Eventually many children with (this condition) require hormonal and surgical treatment after entering adolescence. However, in preadolescent patients treatment is generally restricted to social and psychological treatment.

It is imperative to the health and wellbeing of children with this complex condition that they be allowed to live life fully in the appropriate gender role. In John's case this requires that he be allowed to participate in appropriate activities, as any boy his age would.

When children are gender-segregated for any reason or activity, it is crucial that John be allowed to participate with boys his own age. Sex-segregating him with girls could potentially cause irreparable psychological damage. John should be allowed to use the boys' bathroom, locker room, and any other sex-segregated facility for children.

It is also imperative that John's confidentiality be protected. Revealing his transgender status is not only potentially psychologically damaging, it would compromise the confidentiality of his private medical history.

Thank you in advance for your help in providing John a supportive and healthy environment. If you have any questions or concerns, please do not hesitate to contact me at my office or, if urgent, at my cell phone number: xxx-xxx-xxxx.

Sincerely,

(Name of doctor here).

## Ethics and training

Most medical schools (60%) in countries including New Zealand and Australia spend between zero and five hours teaching health professionals about LGBT people broadly, and a smaller portion of that on transgender people or specifically transgender youth (Sanchez et al., 2017). Health professionals should familiarise themselves with the *Standards of Care for the Health of Transsexual, Transgender, and Gender Nonconforming People* (World Professional Association for Transgender Health, 2011), and keep up-to-date with the local laws and industry ethics policies around transgender youth relevant to their role in health service provision. Graduate programmes that prepare future health professionals in medicine, nursing, surgery and other areas should develop and publish clear affirming policies that advocate for non-discrimination and promote justice and fairness for all. Health professionals can contribute to their own personal and professional development by exploring their personal values and ideas around working with transgender youth. Reflect on how your own gender identity and body influences how you respond to transgender youth, and how confident you are in actively standing up in an organisation to effect change supporting transgender youth's health care needs. What would stop you, and how would you ensure that you personally are supported and empowered if faced with organisational barriers? How would you help a young person who is not getting the help they need and is desperate enough to self-harm, self-medicate, use online goods or other people's scripts? You may look into local and international health care professional bodies' resources and professional development events for advice (in Australia these include the Rainbow Tick accreditation course for health service providers and others; in the UK Stonewall provides services, in Ireland belongto is helpful and so on).

## Conclusions and recommendations

The statistics and information on transgender youth's physical health, medical needs and experiences outlined in this chapter have shown how physical health treatment opportunities have in some ways become far more varied and accessible over time. However, it is also true that there are still barriers in place for some transgender youth's health care needs depending on the country context, the age of the transgender young person, the gender identity of the young person, financial resourcing or insurance coverage, support levels from parents/guardians and the education and experience of health professionals. In addition, the history of eugenics in Swedish reproductive care meant that, even though that country was the first to legalise transition for transgender people in legal documentation, its influential choice of sterilisation requirements live on and limit health care options for many transgender youth around the world today. In challenging the assumption behind sterilisation requirements, with a focus on thinking about the fertility of transgender youth, we have to be careful to not push a view of reproductive life as central to every human's existence, but to consider the many options young people will have for both pursuing their variable gender affirmation needs and options to lead lives with or without children.

The shifts in thinking about physical health over time have moved towards an understanding of a diversification of needs, rather than a one-size-fits-all approach. Health professionals and services need:

- to train both pre-service and in-service health professionals about transgender youth

- to provide professional development training for health support staff (i.e. administration staff) on inclusive practice for transgender youth

- to access information about specialist services for transgender health care – especially around issues of gender affirmation including hormone therapies and surgeries – in order to make appropriate referrals when issues beyond their expertise arise

- to display symbols or posters in support of transgender people to subtly communicate that the health service will be responsive to their needs

- to include requests for pronouns preferred on patient intake information sheets

- to promote transgender youth-friendly mental health services and interlink with cross-disciplinary groups of experts

- to address complaints about inappropriate behaviour towards transgender youth in an appropriate and timely manner

- to provide parents of transgender children with information about the danger of preventing transgender youth from seeking medical care, and an understanding of gender affirmation processes as non-elective in some transgender youth's pathways to treating gender dysphoria
- to involve parents in planning about transitions and appropriate ages for life-changing decisions, where they can be a support for the child or even an advocate
- to discuss the full range of options for transgender youth who are considering gender affirmations – such as doing nothing or delaying treatment for a time if that suits their gender exploration or needs, social gender affirmation elements, legal gender affirmation elements, medical gender affirmation elements and the different reasons people do and don't sometimes prefer aspects of these options. It is important to discuss how treatments may or may not have the results the youth envisions, and may have lasting impacts of various kinds, and may nonetheless be useful for wellbeing or impact wellbeing in various ways
- to provide easily accessible health information for these young people on multiple platforms including face-to-face and online
- to help parents/guardians and young people understand the laws and options around health care in their context
- to recognise when a health care issue is and is not directly related to the young person's transgender status, or try to understand and discuss these relationships
- to facilitate opportunities for transgender youth to improve their health knowledge and their knowledge of the dangers of black market or incorrectly obtained treatments, and the complications of taking hormones to be aware of
- to provide opportunities for transgender youth and their parents/guardians to share information about transgender-friendly health providers, practitioners and professionals.

■ Chapter 4 ■

# Transgender Youth, Sexual Health and Sexual Health Services

Defining my sexual orientation has always been somewhat confusing for me personally. As female born and as a teenager, realising I was attracted to girls and then to women, I was a lesbian (hate labels). Now as a mature aged transman who has had top surgery, but still has female sex organs in a way, I guess I see myself as a straight man with a twist. Currently there is no one in my life who rocks my world. ... I am willing if that special someone came along. (Alex, male/trans guy, straight with a twist, 22 years)

I am attracted to men, women, intersex individuals, transsexuals and genderqueer or questioning. Gender is not important for me. I have had sex with men as a female presenting person, and women as both female and male presenting. Before transition I was unable to be touched by hands or mouths on my genitals and was unable to undress in front of others or a mirror. After T and chest surgery, I enjoy an active sex life that involves oral sex as well as penetrative sex. I am no longer uncomfortable being naked in front of others. (Aid, socially male, pansexual, 18 years)

I'm single and probably will be for a long time. The closest thing to a successful relationship I've had was with a girl who, mere hours after realising how we felt about each other, left Australia and flew back to her home in California, where she remained for the duration of our 10-month relationship. She was the only person who has ever shown me any semblance of real love, despite my transsexualism, my ADHD, my depression, and, while we were together, my problems with self-harm, bulimia and alcohol abuse. My most recent relationship was with a 15-year-old bisexual boy. It lasted four days – from the Wednesday that he confessed his 'love' for me, and I admitted feelings for him, to the Saturday when he – despite assuring me that he loved me despite my condition and that as long as he had me, it didn't matter that I wasn't ready for sex *or* that he'd have to give up the casual sex he was having – slept with two other people. At the same time. I often doubt I will ever have sex. That's not what consumes me, though, as doubting I'll ever be loved. I'm the kid you might like…for a little while. … And even if they did, who's going to want to date a transperson? (Reagan, FtM trans, 17 years)

## ■ KEY POINTS

- Sexual health services for transgender youth in many countries around the world, and sexual education efforts at the global level overseen by UNESCO and other bodies, were historically tied to HIV pandemic responses.

- Sexual health services and education efforts for transgender youth will increasingly incorporate mobile phone apps, online websites and inclusive resource approaches.

- Queer and pangender are sexual identity labels often used by transgender youth.

- More transgender youth have some amount of same sex attraction compared to cisgender youth.

- Some of those who were 'lesbian' prior to transition, continue to be attracted to women but refer to themselves as 'straight men' post-transition.

- Some transgender youth are asexual; some are comfortable with a wide variety of sexual behaviours.

- Gender dysphoria and transition could impact use of sexual orientation labels, relationships, libido and engagement in sexual acts.

Changes in marriage policies, sexual cultures, sexual identities and technologies in recent years have been prolific. These changes can make the dating worlds and sexual health risks experienced by modern transgender youth unrecognisable from those once experienced by adult sexual health workers and sex educators. How can this gap be bridged by services, professionals and practitioners? This chapter addresses past treatment of sexual health issues for transgender youth, and the development of a key contemporary view of these young people as needing inclusive approaches and the opportunity to be considered agents for their own sexual health. It includes statistics on the marriage and relationship options open to transgender youth, their romantic and sexual attractions, use of sexual identity labels, and the impact that gender dysphoria and transitions can have on their sexual lives. It considers issues of sexual protection, STIs and pregnancy, partner violence and sexual abuse. Deficiencies in sexual health services and sex education are outlined, as well as the features associated with helpful sexual health professionals and sex educators. Useful methods for contending with cisnormativity and cissexism in sexual health services and sex education are offered, alongside issues in ethics and training for professionals. Steps to be taken for developing services and professionals are listed.

## Historic sexual health service and education: Sex worker tropes and HIV risk

Since the emergence of the HIV/AIDS crisis in the 1980s, there has been an increased focus on sexual health, human rights, and identity politics around transgender youth (Altman, 1997; Binnie, 2004). Global pandemics of sexually transmitted infections (STIs), with global impacts such as HIV pandemics, were a catalyst for international human rights bodies and health organisations (such as the United Nations and the World Health Organisation) and many governments paying more attention to transgender people's sexual health risks and needs. These bodies started realising they could no longer ignore sexual and gender issues once allocated to 'private' individualist realms rather than public collective realms of ethics and morality – HIV may even be seen as a kind of metaphor for the global recognition of transgender and other diverse identities (Altman, 2013; Binnie, 2004). The creation of UNAIDS has particularly enabled a global focus on the development of sexual health services and resources for high-risk populations, indirectly and directly including transgender youth, who were often considered under 'homosexual'/LGBT groupings and sex worker groupings. In many countries, these youth have turned to sex work as a matter of survival when facing rejection and homelessness, and this has become a negative trope (or stereotypical model) of transgender young people in some sexual health literature. It is important to remember transgender youth who engage in sex work may enjoy other occupations if they were accessible, or alternately may engage in the profession willingly and not wish their profession to be viewed as disempowering.

HIV and sexual risk education acknowledging at least some information of relevance to transgender youth (such as STI information) has been pushed in some countries since the HIV/AIDS crisis of the 1980s, but there has always been a push against this by conservative sexuality education proponents (Elia, 2005; Irvine, 2002). Since modern history began, conservative approaches have been favoured in many countries' sexuality education messages about transgender youth, and these sometimes remain influential to this day. These approaches have especially included sexual morality approaches, which are tied to religious institutions that often hold a considerable stake in education governance and curricula around the world. Sexual morality messages about transgender youth have portrayed transgender youth as being 'sinners' and 'deviants', acting in worldly ways against Judeo-Christian and Islamic sexual ethics, which rely on a procreative logic for sex, and the idea that sexuality should only occur between traditionally submissive feminine women and dominant masculine men within the context of religious marriages (Elia, 2005; Irvine, 2002).

Physical hygiene approaches have also been dominant in some contexts since the 1940s within efforts against venereal diseases, and are also still seen in a range of contexts today. They cast transgender (and gay) people as abnormal abominations to be avoided sexually, so that 'normal' cisgender people avoid becoming like them (Jones, 2011a). A Vietnam study of 3698 survey participants, 48 focus groups and 85 in-depth interviews with students, school staff and parents showed some staff were influenced by physical hygiene approach constructions of transgender people as diseased, potentially contagious and as carrying sexual diseases – a message sometimes directly taught by some within sex education (UNESCO, 2016d). One male student noted: 'because teachers do not have a good understanding of that issue (LGBT), they just disseminate wrong information to our non-LGBT peers.' These historic approaches have also been seen recently re-emerging with greater vigour alongside increased idealisation of nationalist and family values in Russia, Egypt, Chechnya and several other countries (Jones, 2016b; UNESCO, 2016b).

Newer neo-conservative approaches to sex education for transgender youth within the ex-gay/ex-transgender movement and America's Christian Right's sex education efforts have also emerged in recent decades and harken back to these basic approaches by centralising religion and a sense that transgender identities cannot be lived out in full (Cloud, 2005; Hardisty, 1999; Irvine, 2002). These approaches have been reinforced by the American Government's Trump Administration's policy rescindments around the recognition of transgender youth in school sexuality education (Jones, 2017c). There have also been smaller offshoots of evangelist education efforts of this kind within Australia, England and other countries. Advocates include ministries such as Exodus International (Scott Davis and Exodus Youth), Inqueery, HOPE Ministries, P-Fox and Love in Action. The programmes, speakers and materials promoted through Exodus Youth and P-Fox propound this discourse. In this approach, there is an objective of making Christianity more appealing to transgender youth so as not to 'lose' them through judgement – of couching ideas on gender complementarity (heterosexual cisgender sexuality as 'God's path') in discursively rich terms such as 'pride' to initially appear more accommodating towards them (Cloud, 2005). However, at the same time, direct anti-globalist anti-human-rights backlash efforts are made to attack any real acceptance of, or sexual possibilities for, transgender youth beyond options of cisgender conformity and heterosexual reproductive sex within marriage. So in a sense, it is the same message dressed in a slightly more colourful outfit. These perspectives are linked to conversion therapies and have been widely denounced (APA Task Force on Appropriate Therapeutic Responses to Sexual Orientation, 2009).

## Contemporary sexual health service and education: Sexual health agents and inclusivity

The increased development of a human rights agenda relating to sexual health has meant that transgender youth are now regarded by UNESCO and the WHO as having the right to good sexual health and up-to-date sexual health information (Hillier *et al.*, 2010; UNESCO, 2009; World Health Organisation, 2006). Some research has highlighted that transgender people remain at significant risk for HIV (Bockting, Robinson & Rosser, 1998; Garofalo *et al.*, 2006; Stieglitz, 2010). Several studies have identified sexual risk factors around sexually transmitted infections including HIV/AIDS specific to transgender identity, such as the prevalence of prostitution in homeless and rejected youth populations, shame and isolation, compulsive sexual behaviour, secrecy and sharing needles whilst injecting hormones (Bockting *et al.*, 1998; Stieglitz, 2010). However, transgender youth have often been managed with sexual health programmes treating STIs including HIV in ways developed for gay students, which overlooked transgender identities and needs (McGuire *et al.*, 2010). In addition, transgender youth can mediate their use of sexual health services due to the sense of public surveillance by known acquaintances particularly in rural and remote areas/small towns (Jones, 2015a).

The advent of greater access to the Internet and mobile phones with video cameras has meant transgender youth often engage in informal sexual health knowledge practice and information circulation. This can occur through their social media, discussion boards and YouTube clips tracking their experiences of dysphoria and gender affirmation progression. These informal information dissemination practices can challenge and reform professional sexual health and sex education approaches in multiple ways (Byron & Hunt, 2016; Riggs & Bartholomaeus, 2017). On one hand, they provide positive framings moving well beyond approaches which position transgender youth as sexual health 'risk subjects' and use new terminologies in affirming ways. On the other hand they affect issues of information control: misinformation may occur when youth become 'health agents' in unmediated environments. Analysis of discussions of intimacy from the perspectives of transgender young people as narrated in a sample of YouTube videos can be extremely useful in thinking about sexual health and sexuality education (Riggs & Bartholomaeus, 2017).

Riggs and Bartholomaeus (2017) posit that these clips suggest the need for approaches to sexuality education that largely eschew the gendering of body parts and gametes, and which instead focus on their sexual or reproductive functions, to address the needs of transgender youth (who may find normative discussions of genitals distressing) and provide cisgender young people with a more inclusive understanding of bodies and desires.

Sexual health services now are increasingly encompassing more inclusive phone application and online services which don't demand a physical meeting at times, including the hugely popular chlamydia and gonorrhoea screening programmes in the UK using home testing through which individuals take on the 'health agents' role and become more empowered to be responsible for their sexual health testing and practices (Baraitser *et al.*, 2015). These apps, online services and home tests can be useful based on fulfilment of the key assumptions that:

- users have access to private Internet access (including, for youth, via mobile phones with Internet access)
- individuals have some existing sexual health literacy
- users are willing to take on new responsibility for their own sexual health care
- online services are convenient and discrete
- online services are cost effective
- remote support will enable new online users to engage in sexual health care
- clinic processes will adapt to the new online service provision
- people can accept the loss of a consultation session or sessions with sexual health professionals.

Whilst most of these assumptions are supported by evidence from many interventions and relevant sources, there is no data on the acceptability of loss of health professional contact and this can even be seen as a disadvantage, particularly with testing for HIV which might involve deeply confronting human psychological and emotional experiences due to the seriousness of potential diagnoses (Baraitser *et al.*, 2015).

Therefore, the move towards increasing app and online sexual health care service provisions potentially offers transgender youth some exciting wins and some palpable losses. For some transgender youth populations who have either had past bad experiences with in-person sexual health services or are worried about issues such as discretion about their identities and bodies, their visibility in accessing sexual health services and the potential for discrimination, these alternative options for sexual health care can offer a welcome change – so long as they have access to mobile apps and service websites and are literate enough in sexual health issues to know to access them. This sexual health literacy could be enhanced through collaborations with popular transgender youth YouTubers and online forum facilitators, for example, who could disseminate videos with sexual health professionals or link their networks into using available services. However, since transgender youth are disproportionately affected by HIV, there may be some significant losses for young people who rely on the emotional and psychological support of their sexual health providers and professionals.

It will also be especially important to consider the isolation experienced by transgender youth, for example, in considering a lessening or abandonment of face-to-face and phone call contact services where these youth get to speak to adults on sexual issues and education (Jones *et al.*, 2015; Smith *et al.*, 2014). Online service introduction should ideally be considered as part of a dynamic sexual health economy and not a stand-alone service, particularly for meeting transgender youth's diverse needs (Baraitser *et al.*, 2015; Jones, 2015a). Clinics will need well-trained staff and processes available to respond as clients move between the online, telephone and face-to-face service for different elements of sexual health care. Efforts should be considered not as additional add-on services, but as part of the sexual health service systems' holistic evolution in provision to transgender youth; different parts of the system will need to test how provision particularly impacts transgender youth care compared to other clients.

Transgender students are still rarely provided with relevant sexuality education in schools (UNESCO, 2016b). There are, however, several new approaches to transgender youth seen in modern sex education curricula and programmes around the world; the two main ones that will be discussed here are inclusive approaches and neo-conservative approaches (Jones, 2011b). In UNESCO's sexuality education technical guidelines and most Western OECD (Organisation for Economic Co-ordination and Development) countries' policies

– including Australia, England, the US and New Zealand – inclusive education approaches demand notions of 'inclusion' in sexuality education (OECD, 2003; UNESCO, 2009, 2011, 2016b). The aim is to supply equitable provision for diverse students, including transgender youth, and the approach maintains that to be excluded is to be disempowered and constituted as 'abnormal' (Barton, 1997, p.233). There is a belief that segregated schooling should not exist due to the divisions created socially and the barriers created to democratic participation, including special schools that deal with disabilities or schools that cater specifically for transgender and sexually diverse students. Transgender youth are instead seen as 'at risk of educational failure' if their needs are not met in the regular classroom. The sexuality framework incorporates sexual 'others', to prevent these others becoming 'at risk' (Robinson, 2002, p. 428). For example, Australia's *Health and Physical Education (F–10)* national curriculum highlights 'gender-diverse students' for special consideration within inclusive sexuality and sexual health education lessons:

> All school communities have a responsibility when implementing the Health and Physical Education curriculum to ensure that teaching is inclusive and relevant to the lived experiences of all students. This is particularly important when teaching about reproduction and sexual health, to ensure that the needs of all students are met, including students who may be same-sex attracted, gender diverse or intersex. (Jones, 2017a, p.413)

## Current and future marital options

The marital futures of transgender youth have been a source of concern historically for parents and families and marriage is sometimes a key issue brought up against transgender status; a parent's dream of a child's future marriage can be a complicated phenomenon. *Being married* in itself is not an unproblematic social 'good' or the goal for all people; however, *the right to marry* is a 'good' in terms of its symbolic nature indicating equitable status and from a standpoint of non-discrimination in citizenship (Jones, 2009; Weeks, 1999). Times are rapidly changing on this issue. The marital options of transgender people now vary from country to country, and year to year. Where genderless marriage is legal, transgender youth can consider marriage a realistic future option if they desire it – countries like Norway and Sweden have been early and enthusiastic adopters of genderless (or sexless) marriage policies where the gender of partners in identity documents were inconsequential to their ability to marry (ILGA Europe, 2009; Jones, 2009). Where same sex and male–female marriage is legal, such as in Germany and Spain, transgender youth can also rest assured they will face fewer restrictions, although the specifics of the laws may necessitate identity documentation fitting male or female sex (Jones, 2009).

Where only male–female marriage is allowed, transgender youth may or may not be able to look forward to marriage. In Iran there is a requirement for full transition surgeries for transgender people to be able to participate in marriage as males or females only; however, it is difficult to marry due to resistance from in-laws refusing transgender family members (Outright Action International, 2016). There are still countries particularly in parts of Europe (e.g. Switzerland) and Asia (e.g. Japan) where transgender youth may be required to be sterilised to marry as a legally recognised 'man' or 'woman' (H, 2017). Other criteria may be taken into consideration, depending on the country, such as sex allocated at birth, life experiences, self-perception 'as man or woman', sex reassignment procedures undertaken, sex/gender of partner and characteristics at the time of marriage.

Two thirds of Australian transgender people aged 16+ had never married, 18 per cent were in de facto relationships, 8 per cent were married, 5 per cent were divorced, and 2 per cent were separated (Jones *et al.*, 2015). This was likely partially affected by the young age of many participants and the lack of genderless and same sex marital options at the time of the study. There were, however, individuals within the de facto group who were engaged to be married in the future and were awaiting non-discriminatory developments to marital laws that have since arrived. There were transgender Australians living in the state of Victoria who not long ago had to be sterilised to marry; this is no longer the case. Sexual health professionals and sex educators need to educate youth and their guardians on the changing nature of marital laws around the world, and how it may be worth putting off (unwanted) enforced sterilisation in contexts where the laws may soon change if the sterilisation is mainly sought for marriage eligibility. Sterilisation itself is not a 'bad thing' and may be a wonderful option, but only when chosen and wanted by a mature individual whose aim is to become sterilised. Conversely, unwanted sterilisation, if obtained for potential marital or identity purposes during a period of change where it may soon be an obsolete requirement, is worth questioning. It is unfair that transgender youth in several contexts must endure difficult life-altering decisions like choosing between being able to reproduce more easily or being able to be recognised within identity documents and marital laws – these options are not mutually exclusive. Sexual health services should *advocate against enforced sterilisations* in countries where these are pushed.

## Relationship status and futures of transgender youth

Clichés from old movies about lonely transgender people necessarily never experiencing romance only provide a mythical vision that torments transgender youth. In a study of 160 adults, the key difficulties in negotiating romantic relationships as transgender reported were: (1) anxiety over potential responses; (2) discrimination from potential partners; and (3) lack of self-acceptance (Riggs, von Doussa & Power, 2015). Younger people in the study were more likely to perceive that at some point in their life they would experience an ideal relationship. Romance is indeed an increasing reality for transgender youth living in contexts where acceptance is improving. Sexual health workers in these contexts are likely to discover in their fieldwork that transgender youth actually have many romantic experiences, and the research evidence supports this (Bungener *et al.*, 2017; Smith *et al.*, 2014). A Dutch study compared the romantic experiences of 137 transgender adolescents with data for 8520 same-aged cisgender youth (Bungener *et al.*, 2017). Of the transgender adolescents, 77 per cent had fallen in love, and half (50%) had had a romantic relationship. Whilst in comparison with the general population, it was true that transgender adolescents were romantically less experienced, most had some experience.

Participants in an Australian survey of 189 transgender youth (Smith *et al.*, 2014) were most likely to be in a monogamous relationship (29%), followed by single and looking for a relationship (28.6%), single and not looking for a relationship (24%), in a non-monogamous (open) relationship (7%), in a polyamorous relationship (consensual relationships with multiple people or more than one person; 4%), or other (7%). Those who were single and looking often had elaborate visions of partners within delightfully utopic future dreams:

> I hope that I'll find someone who'll stop making me care about who I identify as and come to an acceptance of the limitations of my body and the freedom of my mind. I want to do something big in the world and I promise you that I'll make it happen. I want a change in the way we view sexuality and gender not only in the Western world but in countries [in] which discrimination is still a pervasive part of everyday life. I want to write, act and essentially be an outspoken humanitarian and advocate of human rights, sexuality and gender identity, to both challenge and unify people all over the world and make a better and more accepting world for my children and anyone who has gone through the pain and anguish of institutionalised discrimination. (Willow, gender questioning, 17 years)

Almost two thirds of the transgender people aged 16+ in another study were in a relationship: 43 per cent were in a monogamous relationship, 12 per cent were in an open relationship, and 5 per cent were in a polyandrous relationship (Jones *et al.*, 2015). In addition, 8 per cent were single and dating, and a third (33%) were single and not dating. Some participants had met their partner before they started transitioning. They transitioned during the course of the relationship and remained together, with the other partner being supportive throughout the process. For example, Maddox (male/FtM/trans man, queer/heterosexual, 21 years) had found that this romantic and sexual dynamic with his girlfriend remained unchanged, despite the way the labels around it might have:

> I am in a long-term relationship with a woman. It is every bit as normal as any other heterosexual relationship; we have very heterosexual sex and always have. We have been together two-and-a-half years, I have just moved interstate to be with her. We were together while I redefined my gender identity, so for the first two years we were titled 'lesbians', but she has always felt I was her boyfriend and has always known this path would be the one I ended up on so she was ready for it. She has been one of my main supports.

Nikozilar (male, bisexual/pansexual, 20 years) had felt particular support from his long-term boyfriend during the harder parts of transition:

> Aged 17, I started dating my current partner (a male). We met at a LGBTI event and he saw me as male from the start. It's taken a while, but I feel very comfortable having sex with him. We've happily been together for years now and he helped me stay sane during the long wait to start testosterone.

Others, like Amy (MtF transgender, 18 years), found the transition or the social response to it brought their dating with an established partner to an end:

> I have always known I wanted to be a girl, always. I guess I consider myself a lesbian, even though right now I have a penis... lame. I got engaged, to a beautiful and nice girl I was with for a very long time. Everything was good ... eventually I came out as trans, she knew I was bi already, she was supportive and was still ok with it...until she told her parents and after that she told me it was off, that was the end of that.

Sexual health workers and sex educators should educate transgender youth, their parents and guardians, and other youth broadly on the wide range of relationships (including also traditional heterosexual marriages) that transgender people engage in to dispel any myths of their incompatibility with romance, and support youth through dating ups and downs.

## Romantic and/or sexual attraction

Transgender youth are more likely to experience some same sex attraction than the cisgender youth population according to several studies (Clark *et al.*, 2014; Jones *et al.*, 2015; Smith *et al.*, 2014). A New Zealand study found approximately 40 per cent of transgender students were not exclusively opposite sex attracted, compared to less than 7 per cent of cisgender students. Similarly, Figure 4.1 shows how over one third (36%) of Australian transgender people aged 16+ reported being sexually attracted to people of both sexes; one quarter (25%) were exclusively attracted to the opposite sex, 15 per cent reported they were exclusively same sex attracted, 14 per cent expressed that their sexual attraction changed and a tenth were uncertain (Jones et al., 2015). On the discussion board forum blog for the study, the participants delivered a variety of sexual attractions which could be grouped under categories of attraction towards: 'male-born men and transmen'; 'female-born and transwomen'; 'only women'; 'only men'; 'both sexes'; 'all gender expressions' and 'specific persons regardless of their anatomy or gender identity'. One transgender person expressed being 'undefined' in regards to sexual orientation. Others expressed a sexual orientation for which single labels were not available. For example, a transgender FtM person said:

> I am attracted to both sexes, but mostly only gay people in those categories, and only the more 'masculine' in demeanor of those categories. Some gay males, some 'butch' lesbians. Also some androgynous-type of people – again, those who are more 'masculine' in demeanor. ... Seems that a 'queer' energy twist is key, along with masculine-type energy.

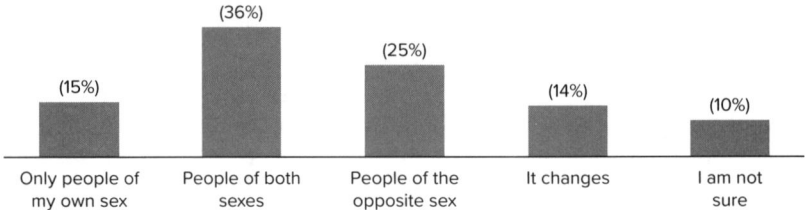

Figure 4.1: *Romantic/sexual attractions of transgender people aged 16+ (n=212)*

Many participants referred to fluctuations in their choice of sexual partners. Some expressed that despite always having been in relationships with women (pre- and post-transition), they would always identify as 'queer' because they were attracted to all expressions of gender despite their current or past circumstances in relationships. For example, Ramir (transgender, homo/queer, 25 years) was open to falling for anyone, but thus far had only been with cis-women. He was now in a long-term relationship, and hoped to be with her 'for the long run'. However, he reflected, 'I feel strongly that I am not straight even if I am in a guy–girl relationship. My lesbian community is a big part of my life.' He said he considered himself 'queer 100%', and his current girlfriend 'accepts me for the person that I am, and that includes treating me accordingly in the bedroom according to what I am comfortable/uncomfortable with'.

Another Australian study found that some transgender youth made a distinction between romantic attraction and sexual attraction in their open-ended responses (Smith *et al.*, 2014). As one young trans man/boy (25 years) explained, 'I am romantically attracted to women and transmen and sexually attracted to all genders including cismen.' Another transgender youth elaborated:

> I am romantically, emotionally and physically attracted to males and females in whatever form be they cis, trans, intersex and especially androgynous. I would marry a male or a female depending on who I fell in love with. I am equally attracted to both genders romantically though I am more sexually attracted to females. (questioning, 18 years)

Another said:

> I class myself as panromantic I like to have romantic relationships not sexual. (gender-fluid, 21 years)

Transgender youth can discuss romance or themselves as romantic participants in ways that do not denote the gender(s) of either the object of their attractions or themselves. In doing so, they creatively carve out spaces for themselves where they were able to experience sexual desire, pleasure, attraction and identity in ways that do not pin them down to restrictive gender identities or expressions. They can create new identifications that very specifically described their experiences. For example, Eden (genderqueer, 21 years) said:

> I consider myself a gay male woman. I am comfortable with my male anatomy, am primarily attracted to (effeminate) men and consider my relations to be 'same-sex'. However, I expect others to call me 'she' and see me as female in all other areas. Occasionally, when I am attracted to women, I am attracted to them on the basis of the female aspects of myself. So attraction for me is always, in some sense, same-sex. I am also attracted to non-binary people or people who push the binary.

Sexual health providers and professionals, and sex educators, need to understand that such unique identities *do not mean that transgender youth are confused*. On the contrary, *some might consider sexual health providers or educators who insist on binary explanations of romance as suffering from outdated thinking*. They may consider old-fashioned limitations to be done away with, alongside normative gender and romance ideals.

## Transgender youth's use of sexual identity labels

Most transgender youth have strongly privileged the use of sexual identity labels that did not denote the gender(s) of either the object of their attractions or themselves in recent Australian studies (Jones et al., 2015; Jones & Hillier, 2013; Jones, Smith et al., 2016; Smith et al., 2014). Half used either 'queer' or 'pansexual' (50%), over 10 per cent used 'bisexual' (Jones, Smith et al., 2016; Smith et al., 2014). Figure 4.2 shows how labels like 'questioning' and 'other' are also especially popular with transgender youth aged 14–25 years, whereas more mainstream concepts (heterosexual, homosexual) are less widely used (Jones, Smith et al., 2016).

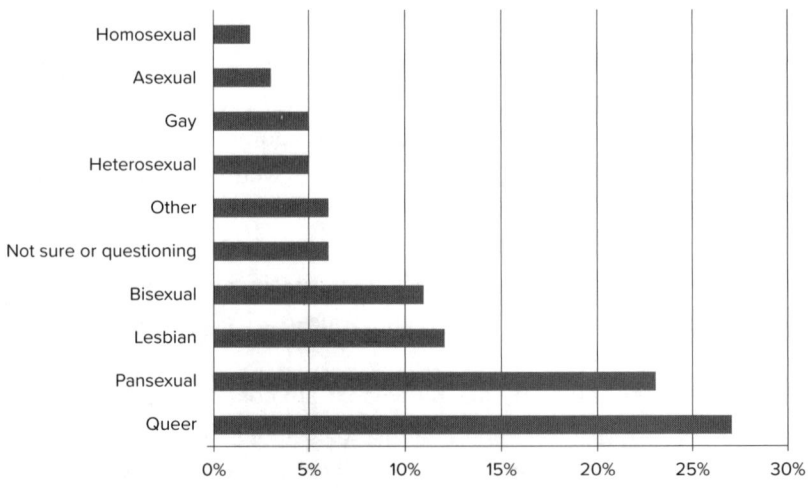

*Figure 4.2: Sexual identities of transgender youth aged 14–25 years (n=189)*

Transgender youth showed they understand their sexual identities in highly personal and self-reflective ways (Jones et al., 2015; Jones & Hillier, 2013; Jones, Smith et al., 2016; Smith et al., 2014). This complexity was evident in the way transgender youth aged 14–25 years understood their sexual attractions, behaviours, desires and identities (Smith *et al.*, 2014). For example, a genderqueer young person (16 years) said 'being queer [was] about rejecting heteronormativity and cissexism'. An agender youth subverted restrictive notions of gendered sexual desire by using the sexual identity label 'pansexual' and noting individual aspects that they were attracted to regardless of their object's sex or gender identity:

> Pansexuality, for me, is not basing my romantic or sexual attraction on gender or sex. There are many other characteristics that prevail in importance such as physical attraction, spiritual connection, intelligence, cultural similarities which decide whether I want to begin a romantic/sexual relationship with someone. (no gender/agender, 17 years)

Transgender youth's use of sexual identity labels was impacted by their age. The 14–21 age group was more likely to choose 'pansexual', the 22–25 age group preferred 'queer'. Pansexual has also been popular in other Australian research when young people were given similar options (Jones *et al.*, 2015), however, some transgender youth liked how 'queer' seemed to offer a subversive approach to life generally:

> Personally, I prefer to identify as queer rather than pansexual, as 'sex' and 'sexual' do not always factor in to who I am attracted to and how I am attracted (e.g. emotionally, spiritually). Queer culture and community are important to me and my sense of identity. 'Queer' feels like less of a label and more of a state of being and interacting with the world. (girl/woman, 24 years)

The labels used could differ as individuals evolved in their gender identities over time. Some participants focused on attraction rather than identity in order to subvert assumptions being made about their gender based on their sexuality. Sexual identity(ies) also came with communities attached to them, and for some young people this affected the categories that they chose to publicly identify with, even if their desires, attractions, and behaviours were more ambiguous. One transgender youth (gay, 25 years), took such factors into account:

> Originally it meant to me that I was attracted to and fell in love with people of the same sex as me. I guess now that I am trans that is no longer accurate for me. I can confidently say I am only attracted to women, so when people ask my sexuality I like best to say 'attracted to women' because that doesn't need my gender to be specific. I suppose I really just identify as queer, however I spent so long in the gay/homo community that I feel very attached to the description and want to keep it!

Transgender youth who use an 'asexual' sexual identity label may experience greater levels of stigma and, as such, may have worse mental health outcomes (Yule, Brotto & Gorzalka, 2013). In the study of the transgender youth aged 14–25 years, 3 per cent used the 'asexual' sexual identity label (Jones, Smith et al., 2016). Whilst this number is small, it is only slightly smaller than the portions of transgender youth using the labels 'heterosexual' (5%) or 'gay' (5%). One transgender youth (17 years) explained that identifying as asexual meant that they were 'not sexually attracted to anyone, regardless of gender', another (21 years) stated:

> I am sex repulsed and uninterested in sexual relationships but recognise that I have sexual appreciation of others.

Being asexual did not mean a transgender youth was a virgin, just that they had less or no sexual desire – they may have sex to please partners, for curiosity or they may avoid it. Being a virgin did not mean a transgender youth was asexual.

An important point to note is that transgender people attracted to the same range of gender expressions could use very different labels. On transgender social media discussion boards, those attracted to 'all expressions of gender' variably described themselves as gay, queer, pansexual or bisexual (del Pozo de Bolger et al., 2014; Jones et al., 2015). Sometimes the terminology used by transgender people attracted to all expression of gender depended on context; transgender youth particularly may erase more complicated elements of sexual identity and history in contexts where people had restricted understanding of identity variance. For example, a genderqueer youth (19 years) used 'pansexual' (with some uncertainty). They were attracted to femininity through to masculinity. They had monogamous relationships with males 'when seen as a straight woman', and monogamous and polyamorous relationships with women 'when seen as a lesbian'. Another FtM transgender person attracted to 'all gender expressions, the whole spectrum of presentations and bodies' described himself as 'gay' generally, as for most everyday people it was easier for them to comprehend given he was accepted as male and his current relationship was with a male. When describing his attractions to others within the queer community though, he used the label 'queer (usually PDQ, pretty darn queer)'. He felt this covered, more accurately, past sexual experience with males, females and genderqueer/trans* people.

Sexual health providers and professionals, and sex educators should understand, therefore, that sexual identity labels may tell you very little about transgender youth's identities. What the labels mean to the transgender young person will be unclear without asking for clarification. It is better, then, *if collecting sexual data for sexual health tests or purposes, to ask directly the precise information you need, rather than relying on assumptions based on a transgender youth's sexual identity label* (remember they may even be using a label with you which is different to one that they use in other environments). If you are unsure, either politely seek clarification (letting the individual know clarification is being sought for a particular reason which you should explain), and let them know that it is safe to discuss the matter (and ensure it is safe by keeping the information confidential and never acting titillated by sexual details). You should understand that sexual details should not be collected where not relevant and that sometimes transgender youth can feel unsafe to share information.

## Gender dysphoria and transition impact sexual life

Transgender youth can be sexually active, but may experience hesitations about this related to their gender dysphoria, body issues or treatment experiences (Bungener *et al.*, 2017; Jones *et al.*, 2015; Smith *et al.*, 2014). A Dutch study compared the sexual experiences of 137 transgender adolescents with data for 8520 same-aged cisgender youth (Bungener *et al.*, 2017). Of the transgender adolescents, 26 per cent had experienced petting whilst undressed, and only 5 per cent had had sexual intercourse. Trans boys had more sexual experience than trans girls. In comparison with the general population, transgender adolescents were significantly less sexually experienced. Despite challenges, transgender adolescents are or do eventually become sexually active, although to a lesser extent than their peers from the general population and sometimes with more initial hesitation related to bodily dysphoria.

A study of transgender people aged 16+ considered the impact of being transgender on sexual life and experiences (Jones *et al.*, 2015). Some transgender people, like Brett, felt it had not affected their sexual life at all. For example, Brett engaged in the same sexual acts – kissing, performing oral sex, receiving oral sex, performing penetrative sex through the front hole (vaginal) on his partner, and wearing a strap on – and was with the same partner in roughly the same dynamic before and after his transition. However, some transgender people said their sexuality had been affected since they became aware of their trans* identity; JW said, 'Null and void: I have had no relationships since being out as trans.' Thewaywesee (trans* male or queer male, pansexual, 22 years) said, 'What sexual life? It was hard enough finding someone when seen as female. Now being a trans* male I don't even know where to begin.' Other transgender people like Junk000 (male, undefined, 22 years) had a change in sexual orientation – he was originally attracted to feminine males and now he could not give a label to his sexual orientation. Transitioning impacted his sexual drive in two ways: first, it had 'obliterated it' and, second, it had changed its direction: 'I suddenly became attracted to women.' Gavin (male/FtM transgender, straight, 23 years) also had a few sexual relationships with men when he was in high school, but once he transitioned he had sexual relationships with women. Aid (socially male, pansexual, 18 years) said pre-transition he was 'unable to be touched by hands or mouths on my genitals, and was unable to undress in front of others or a mirror'. After testosterone treatments and chest surgery, he said, 'I enjoy an active sex life that involves oral sex as well as penetrative sex.' He was now 'comfortable with all'.

There were participants interested in bringing bodies together in all sorts of creative ways, alongside participants who didn't enjoy being touched. Participants described engaging variably in a range of possible sexual acts including:

- none
- kissing

- performing oral sex
- receiving oral sex
- performing penetrative sex through the front hole (vaginal)
- receiving penetrative sex through the front hole (vaginal)
- performing penetrative sex (anal)
- receiving penetrative sex (anal)
- wearing a strap on
- anything
- other acts.

Several participants responded quite positively to the list on the whole. Draconem said, 'I'll go with "anything" including "other". Haha.' Garfield joked that he'd happily engage in 'all of the ones you listed except for "none"'. There were others – particularly those who identified as straight males – who were less interested in experimentation or ruled out receiving penetrative sex. However, there were also straight males interested in receiving penetration. No general rules of impacts on preference for sexual acts can be declared for transgender youth. It is noteworthy, however, that they may engage in a broader range of behaviours (with a variety of partners, with individually variable impacts) than sexual health providers and sex educators might assume from their gender affirmations.

## Sexual protection, STIs and pregnancy

International research has suggested that STD and HIV infection can be high for transgender communities (James *et al.*, 2016; Rowniak *et al.*, 2011; Stephens, Bernstein & Philip, 2011). US research (James *et al.*, 2016) suggested that whilst most US transgender people were at five times the level of risk to the general cisgender US population (1.4% vs. 0.3%), HIV rates were significantly higher for trans women (3.4%). The study found that 12 per cent of transgender women had done sex work at some point in their lives and this may be a contributing factor. The literature overall also mentioned contributing factors such as high-risk sexual behaviours or sex work for some transgender people, hyper-sexuality and genital dryness/bleeding during hormone therapy, the unfamiliar nature of the gay community for boys who had sex with boys, and incorrect assumptions concerning risk.

A Canadian study explored the pregnancy experiences and related health factors amongst 923 transgender youth aged 14–25 years using a national sample (Veale *et al.*, 2017). In total 5 per cent of transgender youth reported a past pregnancy experience; this is comparable to broader Canadian youth population-based estimates. They reported over six times a greater likelihood of having been diagnosed with an STI by a doctor (19%). This suggested they may have experienced a period of not using protection, or some confusion about contraceptive and protective devices at some point over the years, where pregnancies were unintended. It is notable that some individuals may intentionally try to have a baby early to try to conform to gender norms before accepting transgender status or because they intend to transition later, or for other reasons. Therefore, pregnancy and related sexual health services (including prenatal care, abortion, adoptive services and other options) should not be overlooked by sexual health professionals and sex educators working with transgender youth.

A study of transgender people aged 16+ asked how the participants protected themselves during sexual engagements on discussion board forums (Jones *et al.*, 2015). The study showed transgender people were under-prepared for their new level of sexual risk given different types of sexual behaviours, particularly for FtM transgender and gender diverse people entering into gay male communities (who generally had more established knowledge about sexual practices and protection options). Of the 21 who responded to this question, most were not using any protection. One showed typical thinking of the group when he reasoned that with his boyfriend he would no longer need protection 'as that cycle isn't happening any more'. Several FtM transgender boys (who had most recently been in relationships with women before becoming trans) used no protection at all – a practice quite common amongst lesbian communities, and which seemed to be 'exported' from lesbian experiences into FtM sexual lives post-transition. One said that when he had gone to a doctor for an STD test (as an FtM transgender person who had only slept with women), the doctor had laughed and suggested he was at no risk at all. This *simply is not true* – oral and vaginal sex alone can transmit chlamydia and herpes, amongst other STIs. Precise STI protection information and information about pregnancy risk would be useful for transgender youth. Given that they had been seeing sexual health practitioners (in most cases) fairly often for their gender affirmations and transitions, these engagements seemed good opportunities for provision of sexual health materials. However, the lack of transgender-focused information on sexuality was clearly a barrier.

## Partner violence and sexual abuse

Transgender youth face increased risk of physical or sexual intimate partner violence according to US studies (Kussin-Shoptaw, Fletcher & Reback, 2017; Valentine *et al.*, 2017). Research suggests the relationships of transgender girls, however, represent a greater danger to them than the relationships of transgender boys. Studies, mainly from the US and Australia, show that transgender boys and men in romantic relationships had decreased depression symptoms, were affirmed by their romantic partners seeing them as male and could explore a range of sexualities and sexual experiences not previously available to them pre-transition given partners' support (Bockting, Benner & Coleman, 2009; Jones *et al.*, 2015; Meier *et al.*, 2013; Riggs, von Doussa *et al.*, 2015; Schleifer, 2006). However, transgender girls and women may perceive inherent risks when seeking to date cisgender men, experience confidence issues over judgements of their physical appearance, fear rejection by partner upon disclosure of their transgender status, and experience a loss of intimate relations even from supportive female partners if they transition (Hines, 2007; Iantaffi & Bockting, 2011; Riggs, von Doussa *et al.*, 2015).

In the past year 12.1 per cent of transgender women, 9.1 per cent of trans\* individuals with alternate or non-conforming gender identities, 8.2 per cent of gender non-binary/genderqueer individuals and 6.6 per cent of transgender men experienced physical or sexual violence from their intimate partners (Valentine *et al.*, 2017). Further, American studies have shown that transgender women in particular have consistently reported elevated rates of lifetime physical and sexual abuse both within and beyond relationships. Amongst 99 transgender women enrolled in a Hollywood Comprehensive Risk

Counselling and Services programme (Kussin-Shoptaw *et al.*, 2017), 85 per cent reported experiencing physical or sexual abuse at some point in their lifetime, and symptoms of psychological and emotional distress amongst those who reported abuse were more severe than those observed in programmes for cisgender people. In another US study, more than three quarters (77%) of the transgender women who had engaged in sex work experienced intimate partner violence and 72 per cent were sexually assaulted, a substantially higher rate than the overall sample (James *et al.*, 2016). Kussin-Shoptaw and colleagues (2017) argue that this high prevalence of physical and/or sexual abuse amongst transgender women and its associated distress should lead service providers working with this population to be especially sensitive to the abuse history and any need to refer people on to counselling, legal protection servicess or social service provisions.

## Deficiencies in sexual health services and sex education

UK, South African and other international studies point to the lack of knowledge of sexual health professionals and sex educators on transgender issues (Lefkowitz & Mannell, 2017; Muller *et al.*, 2016). A UK study of 20 semi-structured interviews with sexual health service providers and professionals showed five main problematic ideas limited their treatment of transgender youth (Lefkowitz & Mannell, 2017):

- *Binary-only understandings of transgender identities.* Of the service providers and professionals interviewed, many understood transgender within a male/female binary only, and did not recognise other transgender identities.

- *Conflating transgender status with homosexuality.* Of the sexual health service providers and professionals interviewed, many perceived being transgender as being gay or as a sexual orientation.

- *Uncertainty about what sex organs/parts transgender youth had.* There was significant confusion amongst sexual health service providers and professionals regarding what sexual organs transgender youth had.

- *Assuming that transgender youth had unstable mental states.* Of the sexual health service providers and professionals interviewed, most saw transgender youth as mentally unstable and confused.

- *Bias against the age and self-awareness/decision-making skills of transgender youth.* Of the sexual health service providers and professionals interviewed, many service providers perceived that transgender youth are too young to know that they are transgender.

Some of these representations were potentially stigmatising and many conflicted with transgender youth representations of themselves (Lefkowitz & Mannell, 2017).

Some research highlighted that transgender youth are at significant risk for HIV, but are often overlooked in sex education efforts (Bockting *et al.*, 1998; Garofalo *et al.*, 2006; Stieglitz, 2010). Compared to cisgender same sex attracted youth, transgender youth were less likely to report that their sexuality education at school was inclusive of positive messages around gender diversity (Jones & Hillier, 2013). Two thirds of transgender youth aged 14–25 years rated their school's sex education provision *mostly inappropriate*, and under 10 per cent as *mostly appropriate* (Jones, Smith *et al.*, 2016). Those enrolled at Christian schools most often reported that sex education was *mostly inappropriate* (85%); none found it *mostly appropriate*. Over half (55%) of transgender youth aged 14–25 years rated their school's puberty education provision *mostly inappropriate* (Jones, Smith *et al.*, 2016). Nathan (FtM, 21 years) explained, 'sex education class did not mention trans' and Boston (gender questioning, 18 years) noted, 'we are told to be "lady-like"'. Over 40 per cent reported that their school featured an over-reliance on segregation by gender (e.g. single-sex lessons) which impacted the delivery of sex education and sexual health information; making it seem as though sexual knowledge belonged only to particular gender identities or bodies – not to everyone. UNESCO has pointed out the links between inadequate sexual health education coverage for transgender youth and poor outcomes (UNESCO, 2011).

## Helpful sexual health professionals and sex educators

In describing good experiences with sexual health service providers and sex educators, transgender people highlighted *the importance of saying something affirming about transgender people* in sexual health/sexual education sessions (Hillier *et al.*, 2010; Jones & Hillier, 2013). Transgender youth most praised sexual health professionals and sex educators who:

- *understand that transgender people need sexual health services that are directly included in or additional to lgb services*: Transgender youth appreciated when sexual health services and resources were specifically tailored for them. When transgender youth were overlooked, they noticed, and they discussed the issue as a point of contention. Eric (FtM transgender) said, 'The sexual health clinic only deals with GLB issues' (Jones *et al.*, 2015, p.41). Sexual health workers and educators should not consider transgender issues covered under gay issues or services automatically – these should be worked in or given separate coverage.

- *directly affirm gender diversity in sexual health and education messages*: Transgender youth appreciated sexual health professionals and sex educators who taught direct positive messages about gender diversity. A study of 51 Australian transgender youth aged 14–18 years showed sexuality and gender educators reported positivity about gender diversity had correlations with their personal school morale, wellbeing and belonging (Ullman, 2016). However, another study showed less than a third of 3134 transgender and cisgender students received sex education that taught them 'That males don't have to be "manly" and females don't have to be "girly"' (27.39%) (Jones, 2015b, p.111). The 91 transgender youth in the study were less likely than the cisgender youth to feel they had received the message. Transgender youth therefore need a gender diversity message to be *clearly and directly* communicated.

- *facilitate both online, and face-to-face or phone support*: Transgender youth appreciated professionals who facilitated both online support groups and other forms of contact such as phone or face-to-face sessions. Around a third felt better when they accessed information and social contact through online supports, whereas almost half felt better when they talked to a professional offline (Smith *et al.*, 2014). Over nine in ten used the Internet to research this sort of information, and resources can be supplied over sexual health services' websites.

- *look up information and issues they lack knowledge or experience on*: Transgender youth appreciated when sexual health service providers made an effort to understand new sexual issues, transgender issues or STI risks and so on (Jones *et al.*, 2015). For example, Jake (male, 21 years) said:

  > The Sexual Health clinic are great. They sometimes lack a bit of knowledge but are more than happy to look it up or find out for me, etc. ... They have a general understanding but it is not their area of expertise like say an endocrinologist, but they do have one of those on staff who visits from time to time.

## Combatting cisnormativity and cissexism in sexual health services and sex education

Training by transgender people is recommended to help address the misunderstandings common to sexual health service providers and professionals (Lefkowitz & Mannell, 2017).

To directly combat the transphobic and cisnormative/cissexist bias exhibited in the UK sexual health provision, providers and professionals can be actively taught messages which directly overcome the five main inaccurate assumptions of sexual health professionals:

- *Replace 'binary-only understandings of transgender identities' with acknowledgement that transgender youth have diverse binary and non-binary identities.* These non-binary possibilities include genderqueer, gender non-conforming, gender-fluid and other identities. In short, some individuals feel they are neither male nor female in identity; some feel somewhere between or don't conform to the 'norms' expected of their gender; some feel that their gender identity changes constantly, regularly or occasionally. These are all legitimate ways to be as a human being just as feminine and masculine identities are.

- *Distinguish transgender status from homosexuality.* Transgender youth have a variation to their experience of their gender, and that this is not itself 'a sexuality' or 'homosexuality'. Transgender youth may or may not have a diverse sexual orientation; for example, a transgender girl (who was allocated a male sex at birth) might be asexual, straight, lesbian, bisexual, pansexual, unsure or queer. Transgender youth have a broad range of sexual orientations. It is up to an individual to let you as a sexual health professional or sex educator know their orientation, if they feel safe and comfortable enough to.

- *Accept that transgender youth have a range in sex organs/parts and don't make assumptions or judgements about their bodies; discuss them in terms of function or in the transgender youth's preferred words.* Transgender youth have an unpredictable range in their sexual organs. This depends on their age and development, socio-economic circumstances, needs and bodily ideals. Sexual health professionals should ultimately avoid gendering the organs of transgender youth in the words they use when the youth's preferences for language are unknown (Jones *et al.*, 2015; Riggs & Bartholomaeus, 2017). Engage in discussion of their 'gametes' (not sperm or ova), their 'genitals' (not penis or vagina), their 'chests' or use other neutral terms or directly ask their preferences. Transgender youth can also be directly asked their preferred terms for body parts. Transgender youth sometimes maintain the bodies they were born with in full, and sometimes change parts or much of them. It is important to note that a very small portion of people who are transgender may also have an intersex variation, so their bodies or genitalia may (without intervention) be atypical. As a sexual health worker, you will discover that indeed all humans' genitalia and bodies are atypical…we are all unique and should not be shamed for it.

- *Respect that transgender youth are generally of stable mental state and that dysphoria related to gender in particular.* Transgender youth are not in general mentally unstable and confused about most things. Transgender youth may experience dysphoria around their gender (distress over how it does not align with their bodily presentation) – or may not. There is an 'exit clause' to gender dysphoria diagnoses; for many, this is not permanent and it can be relieved through gender affirmation and/or self-acceptance. Some transgender people are diagnosed with depression, anxiety or other mental illnesses; these illnesses can be treated and do not mean an individual is permanently unstable or should be written off by their sexual health service providers. It is biased to assume any one individual is mentally unstable based on their transgender status alone. Further, anyone with specific mental health issues deserves appropriate respectful care.

- *Do not show bias against the age and self-awareness/decision-making skills of transgender youth.* Transgender youth can know a lot about themselves and their gender at a young age. Indeed, gender expression variance may be experienced 'always' or from infancy (Hillier *et al.*, 2010; Martin & Ruble, 2013; Olson *et al.*, 2015); gender identity variance may be known by five years (Jones *et al.*, 2015; Jones & Hillier, 2013; Olson *et al.*, 2015); and transgender status may be known earlier than sexual identity (Jones & Hillier, 2013; Olson *et al.*, 2015).

## Ethics and training

Sexual health professionals and sex educators should familiarise themselves with the basic sexual health concerns and education needs outlined in both the UNESCO *International Technical Guidance on Sexuality Education* (UNESCO, 2009) and the WPATH *Standards of Care for the Health of Transsexual, Transgender, and Gender Nonconforming People* (World Professional Association for Transgender Health, 2011), and keep up to date with the local laws and sexual health industry policies around transgender youth relevant to their role. Graduate and short training programmes are available that prepare future sexual health professionals and sex educators (including all people in education degrees, as teachers may be involved in sex education) to develop and publish clear affirming policies and curricula that advocate for non-discrimination for transgender youth and their sexual health information needs. Sexual health professionals can contribute to their own personal and professional development by exploring their personal values and ideas around the sexual lives of transgender youth, and the realities of sex work as a sometimes more readily available income for transgender youth depending on their support, preferences and countries. Reflect on how confident you are in actively standing up to empower transgender youth's needs and representation in sexual health care organisations and sex education curricula. What resources do you need, where are they available (such as through global UNESCO resources and local resources), what training do you need to be up to date?

## Conclusions and recommendations

The statistics and information on transgender youth's sexual health service and sex education experiences, relationship statuses, sexual identities, sexual expressions and experiences outlined in this chapter have shown how diverse transgender youth's sexual lives are. The chapter also showed the unpredictability of sexual health needs for transgender youth, who engaged in unpredictable sexual behaviours with varying risk levels, revealing a need for tailored sexual health information.

The shifts in thinking about sexual health and sexuality education over time then have privileged greater inclusivity for transgender youth. Sexual health professionals and services, and sex educators need:

- to train both pre-service and in-service sexual health professionals and sex educators (therefore, all teachers, who may potentially be placed in charge of sex education programmes) about transgender youth

- to provide professional development training for sexual health service support staff (i.e. administration staff) on inclusive practice for transgender youth

- to compile specialist mental health, health and domestic violence services information for transgender youth in order to make appropriate referrals when issues beyond sexual health arise, or sexual health sites are the first point of service contact for an individual

- to increasingly consider whether to and how to disseminate sexual tests, sexual information on transgender youth sexual risks and arrangements for face-to-face and phone contact through mobile phone apps and Internet websites

- to advocate against enforced sterilisations of transgender youth in any country where these are pushed as a reproductive and sexual health rights issue

- to educate transgender youth, their parents and guardians, and other youth broadly on the wide range of relationships (including also traditional heterosexual marriages) that transgender people engage in to dispel any myths of their incompatibility with romance

- to understand that transgender youth's more unique romantic and sexual attractions and sexual identities, and their different alignments with unpredictable choices in sexual acts and partners, do not mean that transgender youth necessarily feel confused. Some simply have complex ways of thinking about gender and sexuality

- to note that transgender youth have individually variable gender identities, variable impacts from their gender affirmations, variable body part combinations and are individuals. They are generally mentally stable and able to understand and decide about their own gender more than anyone else can

- to use neutral language about body parts describing them in terms of function and not gender, or ask for transgender youth's own preferred terms

- to ask directly for the precise information needed if collecting sexual data for sexual health tests or purposes, rather than relying on assumptions based on a transgender youth's sexual identity label

- to discuss the full range of sexual practices, sexual risks, protection and contraceptive options, and partner violence protections available for transgender youth. It is especially important to discuss how hormone and surgical treatments may or may not impact libido, sexual function or performance, fertility, and how these treatments are absolutely not sexual protection from STIs. It is also important to discuss the need for sexual toys (such as butt plugs) or sexual/bodily aids (such as dildos and strap ons) to be treated as potential distributors of STIs through shared contact across partners or lack of appropriate hygiene, and how such tools or body aids should be cleaned

- to provide sexual health information online, via apps and in other forms especially for transgender youth or incorporating established transgender youth online efforts.

## ■ Chapter 5 ■

# Transgender Youth and Education

I don't think any teacher in that school even knew that you could be Trans* and be under the age of 18. (Turbogroove, genderqueer, 25 years)

I was called a fucking faggot, fag, bitch, just the usual really by people in higher years... I managed to avoid the beating up mostly, or I beat them as I always was pretty popular actually, which made it eventually that no one could ever say anything without a mass backing me, so no one said anything again. As of Year 10 I could even cross-dress as I pleased and no one opposed it, they all just told me how much balls it took to do that and high-fived me. (Amy, MtF transgender, 18 years)

I go to an all-girls school, which causes me lots of distress. ... I plan to come out after graduation, so I'll have been an adult for a while. I also feel that I'm a little unprepared for any questions, so I want to make sure that I can give them a solid understanding of what's going on. I'm overwhelmed by a lot of stuff too right now, school, family, friends, out of school activities... The silence has a huge impact on me daily. I feel a huge weight and pressure from it. I hate being closeted because I can't be who I am. ... I just want to scream out that 'I'm male!' There was a very heated discussion about a transwoman in English which had me trembling from the strength of my emotions. I wonder what they'd say if they knew I'm also transgender? (Charredmarsh, male, 17 years)

## ■ KEY POINTS

- Education systems have historically been systems through which gender norms are communicated to populations. Feminists have particularly pointed out the many ways this occurs.

- Education service providers and professionals are urged by international human rights legislation and a recent ministerial call to action to create inclusive, safe and supportive education institutions for transgender students.

- Schools' structural supports and information provision vary from location to location, but are often underdone.

- Support features can include flexibility in gender segregation and facilities use, provision of access to appropriate sexuality and puberty information, education staff use of appropriate names and pronouns and many other features impacting the daily lives of transgender youth.

- Bullying and violence against transgender youth are prolific, and need to be adequately addressed through policy provisions and educational efforts.

- A major deficiency in educational spaces, from which many other deficiencies stem, is the effort made to prevent transgender youth from being themselves, whether directly, or indirectly through structurally promoted gender normativity.

- Helpful education professionals are those who provide affirming messages about transgender youth diversity, support transgender youth including their activism and causes, make an effort to use the correct language for transgender youth identities, and respect the privacy of any individual's transgender status and related information.

School provisions for transgender students – especially bathrooms – have become increasingly debated around the world. This education-focused chapter considers the broad history of the treatment of gender in schools, and the development of international human rights legislation and policies to promote transgender students' inclusion.

The transnational politics behind efforts at developing or rescinding policies about transgender youth are explained. The chapter includes statistics on transgender students' education attendance and attainment levels, experience of structural supports and school uniforms, and experiences of bullying and violence. It shows how the media drama in many countries surrounding their school bathroom use stems from a broader use of bathroom access as a symbol of social status by which segments of society are marginalised. It lists the many benefits to direct education policy protection for transgender youth and advises on policy framings. Deficiencies in textbooks and opportunities for self-expression in schools are discussed, alongside traits of the most helpful education professionals for transgender youth. This chapter finally describes how to combat cisnormativity and cissexism in education settings and training for professionals. Vital steps for improvement are listed for education services and professionals.

## Historic education and services: Gendered conformity

Since the beginning of modern history, education around the world has been highly gendered, sometimes only available to boys from higher socio-economic classes and often completely gender-segregated (Jones, 2011b; Tait, 2012). Where first-wave feminism from the late 19th century focused on women's right to vote and participate in citizenship, second-wave feminism from the 1960s and 70s challenged biological determinism through efforts focused on challenging gender role normativity in schools (Egan & Hawkes, 2010; Jones, 2011b; Tait, 2012; Tuttle, 1986). Tait (2012) described how their efforts pointed to the role of mass education schools in reproducing unequal power relations between the genders and constituting a 'gender regime', through:

- single sex schooling, which assumes males and females are very different
- the differences in the gendered mottos at schools for boys (which value strength, courage, conquering) and girls (which value love, faith, sweetness, less assertive concepts)

- subject enrolment trends which were dominated by hard sciences and physical education for boys, and soft sciences and humanities for girls
- the ways girls have been more likely to be punished for (boisterous) behaviours accepted in boys
- the greater teacher time given to boys than girls in co-educational environments
- dress-codes and the ways boys are allowed more practical clothing
- boys' increased resource access and sports funding
- classroom texts' greater representations of boys and male characters
- the greater numbers of female staff as teachers caring for younger kids and male staff in leadership positions or teaching 'hard' subjects for older kids.

In such highly gendered environments, transgender youth had little choice but to attempted to blend in, bear punitive responses to their gendered presentations or behaviours, or leave education settings when possible (Stone, 1991). Reed Erickson, a US transgender FtM man, had graduated from an all-girls' school, for example, before he inherited the family business and was able to live out his gender identity; he founded the Erickson Educational Foundation (EEF) in 1964 (Devor, 2013). EEF supplied information at no cost to transgender youth and their family members, and professionals where possible. EEF also funded the earliest symposia for professionals who worked with transsexuals which led to today's World Professional Association for Transgender Health, funded the publication of seminal texts by researchers John Money and others, and ensured events were held around the world including in the UK, Yugoslavia, Denmark and other countries (Devor, 2013). Reforms around transgender youth were not large-scale in education and only ad hoc grass-roots efforts were seen, with attempts at attachment to other critical education movements sometimes unwelcome. For example, some feminist and gay liberation education movements sought to avoid the additional controversy attached to transgender youth (Jones, 2011a, 2011b; Moran, 2000; Raymond, 1994; Stone, 1991).

## Contemporary education and services: Safe and supportive schools vs. backlash

Since 2010, advocates for transgender youth, education access and human rights in education broadly from every global region promoted protection of gender identity and expression in international human rights legislation (Vance, 2011). The shift to an inclusive, safe and supportive schools approach for transgender youth was promoted by United Nations (UN) Secretary-General Ban Ki-moon (Jones, 2016b). He named transphobic bullying in schools 'a public health crisis' in a speech to 200 UN Member States who convened to combat it (UN Secretary-General, 2011), influenced by education research showing the prolific bullying transgender and other minority youth experienced. The UN's *Born Free and Equal* policy clarified transgender youth rights to non-discrimination in education and access to a safe education (United Nations, 2012). UNESCO's first international policy consultations on transphobic bullying in schools were conducted in Brazil, where education policy guidelines were developed by academics, education representations, governments and members of human rights organisations and NGOs – including the author of this book (UNESCO, 2011, 2012a, 2012b). The Global Network Against Homophobic and Transphobic Bullying in Schools formed and met annually in different global regions to further policy goals (Kosciw & Pizmony-Levy, 2013).

Transgender youth experiences of negative educational, physical and mental health outcomes from transphobic violence in education settings had been recorded in the US, Australia, New Zealand and UK (GLSEN, 2012; Jones & Hillier, 2013; Jones, Smith *et al.*, 2016; Russell *et al.*, 2011; Smith *et al.*, 2014). Over time transnational UNESCO, Human Rights Watch and other global organisations' consultations facilitated similar student research within Africa, Asia and the Middle East (Human Rights Watch, 2016, 2018; UNESCO, 2015, 2016b, 2016d). Global and regional bodies including, for example, the UN's various arms (UNESCO/UNAIDS/UNDP) and the World Health Organisation promoted transgender youth's rights in education to governments (UN Human Rights Office of the High Commissioner *et al.*, 2015). A Ministerial Statement committing to transgender student protection in educational institutions was released (UNESCO, 2016a). Several countries (Chile, the Netherlands, South Africa, the US and Thailand) and conglomerates (UNESCO, GALE (Gay and Lesbian Education) and the EU) had roles supporting transnational policy rollout – however, the nature of their roles were subject to change depending on changes to governments' administrations (Jones, 2016b, 2017c).

Education is controlled by governments and international religious organisations; it is thus an industry where political battles over transgender youth are fought. It is essential for education providers and professionals to understand the political nature of countries' resistance to (and rescindments of) support for transgender youth in schools, and the fact that *seemingly external international political power expansion efforts may influence how transgender students are attacked by media in their own country*. When Russia, Uganda and Nigeria banned LGBT education advocacy altogether (Malkin, 2014; Onuah, 2014; Rogers, 2014), key informant interviewees noted that such backlash is in part nationalist resistance to the influence of global bodies, influenced by anti-LGBT conservative/traditional family protectionist groups and global politicking that has little to do with 'transgender youth' and much to do with power (Jones, 2016b, 2017c). For example, the Russian Kremlin has sought to destabilise liberal democracies by aiding foreign anti-LGBT political and pressure groups for decades (Dugin, 1997); and also influences the voting behaviour of both pro-LGBT and anti-LGBT groups in Western countries through hundreds of fake social media websites discussing student gender diversity (e.g. Facebook site LGBT United and Twitter account @LGBTuni), stories and ads on transgender students, and inflammatory comments on foreign news media coverage of transgender students (Isaac & Shane, 2017; Leonnig, Hamburger & Helderman, 2017; Shane & Goel, 2017).

The US has also lead *both* transnational protections for transgender youth under the Obama Administration, *and* attacks on transgender youth's rights under the Trump Administration and through transnational evangelical groups' efforts (Jones, 2017c). On the one hand the US Government's Obama Administration (2009–2016) sent an eight-page *Dear Colleague Letter* to all education sectors advising Education Departments to:

> treat a student's gender identity as the student's sex for purposes of Title IX and its implementing regulations. This means that a school must not treat a transgender student differently from the way it treats other students of the same gender identity. (US Department of Justice & US Department of Education, 2016)

It was accompanied by a 25-page document containing examples of inclusive approaches (US Government, 2016); and efforts towards trans students' inclusion overseas through diplomatic pressure, boycotts and aid-restriction (Kosciw & Pizmony-Levy, 2013; Leroux-Nega, 2014; New York Times Editorial Staff, 2016). On the other hand the US Government's Trump Administration (2017–) sent a two-page *Dear Colleague Letter* to educational institutions rescinding protections for transgender youth:

> a federal district court in Texas held that the term 'sex' unambiguously refers to biological sex ... the Departments believe that, in this context, there must be due regard for the primary role of the States and local school districts ... and rescind the above-referenced guidance documents. (US Department of Justice & US Department of Education, 2017, p.1)

This repeal was inconsistent with many US laws, so in May 2017, the 7th Circuit Court of Appeals affirmed the rights of trans student Ash Whitaker (represented by the Transgender Law Centre) to use the bathroom matching his gender identity in a Wisconsin school (Trotta, 2017), typifying grass-roots transgender youth and NGO efforts to combat education discrimination through courts and campaigns. US-based evangelical Christian organisations and figures (C-Fam, Focus on the Family, the Saddleback Church, The Family Ministry, Family Watch International, Republican Senator James Inhofe) have also systematically funded 'hundreds' of anti-trans legislative efforts including repealing existing trans student protections and pushing Uganda's LGBT education 'propaganda' ban (Alsop, 2009; Edwards & Tencer, 2009; Jones, 2016b; Parke, 2016; Sprigg, 2016). Several promoted gender complementarity curricula through transnational outreach into the Dominican Republic, Brazil, Canada and England (Parke, 2016).

Messages about transgender students to education service providers and professionals at the international, national and local levels have thus been substantial, contradictory and destabilising. Interviews with key informants from many education systems around the world suggested that some education systems responded by lessening their support for transgender youth in education; others by fortifying it (Jones, 2017c). For example, Swedish students are given pro-LGBT messages in their curricula and are taught to spot fake news stories and media from their first year in primary school

(Roden, 2017). Education service providers and professionals may fear backlash for supporting transgender youth, but they must realise that their transgender students now have rights to non-discrimination, safety, and access in educational institutions *recognised in international human rights legislation and policies* and promoted in a global ministerial statement. Education service providers and professionals need to stop fearing the transphobic backlash that these young kids have had to bear on their small shoulders for too long, and need actively to avoid being influenced by intentionally disruptive fake news about transgender students being 'the problem' in schools. The problem in education is transphobia; it should be comprehensively addressed using the inclusive approaches discussed by UNESCO and outlined below.

## Education attendance and education attainment levels

Transgender youth attend every education setting including primary school, high school, higher education and vocational education, government schools, religious schools, performing art schools, online and radio schools and home schools (Jones, 2015b; UNESCO, 2016b). The length and level of their attendance is not necessarily the same as for cisgender students, however. Transgender youth reported lower academic attainment in Argentina, China, Denmark, El Salvador, Italy and Poland (UNESCO, 2016b). In Argentina, 45 per cent of transgender students dropped out of school altogether (Ferreyra, 2010). In Australia educational attendance and attainment was more complicated.

A higher portion of transgender Australians had a post-secondary schooling qualification of some kind (almost 70% depending on the study; Couch *et al.*, 2007; Jones *et al.*, 2015), a higher portion than in the general Australian population (57%; Australian Bureau of Statistics, 2012). Conversely, a portion of participants had only completed primary school (4%), and this was twice the portion of the general Australian population who had not attained their high school certificate (2%, Australian Bureau of Statistics, 2012). Given that by law Australian young people are required to stay in schools until 15–17 years of age (depending on state and territory laws), this likely reflected other Australian findings (Hillier *et al.*, 2010; Jones & Hillier, 2012) that transgender youth were more likely to have moved schools or dropped out due to discrimination and bullying than same sex attracted youth. Overall, 25% of 189 Australian transgender youth surveyed reported that they avoided their schools because they cannot conform to the gender stereotypes dominant within these contexts, including 50% of those in Christian schools (Jones, Smith et al., 2016). In addition, young people had noted that post-school education contexts (universities, TAFE) were often less homophobic and transphobic than secondary schooling contexts, and placed fewer restrictions on one's gender expression generally (around uniforms, gender-based rules and so on). Education providers and professionals need to understand that universities, schools, colleges and other settings can become supportive sanctuaries that build up transgender youth and allow them to become highly educated citizens over the most difficult periods of change in their lives…or they can instead be the very locations from which transgender youth are forced to flee, losing significant educational opportunities.

## Structural supports and information provision

Transgender youth need structural supports at school for their practical daily needs such as uniform use, bathroom use, getting changed and incorporation into activities. Australian researchers asked transgender youth to rate such support provisions at their school. The choices were 'mostly appropriate', 'mostly inappropriate' or 'don't know/not applicable' (Jones, Smith et al., 2016). Overall, participants indicated that their schools' provisions were mostly inappropriate (see Figure 5.1).

Over 40 per cent of the survey participants felt that gender segregation (such as lining up in rows of boys and girls, or segregation for learning, etc.) was too often applied at their school. Karen (trans girl, 18 years) said she wasn't 'out' at school, but because it was a very gendered environment in which she faced discrimination: 'I was routinely ridiculed for doing things that were considered "inappropriate" for my presumed gender.' Interviewee Theo (transgender, 14 years) said that whilst he felt that school was generally 'pretty great', it was hardest in physical education 'cause EVERYTHING is split into "boys" and "girls", and me and my best friend (who is also transgender) have considered just not going to that class'. With respect to sexuality education, two thirds of survey participants rated their schools' provision as mostly inappropriate, and less than 10 per cent as mostly appropriate. Students at Christian schools were most likely to indicate that their sexuality education was mostly inappropriate (85%); none found it mostly appropriate. In relation to puberty education, over half (55%) of the survey participants reported provisions were mostly inappropriate. Boston (gender questioning, 18 years) noted that provision for gender diversity in sexuality and puberty education in their all-girls' school were very limited: 'we are told to be "lady-like", our sex ed was appalling'.

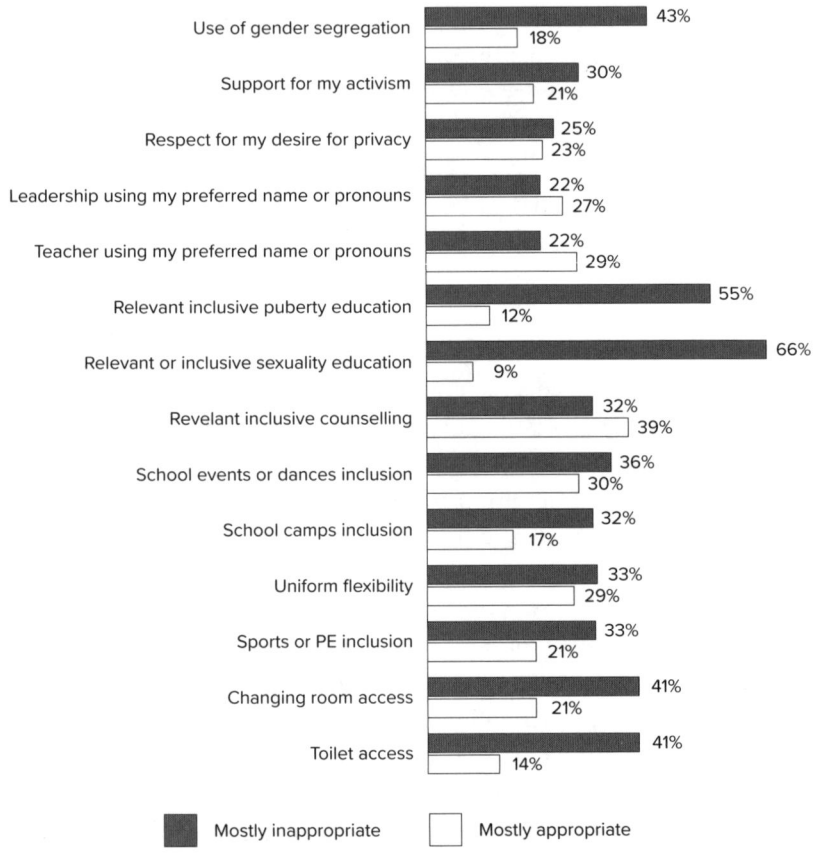

*Figure 5.1: Transgender youth aged 14–25 years on the appropriateness of their schools' support provisions*

Younger survey participants (14–17-year-olds) were more likely to have been provided with trans-inclusive counselling at school (67%; compared to 37% of 18–21-year-olds, and 22% of 22–25-year-olds). This may suggest a story of changing attitudes for school counsellors in recent years, reflecting changes in psychological framings of gender difference and diversity. Participants who attended government schools were more likely to indicate that counselling provision was appropriate for them compared to those from Christian schools. Timothy (trans boy/man, 22 years) commented, 'the only counselling that I knew of in school was from our school Chaplain [who was] the last person I would feel comfortable talking to about my gender identity'. There was no particular trend to the data on the perceived appropriateness of school uniforms. Martin (transgender boy, 16 years) described how depressed he was being 'forced to wear a dress/skirt' at school. Over a third of the students surveyed felt that the changing rooms (41%) and toilets (44%) at their school were mostly inappropriate. The topic of toilets/bathrooms is given its own section in this chapter, because it is such a sensitive issue in media coverage. However, the overall message of this research is that schools, universities and colleges (or other educational settings) must try harder to ensure structural supports for transgender youth are provided.

## Uniforms and clothes are for comfort not discipline

In some countries, such as the UK and Japan, students are required to wear a uniform. Whilst the purpose can be to communicate belonging or ensure conformity, the gendered nature of some uniforms can make it difficult for a transgender young person to wear the outfit consistent with their gender identity without it being markedly noticeable. Even in countries like the US where uniforms are rarely mandatory, over half of transgender people were discouraged from wearing clothing that fit their gender identity at school (James *et al.*, 2016). Transgender youth in Australia where uniforms are mainly mandatory were asked if their school had unisex uniform options (outfits someone of any sex/gender identity could wear; Jones *et al.*, 2015). No participant attended a school where a specifically unisex or gender-neutral uniform was standard. Some emphasised that they instead attended single sex schools in their youth where feminine styles such as dresses, skirts and stockings were mandatory. There were sometimes punishments meted out to those who tried to wear their sports shorts, pants and jerseys outside the context of sport; Gavin (male/FtM transgender, 23 years), for example, noted, 'Lunch time detention was awarded to those who broke the rule consistently…Catholic girls' school.'

Some participants, however, did attend schools where, whilst there were not unisex options as such, there were a range of options for girls which they benefited from greatly. For example, Darkneko said, 'No unisex options were available, but girls were allowed to wear long pants and shorts instead of skirts.' Brett (male/transgender male, 27 years) recounted how he deftly machinated some advocacy towards a greater range in girls' uniforms, not as a trans issue but as a women's issue, making use of the structures available to him at the time to support his needs: 'As part of the student committee I got trousers in for girls in high school. Although I was the only one wearing it.' Education service providers and professionals could create more flexible uniform options for both transgender youth and girls in general by not enforcing females to wear skirts and dresses only (perhaps offering an option of pants, shorts or kilts regardless of gender identity), and by allowing for flexibility in the event a young person wants to adapt the uniform in other ways to their gender expression.

## Attitudes towards transgender youth in education settings

Schools were not seen as environments with trans-positive attitudes. In Japan, transgender students said approaching school staff with questions on gender identity can result in censuring or outright bullying (Human Rights Watch, 2016). The Japanese proverb that the nail that sticks out gets hammered down applies for transgender youth in schools. The strong cultural desire to 'maintain harmony' means that even teachers who do try to support LGBT students can be left, as one former teacher put it, alienated in their own compassion. In an Australian study of transgender people aged 16+, participants argued that single sex schools particularly offered no other option than to act like the intake gender, or that there was a sense that alternatives simply did not exist (Jones et al., 2015). Aid (socially male, 18 years) summed up the general attitude to his gender identity at school as, 'Not accepted. You had to stick to strict gender norms or teachers involved your parents.' This reflected other findings about the prevalence of transphobic attitudes at many schools (Hillier et al., 2010).

A Vietnam study asked school stakeholders if they agreed that 'Teasing feminine male students or masculine female students is harmless' (UNESCO, 2016d). School staff most strongly disagreed (84.9%), followed by parents (69.5%) and students (64.1%). Almost a fifth of students appeared to think it was not problematic. This showed that there was some confusion particularly amongst students over whether teasing on the basis of gender was inappropriate or appropriate. Some teachers described their gender non-conforming students in a positive light, as talented and popular. One teacher from an upper secondary school said they were 'very sociable with good communication skills … this is normal, because this is common now'. One lower secondary school teacher even described appreciation of a popular male student with feminine characteristics who had a 'good relationship with both male student friends and girlfriends since he is very hard working and talented', and who could be relied on to contribute to class tasks through volunteering to help out, regardless of whether a task was considered 'feminine'. Education professionals need to learn from these affirming perspectives which are not always held by students, showing students that gender non-conforming students can be accepted and even celebrated.

## Bullying and violence against transgender youth

There is data from all regions of the world that shows transgender youth experience substantive transphobic discrimination, bullying, harassment and violence in educational settings (UNESCO, 2015, 2016b). Such transphobic abuse targets students who have declared or are perceived to have a transgender status (Pinheiro, 2006). It can also impact cisgender heterosexual students, or cause distress to them when they come into contact with it, as uncovered in a Canadian study (Taylor & Peter, 2011). It can start from infancy in climates where very small children are given strict gender roles (Martin & Ruble, 2013; Olson et al., 2015). Transphobic abuse is grounded in the fear, discomfort, intolerance or hatred of transgender diversity and people perceived to transgress gender and sex norms (transphobia and anti-intersex bias; UNESCO, 2016b). It occurs in education-related environments such as classrooms, playgrounds, toilets, changing rooms, around schools, on the way to and from school, and online. It can involve:

- physical violence, including hitting and shoving

- psychological violence, including verbal and emotional abuse and humiliation

- sexual violence, including rape, coercion and harassment
- bullying, including cyber bullying (UNESCO, 2015, 2016b).

Research has repeatedly shown links between transphobic violence in educational settings and both general school violence and bullying, school-related gender-based violence and homophobic violence since it is perpetrated as a result of existing gender norms and stereotypes (UNESCO, 2015, 2016b, 2016c, 2016d).

Transphobic violence affects the students who are targeted by violence, as well as the perpetrators and bystanders. It negatively impacts:

- education outcomes
- employment and lifestyle prospects
- wellbeing outcomes (UNESCO, 2016b).

Over three quarters (77%) of 27,715 transgender people in a US study (James *et al.*, 2016) who were out or perceived as out as transgender between kindergarten and grade 12 experienced mistreatment. This included being disciplined more harshly (20%), verbal abuse (54%), physical abuse (24%) or sexual abuse (13%). Almost one in five faced dropped out of school as a result. In addition, nearly one quarter (24%) of US transgender people who were out as transgender in college or vocational schools were verbally, physically or sexually harassed.

A Buckland Foundation-funded Australian survey of 3134 same sex attracted students aged 14–21 years included a group of 91 transgender youth (Hillier *et al.*, 2010). The data for these two groups were contrasted (Jones & Hillier, 2013). Transgender youth were significantly more likely than same sex attracted students to have disclosed their diverse identity to a range of people in their lives, including at school – meaning their visibility to bullies was increased. They were also significantly more likely than same sex attracted students to have suffered discriminatory physical assault – being beaten up, punched or kicked by individuals or groups (31 vs. 18%); for both groups, 80 per cent of their experiences of abuse occurred at school. Over twice as many of the transgender youth group compared with the same sex attracted group reported that as a result of discrimination they had been:

- unable to use the changing rooms at school for fear of attack (34 vs. 14%)

- unable to use the toilet at school for fear of attack (22 vs. 8%)
- compelled to move schools (21 vs. 9%)
- compelled to leave school altogether (22 vs. 7%)
- more likely to self-harm (46 vs. 30%)
- more likely to attempt suicide (28 vs. 16%).

These findings echoed international research that showed spoken and corporeal abuse were common for transgender youth and suicide risks were high (Haas *et al.*, 2011; UNESCO, 2016b; Varjas *et al.*, 2008) and thus suggested that schools have an ethical onus to act to better protect these students – alongside existing legal, policy and curricula requirements.

A Vietnam Ministry of Education and Training collaborative study of 3698 survey participants, 280 focus group participants and 85 interviews (with students including LGBT students, school staff and parents) showed 71 per cent of LGBT students were physically abused and 72.2 per cent were verbally abused. Gay, bisexual and gender non-conforming male and male-to-female transgender (GBT) students faced highly significant increases in risk for all kinds of violence (56.5% of GBT students compared to 36.3% of LBT students). Contributing factors included perpetrator motivations of punishing 'feminine' expressions on 'male' bodies, and an increased respect for 'masculine' expressions (even on 'female' bodies) – within a Confucian culture privileging masculinity (UNESCO, 2016d). This reflected relationships between increased physical school violence against people with 'male' bodies and the punishment of 'feminine' characteristics in studies of countries where females can be assigned lower/passive status including Cambodia, Indonesia, Nepal and Pakistan (Plan International Thailand & International Center for Research on Women, 2015).

Transgender children who reported bullying and harassment to school officials in contexts where they are not supported in policy (including schools in Japan and Ghana) risked punitive responses towards themselves (Human Rights Watch, 2016, 2018). Rather than thinking in terms of punishments of either perpetrators or victims (which may increase transphobic tensions), school professionals should aim at enhancing safety and supportiveness for all students through anti-bias education programmes, strong affirmation of all student diversity and belonging, and drawing on local cultural values to highlight the need to embrace others (Jones, 2016b). In China, for example, Aibai has drawn on the way family relationships are respected through anti-violence efforts that incorporate mothers talking about their gender diverse children to schools and universities. In America, Gay Straight Alliance networks have drawn on student social alliances to show support for individuals suffering transphobia through creating friendship networks and social campaigns. In South Africa, singing and dancing troupes express stories of the emotions stirred by social rejection and social warmth to LGBT people. In India, the Tagore school is famous for educational anti-homophobia and anti-transphobia campaigns which are entirely driven by the students themselves, showing their hard work and leadership initiative. Individual Indonesian education professionals have reported sending students for counselling against violence. These educational efforts – though sometimes ad hoc and disparate – show there are many non-punitive ways educational professionals can deal with transphobic violence, whether alone or by working with other professionals, which are sensitive to even very difficult contexts.

## Bathrooms as tools of social status

Access to public bathrooms is a major human rights issue. Bathroom access is often denied to groups when their marginalisation has become systematic – for example, people of colour were denied access to bathrooms during Apartheid in South Africa, slaves were denied access to bathrooms in the US, and so forth. Education policies and the media have made much of cases wherein transgender kids wished to use bathrooms congruent with their gender identity at school (Dibben, 2013; Jones, 2017c; Starnes, 2013). There can be efforts by conservative extremist media to pretend that transgender youth put other students at risk in bathrooms, cruelly suggesting that little trans girls wishing to relieve themselves are rapists of other little girls. There is no data to support this; data shows instead that transgender students are at more risk from cisgender students and staff when they use the bathroom. Over half the 27,715 participants in the US transgender survey had avoided public restrooms in the past year (59%) for fear of confrontations (James *et al.*, 2016). Nearly a third (32%) limited what they ate and drank to avoid needing to use the bathroom, and

8 per cent developed a urinary tract infection, kidney infection or kidney-related problem as a result.

Transgender students in the Vietnam study reported that they were especially likely to have experienced violence in bathrooms and changing rooms, because bathrooms are such highly gendered spaces and therefore spaces where transgender people are more likely to be policed (UNESCO, 2016d). Transgender people aged 16+ were asked if there had at least been some unisex bathroom options (toilets someone of any sex/gender identity could use) at the schools they attended (Jones *et al.*, 2015). The respondents all answered 'no'. Maddox (male/FtM/trans man, 21 years) noted, 'We had two sets of disabled toilets, but they weren't accessible to able-bodied students.' Maddox's distinction about able-bodied students is important to remember in light of the fact that he *did not* identify as having a disability. Some schools have sought to let transgender students use the disabled toilets as a kind of temporary solution during transition periods, for example. But this is not useful long term for someone who does not identify as having a disability and is recognisably able-bodied in the minds of other students, compared to having a unisex bathroom. Unisex bathrooms are common in some parts of Europe. Anyone can access them without the need to declare any particular identity, and these options – or allowing students to use the bathroom congruent with their gender identity – can actually allow for much less fuss than forcing someone into the wrong space or a space they simply can't use.

## Policy protection for transgender youth

Directly worded anti-discrimination policy protection of transgender youth should be a standard expectation across education sectors, at the national, state level, individual school and classroom level. Direct school-level policy protection against homophobia and transphobia is associated with:

- greater promotion of the message that 'males' don't have to be 'manly' and 'females' don't have to be 'girly'
- greater use of posters about diversity
- links with support groups and services
- increased reports of library resources/books about diversity

- students who speak up against discrimination
- better social treatment of LGBTIQ youth
- halved bullying rates for LGBTIQ youth
- halved suicide rates for LGBTIQ youth (Jones, 2015b).

Policies should directly describe transphobic abuse (verbal, physical and otherwise) as banned and should outline management and support ideals for transgender youth in the event of transitions, for example. Not all policies aiming at a supportive direction are equally affirming of transgender youth; a Japanese study found the non-binding suggestions on gender diverse students issued in April 2016, predicate respect and accommodation for gender identity on the basis of diagnosis of a mental disorder only – requiring a pathologising view of the group as being 'disordered' despite the progress to gender dysphoria diagnoses in modern psychology (Human Rights Watch, 2016).

In South Australia, the focus is not on 'managing' the student, it is on 'managing' and guiding the educational context's *support* for the student so that their gender affirmation is supported in the least disruptive and most beneficial way for the individual (depending on their varying individual need or preference around such areas as privacy, change in documentation, amenities access and/or other adaptations as relevant). The South Australian policy particularly ensures transgender students can use their preferred first name and pronoun, such as she, he or they; access toilets and changing rooms that match their gender identity; choose from all uniform options available at the school; share sleeping quarters on excursions corresponding to their gender identity; and take part in Physical Education lessons and most sports as their identified gender (South Australia Department for Education and Child Development, 2017).

## Deficiencies in education: Textbooks and self-expression

One area of deficiency is textbook representation of transgender youth. Two US studies (Macgillivray & Jennings, 2008; Young & Middleton, 2002) and one from Canada (Bazzul & Sykes, 2011) considered textbook guidelines for addressing LGBT educational content using content analysis. All studies revealed little or no mention of transgender youth in the texts, reflecting other literature arguing gender identity is largely ignored in sexuality education efforts (Bockting *et al.*, 1998; Garofalo *et al.*, 2006; Stieglitz, 2010). Professionals' reports suggested that transgender students were under great pressure not be themselves at school (Brill & Pepper, 2008; McCredie, 2008; UNESCO, 2016b). This pressure was exerted upon transgender youth both by people advising them outside of the school (families, parents and external service providers) and the people working within it (principals, teachers and so on).

Transgender youth aged 16+ unfortunately confirmed the existence of pressures to conform in an Australian survey; when they often commented that it was simply not possible to be themselves or express their identity at school (Jones *et al.*, 2015). Turbogroove (genderqueer, 25 years) emphasised that attempts to be himself were 'Strongly Discouraged'.

Just under one tenth of transgender youth aged 14–25 years surveyed had formally changed their gender on their school records (Jones, Smith *et al.*, 2016). A further 41 per cent reported wanting to do so. Thus about half of the group felt that changing their gender on their school record was a key part of their educational experience, but had not been able to. One interview participant, Charlotte (24 years), reported maintaining a silence about her gender identity to avoid affecting a family member's career: 'I was at a Christian school and my mum worked there as a teacher. So, I always had this fear that if I told one of my friends my secret, it would cause my mother to lose her job.' Education professionals should therefore understand that their support for people to be themselves can be an incredible shift in thinking in their school, and that just because they do not 'see' transgender kids in their classroom, it does not mean they are not there and very carefully weighing the support for non-conforming gender expressions that is shown.

## Helpful education professionals

Good experiences with social service providers involved professionals who, conversely, *supported transgender youth to be themselves to the extent it was currently possible to be* (Jones, 2017a; Kosciw *et al.*, 2014; UNESCO, 2015). Transgender youth most praised social service professionals who:

- *affirm messages on gender diversity*: When asked to explain how schools could better support them, the strongest theme in 3134 same sex attracted and transgender youth's (aged 14–21 years) responses was that they wanted the sexuality education curriculum messages to be diversified: more inclusive of same sex attraction and gender diversity, more detailed and complex, less conservative (Jones, 2015b). Samara (female, 15 years) was part of this group who typically wanted schools 'teaching that homophobia is wrong and shouldn't be tolerated'. Hamish (male, 18 years) similarly wanted his school to start 'including sexual diversity in the sex ed courses'.

- *publicly support transgender youth broadly and individually*: The survey of Australian youth aged 14–25 years showed that social support from staff and peers made significant differences to transgender youth's outcomes (Jones, Smith et al., 2016). Transgender youth in this study who received teaching staff support were significantly less likely to drop out of school (5 vs. 23% without staff support) and hide at lunchtime (23 vs. 50%). Transgender youth with teaching staff support were also at decreased risk of experiencing bullying by mobile phone (8 vs. 27%), written abuse (11 vs. 27%) and discriminatory language from friends (31 vs. 62%). Support for transgender youth can involve supporting whole school and whole class efforts at actions to show support for transgender youth generally – such as activities inspired by the campaigns on 'Wear it Purple' or 'International Day Against Homophobia, Transphobia and Biphobia' or other events.

- *use the appropriate pronouns, name and gender identity for their transgender students*: A survey of transgender youth aged 14–25 years showed that where teachers' use of students' pronouns/name/identity was 'mostly appropriate', students were less likely to struggle to concentrate in class (22 vs. 54% of those whose teachers used inappropriate pronouns/name/identity), drop marks (16 vs. 54%) or drop out (6 vs. 22%; Smith et al., 2014). They were less likely to experience inappropriate language use from their peers, who mimicked the teachers' modelling. They were less likely to experience written abuse and graffiti about them. They were less likely to experience being humiliated or socially isolated at school.

Bailey (trans boy, 16 years) discussed the difficulties he experienced in having his principal refuse to use male pronouns: 'It makes me depressed so much that a lot of the time I can't focus at school. Sometimes I really hate myself for this, and I want to die.'

- *respect the privacy of transgender youth*: Transgender youth who reported that the respect for their desire for privacy around their transgender status and related issues was mostly appropriate were less likely to experience harassment and abuse (Jones, Smith *et al.*, 2016), compared to those who felt their privacy was mostly handled inappropriately (see Figure 5.2). Conversely, participants who had experienced harassment, discrimination or abuse at school (38% of the total sample) were twice as likely to have PTSD (21% compared to 10%).

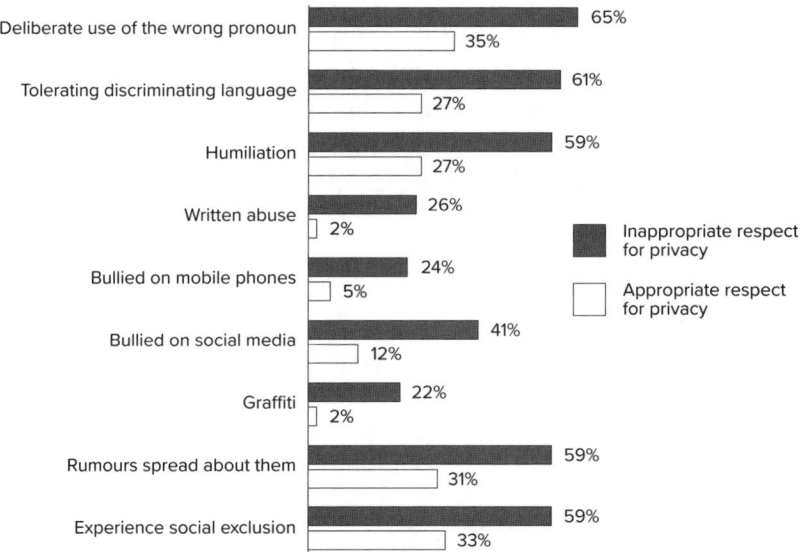

*Figure 5.2: Percentages of transgender youth experiencing social abuse type by appropriateness of teacher support for their privacy around their transgender status*

# Combatting cisnormativity and cissexism in education

Most transgender youth aged 16+ in a survey reported that they wanted to see more education and information provision on the concept of transgender – that it exists, what it can mean, that it's an affirmed and protected set of characteristics in law and part of broader diversity (Jones *et al.*, 2015). For example, Doc79 said, 'If they can teach that some kids have two mums, or two dads, then surely they can teach that not everyone who was born one sex will remain that sex…' Unisex options for the school uniform were another key theme. Gavin remarked, 'Let me wear the sports uniform, I looked awkward enough in their frilly dress!' Other features such as supportive school counsellors and other topics explored above were mentioned; Maddox added, 'the education system I experienced did not mention gender or sexuality differences. That is a shame and it should be changed. These educational changes will save lives.' Other ideas included stricter, clearer rules against transphobia and homophobia, more inclusive sex education and queer spaces.

The research in this chapter points to the vital role that supportive leadership, teachers and classmates can play in the mental and general wellbeing of gender diverse and transgender young people. It suggests the need for greater sensitivity to the many ways in which schools can be oppressively gendered environments. If whole-of-school supports are put in place, it is possible to create inclusive and respectful educational environments where transgender youth can thrive and experience protective factors from further negative wellbeing outcomes (Smith *et al.*, 2014). Whole-of-school approaches to creating inclusive schools for transgender people include (Bartholomaeus & Riggs, 2017):

- philosophy and ethos
- policies, procedures and guidelines
- leadership
- record keeping
- practices and language use
- resources and training
- support for school community
- curriculum/teaching and learning
- transgender-specific initiatives.

## Ethics and training

Education professionals should be given pre-service, in-service and professional developments on transgender youth and LGBTIQ themes. Pre-service training on LGBTIQ issues occurs nationally or sub-nationally in Argentina, Australia, Belgium, Brazil, Canada, Mexico, the Netherlands, the United Kingdom and the US – sometimes not in systematic ways and often due to individuals' passion (Carman et al., 2011; UNESCO, 2016b). The overwhelming majority of LGBT teachers surveyed (79%) had felt uncomfortable whilst working at a school because of their gender or sexual diversity (Gray, Harris & Jones, 2016; Jones et al., 2014). It is essential that it is not left to transgender teachers to deal with transphobia in education sectors – it is the role of all education providers and professionals. Swedish National Agency for Education and RFSL (the Swedish Federation for LGBTQ Rights) organisations train education professionals and develop support materials (Jones, 2016b). The curriculum addresses a 'norm critical' approach examining how 'social norms' marginalise people, rather than focusing on one marginalised group in particular. An in-service case study from Uruguay is an example of training efforts incorporating all education professionals to directly foster a direct openness to transgender youth:

> Uruguay's comprehensive education policy to combat homophobic and transphobic violence and discrimination is part of the National Programme for Sexual Education. It teaches trainee teachers about: self-awareness; gender and identity in the family; gender and domestic violence; social stereotypes; and the role of media and advertising stereotypes. In order to train teachers, the education sector relied on partnerships not only between different sectors of government, but also with concerned public services and civil society organizations. Teacher training for sexuality education was delivered in partnership with NGOs, which was particularly helpful for demystifying and discussing topics linked to sexual orientation and gender identity/expression, including violence. (UNESCO, 2016b, p. 96)

## Conclusions and recommendations

International human rights legislation, national and state anti-discrimination legislation, various education policies and curriculum require education service professionals to support equal access for transgender youth. Research showed that there was an urgent need to respond to transphobic violence and the dearth in support features in schools for transgender youth. The data also showed that schools could make a difference for these students in several ways. Specifically, encouraging social support for transgender youth from educational professionals and students (including correct language use, for example) can contribute to contexts in which these students are less likely to be bullied or drop out, and more likely to have improved educational outcomes.

Professional development, school-level policies and guidelines could greatly assist leadership and staff in understanding how to approach transgender youth's needs. Safety concerns and conservative backlash are commonly cited as prohibitive obstacles to school supports and activism for transgender youth in other contexts. Key informants from such contexts have suggested that legal, financial and capacity-building aid and virtual (online) supports were more urgent requirements (Jones, 2016b). However, the findings on the value of school supports may be transferable for nations including the Netherlands, UK, Malta, Ireland, Japan, America, Australia and Canada, which have democracies, transphobic bullying rates and developing polity provisions increasingly commensurate to the settings in the research discussed.

The shifts in thinking about gender in education over time then have privileged greater inclusivity for transgender youth. Education service providers and educators need:

- to review current subjects, curriculum and education policies in order to remove prejudiced content and statements that are no longer suitable; add contemporary best-practice protections for transgender students in anti-violence codes and guidelines; and add explanations for terms and concepts related to gender diversity following UNESCO guidelines

- to review and supplement documents, textbooks and library resources related to matters of gender diversity

- to incorporate gender diversity into teacher training curricula, so as to equip future teachers with sufficient understanding and relevant skills related to these issues

- inter-sectoral collaborative research and workshopping between education sectors, health care management agencies, and NGOs
- to create a culture of non-violence and provide safe education settings
- to adopt more flexible regulations regarding school uniforms and aim towards provision of at least some unisex toilet options on campus
- to provide transgender-friendly and privacy-focused school counselling services or referrals
- to supply other structural supports for transgender youth including templates for gender affirmation management plans and diversity affirming posters and pamphlets
- to organise rich and interesting age-appropriate activities on gender diversity, related human rights principles and resources on transgender youth themes
- to use the preferred names, pronouns and language requested by transgender youth
- to work together to prevent transphobia through holistic whole-school culturally sensitive methods appropriate to the school setting.

■ Chapter 6 ■

# Transgender Youth, Social Supports and Social Services

I hope, more than anything – more than health, more than finding someone to love, and even more than happiness – that I become famous. I think the world needs someone in this position to tell them that they're okay. They're normal. They're going to survive it. That they don't have to suffer like I did. That they can't let other people destroy them. That they're worth something. I want to be, for someone else, exactly the idol I needed my whole life. (Reagan, FtM trans, 17 years)

I realise that we can't change everyone's opinion ever, but any reduction whatsoever of people being emotionally or physically abused makes a difference and that difference, however small, is a beautiful and wonderful thing. (Charlie, agender/no gender, 16 years)

I hope to find safe spaces, and feel like an important part of the community, and feel safe expression [of] my gender and sexual identity. (Al, genderqueer, 16 years)

## ■ KEY POINTS

- Social services in many countries around the world have historically been linked to religious institutions, although the creation of welfare states and the professionalisation of many areas of social

- services mean many services now have a secular outlook. The background and ethos of social services can dramatically impact their response to transgender youth.

- Contemporary social services can use feedback from transgender groups, co-design input from transgender youth clients and a range of new technologies to greatly enhance their abilities to meet transgender youth's needs.

- Social attitudes to transgender youth vary greatly across different societies, although some amount of prejudice is seen in all regions of the world.

- Transgender youth were significantly more likely to be 'out' to a range of service professionals than cisgender same sex attracted youth.

- Rates of homelessness, unemployment and poverty were high and these factors could create intersectional complications for a transgender person.

- Many transgender youth faced rejection from school chaplains and particular religions that were conservative and endorsed sex and gender complementarity.

- Transgender youth may particularly appreciate transgender social service professionals and support workers, and opportunities for specific transgender peer support groups or approaches.

Transgender youth have distinct needs for services that could be best coordinated by the social service sector; however, they can easily slip through the provision gap. This chapter provides statistics and stories on the social networks, research and services for transgender youth. It details historic treatment of transgender youth, taking note of the dominance of religious social service provision. It then outlines more contemporary approaches in providing support that privileges equitable access and the input of transgender youth themselves. It includes information on social attitudes to transgender youth in a variety of geographic and familial contexts, their identity disclosures to different people in their social network, and strategies for dealing with social rejection offered by transgender young people. The chapter offers statistics on homelessness, unemployment and poverty for transgender youth; as well as their experiences of underground economies and police mistreatment. Issues of religious rejection are explored. An argument is made for supporting general advocacy for transgender youth as a group, whilst supporting privacy for individual transgender youth. Advice is given on collecting service information data on transgender youth using best-practice questions about their gender identity. The chapter then addresses mistreatment in social services, and discusses the ideal qualities of social service professionals for transgender youth. It discusses how services could engage transgender staff and people directly to help combat cis-normativity and cissexism and aid in training. Recommendations are listed for social service organisations and professionals.

## Historic social services: Religion, survival, homelessness and poverty

Since before modern history, social service provision has been a domain of both the state and major religions (McKay et al., 2015; Seu, Flanagan & Orgad, 2015). Social service professionals and practitioners must recognise and understand the historic centrality and complexity of religious organisations' social service provision for marginalised groups. On the one hand, widespread religions including Christianity, Judaism, Islam, Hinduism, Sikhism and others can have at their core an ethic of care for fellow human beings. Such perspectives have therefore inspired or even demanded the creation of or engagement in not-for-profit organisations or charities, shelters, social work, youth work and youth advocacy organisations' work. This provision has dramatically shaped much of the social service field in terms of the ethos behind provisions, which can have a morality aspect which either actively seeks to provide for all marginalised groups or may explicitly exclude some. For example, the Salvation Army, founded in 1865, is a major provider in youth services and emergency accommodation across many countries which claims not to discriminate; however, it has had a history of being accused by the media of promoting negative attitudes about LGBT populations (Condon, 2012; Salvation Army Media Newsroom, 2014).

The Billy Graham Evangelistic Association is one of the largest charitable organisations in the world and was established in 1950. It has a history of propounding, and at time of writing continued (through linking to transphobic articles on its website) to propound, a perception of transgender status as sinful, featuring links to statements including: 'The reality of human sinfulness explains why there are those who are deeply troubled and confused about something as fundamental as their gender and self-identity' (Mohler, 2017). Historically, members of wholly or partially religious social service organisations were often more convinced of their obligation to promote their personal religion or their own beliefs – including those that transgender identities are sinful in their particular religious view – than of obligations to provide for the desperate needs of particular transgender youth they encounter. It is also true that secular services have historically been or may currently be discriminatory towards transgender youth. It is also true that there are social service professionals and practitioners working within religious organisations who are not religious, or who feel no conflict between their religion and supporting transgender youth, or who actively work to make religious services more tolerant and accepting of transgender youth. However, it is important to note that early religious services were more dominated by providers' notions of themselves as religious people with religious duties, than notions of professionalism (Bessant & Webber, 2009).

Links were created over time between religious organisations and other not-for-profit social service providers and social policy makers (DiMaggio & Powell, 1983; McKay et al., 2015; Seu et al., 2015). As welfare states developed in liberal democracies such as the UK, New Zealand, Australia and other countries, their governments controlled social service provision through delivery directly, or tightly regulated funding agreements with not-for-profit bodies (Spies-Butcher, 2014). The pressure produced by such funding requirements encouraged these social services to increasingly compete and collaborate with and resemble one another, developing new cultures valuing professionalism and professional social service knowledge (Bessant & Webber, 2009; DiMaggio & Powell, 1983). An equitable redistribution of resources and service access amongst citizens underpinned welfare states (Spies-Butcher, 2014), changing how charity and human service practitioners described themselves and their work; privileging the idea of becoming 'professionals' rather than the religious perspectives previously dominant, as evident in the professional codes of ethics developed over the last sixty years (Bessant & Webber, 2009). Early accounts of professionalism, however, had distinguished 'authentic professions' (e.g. medicine) from the 'vocational occupations' or 'semi-professionals' (e.g. social work), casing human service workers as para-professionals due to the remaining influence of older pathways into the industry without qualification or accreditation (Bessant & Webber, 2009). There were decades where social services practitioners struggled to achieve state-sanctioned definitions of their field knowledge in various countries, such that their own reflection of democratic and secular values had to be more deeply considered.

## Contemporary social services: Friendship, feeling good and activism

By the end of the 1980s, many social service associations in liberal democracies around the world had won state support for the regulation of training standards, registration and codes of practice (Bessant & Webber, 2009). Many social workers now claimed 'full professional' status comprised of:

- contributing to the social and moral consensus of a liberal modern society

- possessing the personal values of altruism and service to others

- possessing a high degree of training and skill conferred by university education leading to professional accreditation by professional associations

- an orientation to ethical codes, along with the scientific-theoretical underpinnings of professional practice (Bessant & Webber, 2009).

This redefined their identity and work as 'professional', underscoring the need to abide by liberal democratic professional codes such as non-discriminatory service provision and equity of access for clients; rather than moral judgements. As equity became a focus, religious and non-religious social services developed providing support for transgender youth as an additional or even core practice. For example, the Unitarian Universalist Service Committee has recently taken up supporting LGBTIQ Rights in South Africa and developed the iThemba Lam ('my hope') LGBTI safe house. They actively cater for transgender youth who were rejected by their families and turned out on the streets and those who have suffered 'corrective rapes' (transphobic sexual abuse) or other violence (Global Impact, 2017). There are also international social services like Not All Like That (NALT) Christians, Transfaith Online, Axios, Accepting evangelicals and many others emerging to work against past rejections in service delivery.

There are also significant social services catering to transgender youth run by governments; secular LGBT bodies (like IGLYO); and even transgender youth themselves (like Australia's YGender and Freedom Centre services). Spain's Ministry of Health, Social Services and Equal Opportunities published a guidebook on responding to transphobia for people in social services and education (UNESCO, 2016b). Some Northern countries (including Sweden since 1950) have in place clear-cut non-government organisation (NGO) structures allowing community representation which stimulate the prioritisation of funding for transgender themes from the community itself (Jones, 2016b). Frederik Nilsson, Ombudsman and Head of Administration for Sweden's RFSL (LGBT NGO), commented that each of the 7000 LGBT community members of their organisation 'can text or contact us at any time to voice their views on what we are or should be doing or text us during a congress if they can't be there' (Jones, 2016b, p.10). The organisation included transgender people from 2001 based on its members' calls and had advocated for gender-neutral marriage gained in 2009 and the abandonment of sterilisation processes as a transition requirement for transgender people in 2013. The organisation believed strongly in surveying members' views in 'a kind of social democratic and responsive rule and it very much impacts not only what we do, but how – we always use consultative methods and it keeps us updated and connected to the peoples' realities' (Jones, 2016b, p.11) . Nilsson linked these methods to a long history of socialist government in Sweden, and 'networked structures with connectivity going "up" and "down" from people to leaders and leaders to people…so in a way people are the leaders' (Jones, 2016b, p.11). As transgender youth became more represented, their service needs were better met.

Modern social services in New Zealand (e.g. Evolve) and Ireland (e.g. Belongto) seek now to be a 'one-stop shop' for transgender youth providing holistic, free, youth-friendly wrap-around social support services which place individuals aged 10–25 years at the centre of adaptable models of care (Jones, 2016b; Kondou, 2016). Social workers, youth workers, health workers and administrators work alongside, support and empower youth. Services in both countries also encourage transgender youth and transgender organisations to help design and evaluate their social service provision to enhance its equity and usefulness. A New Zealand social service provider reported positive results from requesting feedback (Kondou, 2016, p.25):

> Evolve has managed to reach its current level of service for young, gender diverse people through listening and responding to their needs and working alongside young people as its services are developed. This includes supporting community initiatives…and hosting the trans* peer support group Tranzform on site. It also means making sure our space is accessible, such as by having gender-neutral toilets and displaying obvious signals that we are a trans-friendly service, eg displaying posters for Tranzform and the rainbow flag on our walls. We also work to provide a culturally competent and culturally safe service to gender diverse individuals. Our new patient forms ask the client about their gender identity. We endeavour to use preferred names and pronouns in our consultations. We work on the assumption that the young person is the expert on their own gender, not us as professionals. Part of Evolve's strength comes from taking responsibility for improving our services, like seeking feedback from the community, having internal training, supporting professional development…and hiring gender diverse staff. We are the first to admit our service is not perfect and that gender diverse people are the experts on their own health and social support needs, and that we need to seek, listen and respond to these needs.

Lisa, an Irish Youth Worker from the social service Belongto, said critical social justice education models sat behind their work with transgender youth, and youth empowerment was so embedded in its structures that she was even interviewed and hired by young people alongside the organisation's managers. The young people 'arrange the external speakers, skills training, internal sessions, peer evaluations and so on. My role is really just to support peer educators to achieve young peoples' goals.' This included their goal to have a Russian LGBT activist guest speaker and hear about how Russian youth were faring. 'For the transgender group we have the least resources and experience so we are spending more time doing trust exercises and team-building than activism. ...it is about working out how they can feel safe and what they feel they need.'

Social service providers, professionals and practitioners from many regions have also discussed the value of online outreach models for engaging with transgender youth (Jones, 2016b). A Swaziland worker mentioned the local 'Fortress' programme for LGBT youth and commented, 'The internet allows us to reach beyond where we can walk, drive or fly. Yesterday I emailed a link to a Nigerian LGBT youth survey online to my networks, to grow their participant numbers' (Jones, 2016b, p.9). An Australian who works with transgender youth said it is possible to gain 'access to transgender young people online whom one might never access in-person, because they are uncomfortable in their body right now or don't have access to transport' (Jones, 2016b, p.10). Resources and services can be disseminated online, mobile phone apps and other tools can be used to increase access and anonymity for service users. This is an especially important new option in contexts where transgender youth have no legal protections against discrimination or laws are actively hostile (Jones, 2016b).

## Social contexts and attitudes

Social attitudes to transgender youth vary greatly across countries, although some amount of prejudice is seen in all regions (Elischberger et al., 2018; UNESCO, 2015, 2016b). It is difficult to rely on formal reporting about social violence or attitudes, because where violence reports are not made or are low, there may either be great support for or no support for transgender youth. Where reports are made, some support is indicated *by the very fact that the issue is considered worthy of reporting*. Data on legal contexts can be helpful in understanding attitudes. For example, in Russia there are efforts to ban people teaching about LGBT issues and, as in Andorra and Albania, transgender people face restrictions on what they can do in law or in practice; this represents a lack of legal support or a potentially punitive response (see Table 6.1). In Azerbaijan, Belgium, Finland and France transgender people are allowed to change their names and gender status, if they follow gender affirmation intervention requirements (e.g. surgery in Azerbaijan) and are officially pathologised as 'ill' – a negative way of offering legal aid.

Table 6.1: Comparison of support for transgender people's legal rights in various countries

| | Yes | Yes, but different in practice | Yes, only in parts of the country | No |
|---|---|---|---|---|
| Change of name or gender marker possible | Argentina, Australia, Austria, Azerbaijan, Barbados, Belgium, Brazil, China, Colombia, Denmark, Estonia, Finland, France, Germany, Iceland, India, Ireland, Israel, Italy, Jamaica, Japan, Kazakhstan, Kyrgyzstan, Latvia, Malta, Mexico, Netherlands, New Zealand, Norway, South Africa, South Korea, Sweden, Switzerland, Taiwan, Turkey, UK, US | Russia | | Albania, American Samoa, Andorra, Antigua and Barbuda, Armenia, Bosnia, Kenya, Namibia, Tanzania, Thailand, Uganda, Vietnam, Zambia, Zimbabwe |
| Pathologisation requirement | Austria, Azerbaijan, Belgium, Brazil, China, Colombia, Estonia, Finland, France, Germany, Iceland, Israel, Italy, Japan, Kazakhstan, Kyrgyzstan, Latvia, Mexico, Norway, New Zealand, Russia, South Africa, South Korea, Switzerland, Taiwan, Turkey, UK | | US | Albania, American Samoa, Andorra, Antigua and Barbuda, Argentina, Armenia, Australia, Barbados, Bosnia, Denmark, India, Ireland, Jamaica, Kenya, Malta, Namibia, Netherlands, Sweden, Tanzania, Thailand, Uganda, Vietnam, Zambia, Zimbabwe |
| Sterilisation/ surgery/ therapy requirement | Azerbaijan, Belgium, Brazil, China, Colombia, Finland, France, Iceland, Israel, Italy, Japan, Kazakhstan, Kyrgyzstan, Latvia, Mexico, Norway, South Korea, Switzerland, Taiwan, Turkey | | US | Albania, American Samoa, Andorra, Antigua and Barbuda, Argentina, Armenia, Australia, Austria, Barbados, Bosnia, Denmark, Estonia, Germany, India, Ireland, Jamaica, Kenya, Malta, Namibia, Netherlands, New Zealand, Russia, South Africa, Sweden, Tanzania, Thailand, Uganda, UK, Vietnam, Zambia, Zimbabwe |

Note. This information was collated from several maps of research-based data openly supplied on transrespect.org (TGEU, 2018)

In Australia, Sweden, Denmark, the Netherlands and Malta transgender youth can change their names and status without any requirements – a more supportive situation, especially in Malta where any pathologisation of transgender youth is actively banned and anti-discrimination laws are strong. This does not mean there is no transphobia in these contexts and laws are certainly not fully indicative of social attitudes; for example, in Thailand there is more cultural support for transgender youth than laws indicate; in China, there is less cultural support than laws indicate given cultural pressure for heterosexual cisgender marriages reproducing one's family line, and one particular Maltese family may be less supportive of their transgender child than another. However, *positive legal contexts signal efforts towards affirming non-pathologising support* which help social attitudes to become more supportive over time. Social service providers, practitioners and professionals should become aware of the legal contexts in which their work sits, or which relate to their clients' backgrounds, to understand the restrictions, familial and social attitudes their transgender youth clients potentially face.

Considering what else influenced attitudes, an Internet-based survey examined general population attitudes towards transgender youth in the US and India (Elischberger *et al.*, 2018). Generally positive, although more highly variable, attitudes towards transgender youth were seen in the US social sample, whilst moderately negative ones were seen in the Indian social sample. *Social conservatism (such as religious and political beliefs) and the belief that transgender status was cultural not biological were the best predictors of negative attitudes* in both US and Indian people. However, gender-specific conservatism (the belief in a gender binary of males and females only) was an additional predictor of US participants' negative attitudes, whilst personal contact with gender minorities had a positive influence in the US. Contrastingly, gender-binary belief played only a minor role for Indian people, and political conservatism and personal contact had no role at all.

It is notable that young children who exhibit gender-variance experience greater negativity in social attitudes because of how societies rarely view children as having the knowledge, agency or skills to make 'good' choices due to their developmental stage (Capous-Desyllas & Barron, 2017). This puts them at particular risk of having their gender identities ignored, actively resisted or punished by their social networks (Carver *et al.*, 2003; Grossman & D'Augelli, 2006; Savin-Williams, 1996; Stieglitz, 2010). Very young transgender children being raised in a 'hostile environment' (unsupportive of their identity claims) will often respond to this 'with symptoms of depression, anxiety, fear, anger, self-mutilation, low self-esteem, and suicidal ideation' (Mallon & DeCrescenzo, 2006, p.217). During 55 early childhoods recalled for a US study, nearly half of the transgender participants remembered seriously contemplating suicide, and more than one quarter recalled attempting it as small children (Grossman & D'Augelli, 2007).

Some of the transgender survey participants aged 16+ from Australia had never experienced discrimination (Jones *et al.*, 2015). However, one such participant, Draconem (FtM transgender, 24 years) said it was a possibility he was 'always aware of' (Jones *et al.*, 2015, p.92). Others had experienced being called names like 'freak', 'faggot' and 'dyke' on the street. There were instances where people were verbally or physically abused by cisgender men in groups:

> I have been physically abused in the street for appearing to be a 'faggot' and verbally abused for appearing to be a 'dyke'. I do not defend my gender identity to strangers, though, so it's not known to them. (Junk000, male, 22 years)

Other participants described being chased by thugs wielding bottles and rocks. Participants' comments suggested that street-based aggressors particularly targeted people who were gender non-conforming or transitioning. This suggested a strong need for social inclusion campaigns around people who look different. Social service providers, professionals and practitioners need to understand the sensitivity of both the social context of the child, and the age and amount of access to online services a client has. A younger transgender child may have less ability to access online trans-friendly supports and resources without aid compared to teenagers familiar with the terms and symbols associated with trans-friendly organisations, for example. Outreach can occur through pamphlets in schools and working collaboratively across a range of services to capture those in need 'where they are' rather than requiring them to have an ability to 'come to you' given the potential barriers of social and familial attitudes.

## Identity disclosures for transgender youth's networks

The decision for transgender youth or their parents and guardians to disclose their transgender status to anyone is laden with the potential for risk or liberation (Brill & Pepper, 2008). This is a complex issue for social service providers, who may need aid from other service providers (mental health providers or school principal); but *are absolutely limited in what they can share to get that aid without their young clients' permission.* It is a mistake for a youth worker to 'out' their client to family or service providers without permission. Transgender youth have suffered greatly when identity disclosure is performed without their approval, without an appropriate plan of action and without resources for crisis relief. One transgender student explained that their youth worker outed them to education professionals who then outed them to their classmates with devastating results:

> I actually didn't come out to anyone…it was done for me. I have been bullied. I have been beat up. I have been sexually assaulted and I have been kicked out of home. (Hillier *et al.*, 2010)

A range of studies have considered identity disclosures of transgender people (James *et al.*, 2016; Jones *et al.*, 2015; Jones & Hillier, 2013).

A majority of transgender people in a US adult study (60%) were out to their immediate family and said their family was generally supportive of their transgender status; 18 per cent said that their family was unsupportive, and 22 per cent said that their family was neither supportive nor unsupportive (James *et al.*, 2016). One in ten of those who came out to their immediate family as transgender reported that a family member was violent towards them because of it; one in twelve became homeless. Over three quarters (77%) of those who were out between kindergarten and grade 12 (K-12) experienced harsh treatment, including being disciplined more harshly (20%), verbal abuse (54%), physical abuse (24%) or sexual abuse (13%). Almost one in five faced such mistreatment they left a K-12 school. In addition, nearly one quarter of US transgender people who were out as transgender in college or vocational schools were verbally, physically or sexually harassed.

Table 6.2 shows how Australian transgender youth aged 14–24 years were significantly more likely to be out to many of the people in their personal lives and many of their different service workers, than cisgender same sex attracted youth were (Jones & Hillier, 2013). The data show they had often discussed their identities with friends and Internet contacts. Transgender youth were particularly more likely to disclose their identities to (or perhaps were unable to 'hide' their identity from) professionals. Where transgender youth had disclosed their identity to one professional, they were also more likely to have disclosed it (or allowed it to be disclosed by a social service representative) to another professional.

Table 6.2: Comparison of identity disclosures made by transgender and cisgender same sex attracted youth (SSAY)

| | Pearson Chi-Square | $df$ | Percentage of cisgender SSAY who disclosed to this person | Percentage of trans-spectrum youth who disclosed to this person |
|---|---|---|---|---|
| Mother (n = 3075) | 6.280* | 1 | 65.91% | 78.65% |
| Father (n = 3032) | 4.151* | 1 | 49.32% | 60.47% |
| Female friend (n = 3087) | 0.069 | 1 | 93.86% | 93.18% |
| Male friend (n = 3061) | 1.591 | 1 | 89.86% | 94.05% |
| Partner (n = 2758) | 1.946 | 1 | 78.39% | 85.14% |
| Someone on the Internet (n=2869) | 1.962 | 1 | 84.78% | 90.36% |
| Doctor (n = 2851) | 22.815*** | 1 | 26.25% | 50.00% |
| Youth service worker (n = 2642) | 15.918*** | 1 | 31.27% | 57.53% |
| Counsellor (n = 2591) | 44.835*** | 1 | 33.88% | 71.05% |
| Teacher (n = 2871) | 2.788 | 1 | 39.48% | 48.75% |
| Student welfare coordinator/Student counsellor (n = 2681) | 38.140*** | 2 | 34.33% | 56.76% |
| School nurse (n=2,470) | 5.394* | 1 | 11.98% | 21.54% |
| School chaplain (n=2,463) | 10.079*** | 1 | 15.13% | 29.69% |

Note. * $p < 0.05$, ** $p < 0.01$, *** $p < 0.001$

# Social support and social rejection for transgender status disclosures

I hope to be able to make trans* and intersex friends one day. I wish for the day that I can hopefully gain medical independence from my parents, and then complete independence so I can live a comfortable life away from the judgemental behaviours of my family. (Quinn, genderqueer, 16 years)

Transgender youth face social and particularly familial negative responses and rejections that may be even more complex than for some youth who are gay, lesbian or bisexual (Grossman & D'Augelli, 2006; Grossman *et al.*, 2005; Jones & Hillier, 2013). A key finding was that transgender youth were more likely than cisgender same sex attracted youth to experience rejection from their disclosures (see Table 6.3), exposing them to more precarious living conditions and the social isolation they often reported (Jones & Hillier, 2013). They were particularly more likely to be rejected by school-based staff (teachers, school nurses, student welfare coordinators/counsellors) – the very people transgender youth would turn to for assistance in the place where transphobic abuse is most likely to occur. This underscores the need for external social service providers to stand by transgender youth when others do not, and act as intermediaries if requested.

Rejection caused anxiety for many youth, as Rihanna (transgender girl, 15 years) explained, 'I'm terrified of rejection, so even at home, where I'm out, I'm too scared to be myself.' Some transgender youth faced rejection with resilience. Ashley (unsure about gender, age 17) overcame their father's rejection through logic: 'I argued with him till he ran out of points... He also says he doesn't like Indians or Americans yet he has close friends from both countries, so his opinions don't bother me.' Transgender youth also overcame rejection by concentrating on supporters they did have. For example, Addison (androgynous, 17 years) comments, 'While my priest hasn't been very supportive, my girlfriend's priest is very supportive.' Jo (genderqueer, 20 years) overcame their mother's rejection through living with like-minded people:

I'm out of home and living in [an urban area] now and I live in a strong and supportive community of queer, trans and feminist people who provide safe spaces for me to live my life and learn how to take care of myself. But this community isn't supported by society at large, it has to support itself.

Table 6.3: Comparison of support and rejection for identity disclosures made by transgender and cisgender same sex attracted youth (SSAY)

| | Pearson Chi-Square | df | Percentage of disclosing cisgender SSAY supported by this person | Percentage of disclosing cisgender SSAY who were rejected by this person | Percentage of disclosing trans-spectrum youth supported by this person | Percentage of disclosing trans-spectrum youth who were rejected by this person |
|---|---|---|---|---|---|---|
| Mother (n = 2038) | 4.256* | 1 | 76.42% | 23.58% | 65.71% | 34.29% |
| Father (n = 1505) | 1.915 | 1 | 73.98% | 26.02% | 65.38% | 34.62% |
| Female friend (n = 2897) | 8.266** | 1 | 97.05% | 2.95% | 91.46% | 8.54% |
| Male friend (n = 2754) | 8.486** | 1 | 94.84% | 5.16% | 87.34% | 12.66% |
| Partner (n = 2167) | 11.856** | 1 | 95.29% | 4.71% | 85.71% | 14.29% |
| Someone on the Internet (n = 2437) | 4.620* | 1 | 95.81% | 4.19% | 90.67% | 9.33% |
| Doctor (n = 768) | 12.171*** | 1 | 90.37% | 9.63% | 73.17% | 26.83% |
| Youth service worker (n = 948) | 6.762** | 1 | 96.25% | 3.75% | 88.10% | 11.90% |
| Counsellor (n = 906) | 0.646 | 1 | 93.54% | 6.46% | 90.74% | 9.26% |
| Teacher (n = 1141) | 30.903*** | 1 | 89.93% | 10.07% | 61.54% | 38.46% |
| Student welfare coordinator/Student counsellor (n = 937) | 13.931*** | 1 | 91.17% | 8.83% | 73.81% | 26.19% |
| School nurse (n = 302) | 16.600*** | 1 | 88.19% | 11.81% | 50.00% | 50.00% |
| School chaplain (n=382) | 3.600 | 1 | 68.32% | 31.68% | 47.37% | 52.63% |

Note. * $p < 0.05$, ** $p < 0.01$, *** $p < 0.001$

Further, Jo negates rejection generally by reframing it as a social problem, not an internal one:

> I'm happy with myself but I'm angry at the way I'm made to live my life within the world. I'm marginalised, discriminated against and made second class by the law.

It can be easy to concentrate on negative statistics and negative experiences. However, those narrative examples from transgender youth showed that with access to alternative logic, support, people and perspectives, transgender youth can find alternative positions to those ascribed to them by social rejections. Social service providers could consider offering training in dealing with rejection to transgender youth (or to youth more broadly), using transgender youth's own strategies of discounting valueless opinions, concentrating on the support one does have, and other ideas described above which offer useful tactics. The quotes can be pulled out of this book and discussed, and these tactics considered for their merits and demerits. It would also be good to do exercises where transgender youth reflect on and share their own positive ideas for handling negative interactions. This puts them in the position of resilient strategists, instead of suffering victims, without ignoring the hard fact that difficulties occur.

## Homelessness, unemployment and poverty

Many studies from around the world have shown that transgender youth are significantly more likely to experience homelessness or be fostered out than other youth (James *et al.*, 2016; Jones & Hillier, 2013; Smith *et al.*, 2014; UNESCO, 2016b). Homelessness can include staying in a shelter, living on the street, living out of a car or under a bridge, staying temporarily with friends or couch-surfing because they can't afford housing. It can be a stress-inducing, vulnerable and frightening experience, particularly for a child. Studies have confirmed a relationship between negative experiences of transgender youth and ongoing economic disadvantage (Badgett *et al.*, 2014; Harris & Jones, 2014; James *et al.*, 2016; Jones, 2016a).

A large US transgender population study (n=27,715) showed nearly one third (30%) had experienced homelessness and nearly one third (29%) reported living in poverty – around twice the portion seen in the broader US population (James *et al.*, 2016). Transgender people were three times as likely (15%) as the general cisgender US population (5%) to be unemployed; one in six had lost a job due to transphobia. Family rejection was a major contributing factor for homelessness in transgender youth. Whilst 27 per cent of transgender people whose families were supportive had experienced homelessness, almost half (45%) of those whose families were unsupportive had experienced homelessness. One in twelve was kicked out of the house when they came out to their family as transgender, and a further one in ten ran away from home. Transgender people without the appropriate identity documents for their gender identity were at increased risk of homelessness (50%), and it was even more difficult to update documentation with no stable address. Seven out of ten respondents who stayed in a shelter in the past year reported being mistreated because of transphobia, and this should be a wake-up call for social service providers. Shelters should ensure protection for transgender youth (using correctly gendered or else separate accommodation options for safety) or consider arranging for transgender-specific shelters in areas of high need.

In the beyondblue-funded Australian survey of transgender youth (14–25 years), many participants were currently students, however, a portion of the older young people were finding it difficult to find employment due to the issues around gender dysphoria, the differences in their names on their transcripts and identification, or having documentation that differed from their current gender presentation (making their job applications appear different or fraudulent). In Argentina, a lack of education completion for almost half of the transgender youth meant their employment options were severely limited and many faced homelessness and poverty (Ferreyra, 2010). Indeed, many issues (lack of correct documentation, homelessness, unemployment and poverty) co-contribute to each other, meaning the individual struggles to fix one or all issues. For example, being in poverty can make it hard to travel to and dress for job interviews, having no job makes it harder to afford documentation fees, having no documentation makes it harder to get a job or a house. Without social services offering assistance, sometimes these factors can create cycles in which the transgender individual suffering one or more of these problems starts experiencing the others and finds it harder to resolve their situation as time goes on. It is important, therefore, for social service providers, practitioners and professionals to seek to assist transgender youth quickly in securing documentation, housing and employment opportunities. Helping with any of the issues may make a difference to other related issues – simple steps include helping a young person fill out documentation change forms, providing them an address for mail, providing clothes for job interviews, providing training, providing computer use for emailing a CV and so on.

## Underground economies and police mistreatment

The US transgender population survey showed one in five transgender adults had engaged in the underground economy including sex work, drug sales, and criminalised work – particularly transgender women of colour (James *et al.*, 2016). Nine out of ten (86%) of the participants who interacted with police whilst engaging in sex work or when believed to be engaged in sex work reported experiencing police harassment, abuse or mistreatment, including sexual assault. Of those transgender people currently working in the underground economy, 41 per cent were physically attacked in the past year and over a third (36%) were sexually assaulted in the past year. Police often assumed that transgender girls were sex workers even when they were not. Over half (57%) of transgender people reported that they would feel uncomfortable asking the police for help if they needed it. Of those arrested in the past year (2%), nearly one quarter (22%) believed it happened because they were transgender. Nearly one quarter were physically assaulted by prison staff or inmates, one in five were sexually assaulted. They were over five times as likely to be sexually assaulted by facility staff and over nine times as likely to be sexually assaulted by inmates as the general US population in jails and prisons.

Social service providers and professionals dealing with transgender youth who are in prison should arrange supportive counselling about these issues, and should advocate for youth to be placed in the jail accommodations in keeping with their age, gender identity or preference. They should seek to understand the difficult and complex cycles contributing to the individual's engagement in underground economies or being suspected of such engagement by police, avoiding ignorant moral judgements. In more trans-friendly contexts, underground economies may be less associated with transgender youth.

## Religious rejection and renewal

Transgender youth can be both directly rejected and actively embraced by religious and spiritual communities; however, the historic tendency has been rejection where sex and gender complementarity is central in the focal faith (Gahan & Jones, 2013; Gahan, Jones & Hillier, 2014; Grimes, 2016; Jones, 2013). Almost one fifth (19%) of US transgender people who had ever been part of a spiritual or religious community left due to rejection (James *et al.*, 2016); of that group over two fifths (42%) later found a welcoming new spiritual or religious community. Significantly fewer transgender people aged 16+ years reported being religious in Australia than the general population; faith community responses to transgender status often directly led Australians to leave their religion (Jones *et al.*, 2015). There were also accounts of public shaming by church communities. In addition, the Buckland Foundation-funded Australian survey showed over half of transgender youth (52%) were rejected by their school chaplain for being transgender (Jones & Hillier, 2013). Some Australian transgender youth rejected by one faith community, particularly Christian and Islamic sects, experienced the warm embrace of another faith community, particularly more liberal Anglican, Buddhist, Bahai and Uniting Church groups (Gahan & Jones, 2013). Toni (genderqueer, 16 years) wished for more support from official figures (Smith *et al.*, 2014); many transgender youth are and would like to remain spiritual or religious. It can be helpful for social service providers, practitioners and professionals to discuss the many regional and online transgender-friendly religious communities available with religious transgender youth in need.

## Supporting group advocacy whilst protecting individual privacy

Social and youth work services need to draw a balance between engaging in advocacy for transgender youth groups broadly, whilst acknowledging the need for privacy. For example, some service providers and professionals from around the world discussed the need to encourage visibility of transgender youth as citizens and family members (Jones, 2016b). A Chinese informant discussed how the organisation Abai facilitated mothers of transgender kids to talk to schools and universities, because 'filial duty is respected and mother's love is relatable to the Chinese' (Jones, 2016b, p.11). A research report from the organisation also mentioned China's national history of acceptance of diversity. The beyondblue study found most transgender youth had performed at least one action for transgender rights; the majority had 'liked' a social media site dedicated to activism, signed petitions, improved understanding through conversations and attended rallies (Jones, Smith *et al.*, 2016). Other studies showed transgender people aged 16+ sometimes took it upon themselves to act as educational advocates about trans-identity (Jones *et al.*, 2015). Transgender youth aimed at gaining social improvements or fulfilling responsibility (Smith *et al.*, 2014); one transgender boy (21 years) said, 'activism is the rent I pay for living on Earth'.

There are complexities to relying on transgender youth as faces of activist campaigns. Gillian, Direct Services Manager, Belongto Ireland, commented that transgender youth in her programmes initially wanted to do all available media opportunities and were of a social media generation that exalted representation, but later may want to erase the memory of transition:

> I always advise our transgender students to be careful about considering any media opportunities available to them early in their transition. (...) It is a complexity particular to transgender people, that being out can be both useful and damaging for them in terms of their personal experiences of gender dysphoria (later on in life). (Jones, 2016b, p.11)

Some transgender survey participants aged 16+ explained they preferred privacy and felt that their gender history, or gender identity, was not public property (Jones *et al.*, 2015). Some spoke of the concept of 'stealth': either passing as their gender without aids, transitioning fully and not telling anyone about their gender history, or presenting as a gender-fluid person without specific explanation or coming out processes. They used phrases like 'need to know basis', 'as stealth as possible', 'I just want to be a normal cis guy' and so on. In the beyondblue study some transgender youth discussed key issues with direct activism (Smith *et al.*, 2014):

> They seem to be mutually exclusive options – activism or stealth. One I hate because it means I can't just live as a normal guy – I always have to be 'trans', and I hate that. The other I hate because it means turning my back on people who really do need all the help they can get. (Noah, boy, 20 years)

It actually makes me feel worse because it means having the current legal status of that community thrown in my face on a day to day basis. (George, boy, 21 years)

I find creating art/writing and participating in loud, angry, activism extremely cathartic in the short term though slightly disheartening in the long term because I know I'm not being listened to by the people who need to hear most. (Angel, genderqueer, 23 years)

The disinterest of any individual in activism should simply be respected. The best approach is supporting whole group advocacy for transgender youth in non-exposing ways, alongside privacy for individuals. Specifically, social services can engage in activism on the behalf of transgender youth to protect their visibility and wellbeing, encourage 'non-exposing' resilience-building activism for transgender youth such as supporting an online poll or anonymous efforts; or use animated representations of transgender youth in campaigns and documents such as the anime art used in Japanese efforts (Human Rights Watch, 2016).

## Deficiencies in social services

Transgender youth are at high risk of being denied equal treatment or service, and of experiencing verbal or physical abuse in public accommodations. Nearly one third (31%) of transgender people in the US survey had experienced transphobic mistreatment from staff or employees, and 14 per cent were denied equal treatment or service (James *et al.*, 2016). Because transgender people feared transphobic mistreatment:

- 31% avoided drug or alcohol treatment programmes
- 22% avoided domestic violence shelters or programmes or rape crisis centres
- 18% avoided public assistance or government benefit offices
- 14% avoided extended care facilities
- 13% avoided Social Security offices
- 11% avoided legal services from an attorney, clinic, or legal professional.

## Helpful social service professionals

Good experiences with social service providers involved affirmation from the social service provider or professional for a disclosure of transgender status – youth workers (88%) were very likely to affirm transgender status disclosures (Jones & Hillier, 2013). Taking positive, welcoming attitudes to a transgender young person improved assistance overall. Transgender youth most praised social service professionals who:

- *use peer support models for transgender youth*: Evaluative feedback on peer support models for transgender youth have been very positive, and organisations like the Freedom Centre apply peer support models using Social Cognitive Theory and group drop in sessions, which they report:

    …basically says that we learn and develop best when we observe our peers and get the right information that's relevant to us and have a safe and respectful social environment to practice and understand what we learn. (Freedom Centre, 2013)

    An FtM transgender boy explained that he appreciated the social connection of peer support sessions (Jones *et al.*, 2015):

    I have loved going to a boys group and making some trans* friends, who are all very different to one another but great friends… I still felt quite isolated about my transness and have found a lot of solace in meeting other guys. It helped me to accept myself more – by celebrating them and their gender identity, and getting to know them.

- *ensure access to transgender staff or services:* The respondents to the Australian survey of transgender people aged 16+ wanted to see more transgender staff and social services (Jones *et al.*, 2015). One directly commented that 'local queer youth workers are needed'. In the beyondblue-funded study, Casey (genderqueer, age 20) like many trans-spectrum youth wished for greater access to trans-aware or trans-run queer-friendly health care and counselling (Smith *et al.*, 2014).

- *provide education on gender identity by giving and facilitating talks to other sectors' organisations*: The respondents to the Australian survey of transgender people aged 16+ wanted to promote support and inclusion for transgender people through educational talks to other sectors (Jones *et al.*, 2015). They offered many useful ideas, and some examples were:

> I would like to see (and be a part of) talks in primary schools about transgender issues and acceptance, and talks in high schools about acceptance.

> ...all government funded agencies/services [should] have to do mandatory gender diversity awareness training.

> I would like to see better (and compulsory) inclusion of trans* and intersex people, our needs and specific health and cultural sensitivity issues in the medical school curriculum.

> I believe *education* is the best form of activism! There should be more education on LGBTQI people in primary and high schools, to help stop bullying...!

## Combatting cisnormativity and cissexism in social services

Transgender youth were significantly more likely than same sex attracted students to have disclosed their diverse identity to a range of social service professionals; approximately twice as many had told their youth welfare workers and student welfare coordinators (Jones & Hillier, 2013). Regarding social service provision, racially representative bureaucracy theory dictates that goals of the bureaucracy are best supported by staff reflecting the social backgrounds of constituents (Kingsley, 1944). Transgender youth may specifically respond to transgender or young social workers where it is possible to include them in the range of available staff; where a service provider has a large transgender youth clientele this may be especially important. Sometimes the concerns of historically marginalised groups may receive a fairer hearing should similarly marginalised persons staff public agencies. For transgender youth, it is important that, at minimum, social service providers separate their religious judgement from the democratic or social altruistic value of serving them (Hakak, 2016). Social service providers could hire transgender staff members or engage transgender organisations or peer leaders in some events, or refer clients on for at least part of their service receipt if their needs will not be adequately met in a mainstream service. The funding applications of transgender services should be supported with helpful written references by those mainstream services using them, and in large-scale funding bids it may be fair to consider apportioning an amount of requested funds from the mainstream service to transgender-specific services they rely on.

## Ethics and training

Social service providers and professionals need to be developed to deal directly with transgender youth so they can support them in their goals, or else recognise (if on a religious restriction or other basis) their service deficiencies and provide referrals. Graduate and short training programmes that prepare future social service professionals should enable them to develop their basic knowledge of how transgender youth engage with their social networks. This includes their engagement with professionals from all the other fields in this book so that the social service provider can act as an advocate and care coordinator for transgender youth – understanding the roles of:

- mental health professionals
- health professionals
- sexual health professionals and sex educators
- education professionals and so forth.

Social services providers should reflect on the need for young people to have at least one person who is their advocate, especially where a parent might not be providing that role, including direct affirmation of their gender identity and expression from this adult. Consider the organisations you can link to which might fulfil some or all of the social service needs of transgender youth who can't be provided for by your organisation. Direct experience of working with transgender youth during training years and practicums is especially beneficial for future social service and other professionals (Brill & Pepper, 2008; Jones, 2016b; Kondou, 2016). For example, a former student discussed the significant impact of having spent a practicum in a New Zealand youth service which has a special focus on transgender youth, for enhancing knowledge skills in working with transgender youth in future (Kondou, 2016, p.25):

I had heard the service was committed to improving health care for transgender young people, an area I am particularly passionate about. As a gender diverse person and trans* health-care activist, I am aware of the many challenges we often experience in wider society and within the health-care system. … The passion and drive Evolve has shown in this area, across our team, from management, administration, clinical and social support teams, has blown me away.

## Conclusions and recommendations

The statistics and information on social services and social networks outlined in this chapter show how little control transgender youth may have over their own social experiences. However, transgender youth can respond to negative social experiences using a range of resilience-building strategies and peer support methods that social service providers, practitioners and professionals could usefully promote. Relevant aid delivered in areas such as housing, employment, poverty, police liaison, religious or spiritual referral, or general advocacy is greatly needed. Further, the involvement of transgender organisations, staff and youth themselves in design and delivery of social services is strongly encouraged.

The changes and reforms in social services over time show moves towards privileging greater equity of service access and resource allocation for transgender youth. Social service providers, practitioners and professionals need to:

- train both pre-service and in-service social service professionals about transgender youth

- provide professional development training for social service support staff (i.e. administration staff) on inclusive practice for transgender youth.

- become aware of the legal contexts, the backgrounds, the opportunities and restrictions, and familial and social attitudes transgender youth clients potentially face

- understand the local laws and anti-discrimination laws particularly about service provision in the given context; anti-discrimination legislation may require a service to be equitably delivered to transgender youth regardless of the service provider's ethos and without discrimination on the basis of transgender status or other traits

- ensure that, where religious exemptions apply or the organisation or individual chooses not to offer services to transgender youth and this is consistent with local laws, or where services are simply inadequate to aiding transgender youth appropriately, your service coordinates needs and service assessments in collaboration with other service providers and professionals in the area. Together, work out a solution for how needs can be best met and by whom, with consideration for context and ethos. *Do not leave transgender youth support needs unmet, even if their needs are not best met by you;* understand the ethical responsibility to ensure that any urgent and/or pervasive needs are met *in some way by someone*. Online or transnational services may even be possible in a crisis; solving these needs gaps is the basic creative work of social services and a professional duty

- compile specialist social services information for transgender youth in order to make appropriate referrals when needs arise beyond an organisation or individual's ability to deliver

- ensure all social services aim at avoiding mistreatment of transgender youth; particularly ensure transgender youth are not mis-gendered and are treated with respect, safety and discretion

- assist transgender youth in securing documentation, housing and employment opportunities

- ensure shelters offer protection for transgender individuals or support the development of transgender-specific shelters in areas of high need

- acknowledge that even very young transgender people are the best person to make statements or decisions about their own gender expression, identity and transgender status right now. At minimum, do not dismiss transgender youth as too young for gender determination – their gender experience is as real to them as yours is to you

- consider whether in the given context face-to-face peer group support, private individual and phone contact, support from transgender or general staff members, or contact through mobile phone apps and Internet websites might be the best option or whether multiple options are applicable

- arrange supportive counselling for transgender youth who are in prison about issues including discrimination, violence and sexual abuse. Advocate for their placement in the jail accommodations in keeping with their gender identity or preferred by them, and understand the complex difficulties potentially affecting their situation

- be aware of the wide range of transgender-friendly religious communities available in different regions and especially online in order to make referrals, where desired

- support whole group advocacy for transgender youth broadly in non-exposing ways, whilst working to support the privacy and choices of individual transgender youth

- engage in education of other services on issues of gender and transgender youth, and support opportunities for transgender youth to contribute in visible or discreet ways

- consider how (where relevant) to supply transgender youth with transgender staff support, design and evaluation opportunities

- combat transphobia, cisnormativity and cissexism in social service organisations and practices (e.g. through hiring transgender staff members, engaging transgender social services or supporting their funding bids as needed).

# Conclusion

There were so many special professionals who stepped in when my parents stepped out of my life. From my foster parents to counsellors, and one time a really kind nurse, I will never ever forget what they did for me. (Dani, genderqueer, 18 years)

The doctor who listened to me, kept me alive. The teachers who stopped the bullies and the librarian who let me eat my lunch with her. I didn't thank them at the time. I want to say 'thank you' and I hope you print that. (Lou, agender/no gender, 16 years)

My youth worker was so excellent that I'm inspired to do social work too! She trained the other people I deal with about being transgender, put in many hours and never walked away from me. When I met her I was a mess, a real angry little drop out and expected her to be like the others and just give up. From her encouragement I am back in a new school and a supporter for someone else in the position I was once in. (Morgan, transgender boy, 17 years)

## What different roles do services and professionals have for transgender youth?

By contrasting the information on the different services, practitioners and professionals discussed in this book, it is possible to distinguish the particular roles that each serve for transgender youth. Whilst it is *sometimes* possible for providers to deliver cross-sector support or 'stand-in' when there is a lack of trans-friendly services from other fields, these distinct roles should *ideally* be met by fully qualified and focused professionals. These roles are discussed in Table 7.1, following the order of the chapters in the book.

Table 7.1: The distinct contributing roles of specific service areas for transgender youth

| Service area | Contributing role |
|---|---|
| Mental health services | • **Diagnosis of and information provision on gender dysphoria**; providing written confirmation of diagnosis for other services<br>• **Offering psychological and counselling support** for the young person and their parents/guardians or family members<br>• **Teaching transgender youth methods for expression and feeling good** (engaging with family support, building other support and information, using creative self-comfort, gender affirmation and trying activism)<br>• **Facilitating opportunities for transgender youth to improve their resilience-building skills** through dedicated sessions |
| Health services | • **Supplying or making referrals to specialist health services for gender affirmation** and other transgender health needs<br>• **Providing parents of transgender children with information about the danger of preventing transgender youth from seeking medical care**, and an understanding of gender affirmation processes as non-elective for some<br>• **Involving young people and their parents or adults in planning about gender affirmations/transitions and determining appropriate ages** for various related actions<br>• **Discussing the full range of options, risks and potential outcomes for transgender youth who are considering gender affirmations** including options such as doing nothing or delaying treatment, social or legal gender affirmation elements, medical gender affirmation elements (and benefits and risks) |
| Sexual health services | • **Advocating against enforced sterilisations of transgender youth** as a reproductive and sexual health rights issue<br>• **Providing myth-dispelling sex education for transgender youth, their parents and guardians, and other youth broadly** on the relationships, romantic and sexual attractions and sexual identities transgender people may have; the many sexual acts they may engage in; and non-cissexist language for body parts<br>• **Asking transgender youth directly for the precise information needed** if collecting sexual data for sexual health tests or purposes, rather than relying on assumptions based on a transgender youth's sexual identity label<br>• **Discussing the full range of sexual practices, sexual risks, protection and contraceptive options, and partner violence protections available for transgender youth** including discussing how affirmation treatments may impact libido, sexual function or performance, gamete production and fertility; how affirmation treatments are *not* sexual protection from STIs; the need for sexual toys or sexual/bodily aids to be subjected to appropriate cleaning practices |

| Education services | • **Reviewing current education policies subjects, curriculum, resources, textbooks and supplementary materials** to remove prejudiced content; add contemporary best-practice protections in anti-violence codes and guidelines; and add explanations for terms and concepts related to gender diversity |
| --- | --- |
| | • **Creating a culture of non-violence and providing safe environments for transgender youth** through engaging in campaigns, holistic whole-school culturally sensitive methods |
| | • **Adopting more flexible regulations and structural supports** around uniforms, bathroom options, counselling services, templates for gender affirmation management plans, diversity affirming posters and pamphlets and many other options |
| | • **Ensuring provision of counselling and anti-bias education efforts for the victims, the perpetrators and bystanders of transphobic violence** to deal with the deeper issues behind it |
| Social services | • **Coordinating overall needs and service assessments** in collaboration with other service providers; tackling how needs can be best met and by whom; fulfilling the ethical responsibility and professional duty to ensure needs are met |
| | • **Educating other services about mistreatment transgender youth clients potentially face**, including through their legal contexts, backgrounds, social attitudes and in service provision |
| | • **Providing assistance and advocacy for transgender youth as needed** in securing documentation, transgender or youth peer support, housing, employment opportunities, counselling, crisis management, information and faith supports |
| | • **Evaluating and improving existing social services and other services provisions for transgender youth** through surveys or external and internal feedback aimed at updating provisions |

# What important themes were repeated across all service provision areas?

By comparing the information on the different services, practitioners and professionals discussed in this book, it is possible to identify *the areas for improvement that repeatedly arose across all service provision areas* for transgender youth. Providers of all kinds should support these improvements. There were five main themes, representing improvement areas continually arising for transgender youth in service provision, detailed in Table 7.2.

Table 7.2: Important themes in areas of improvement for all services around transgender youth

| Cross-sector theme | Improvements to enact |
|---|---|
| Understand transgender youth more | • **Train both pre-service and in-service professionals** about inclusive practice for transgender youth<br><br>• **Provide professional development training for support staff** (i.e. administration staff) on including transgender youth<br><br>• **Understand that youth's transgender status can comprise any or all of gender expression incongruence, gender identity incongruence and/or self-identified transgender status**, appearing from infancy and usually occurring by puberty<br><br>• **Promote demographic information on transgender youth showing them as a diverse range of people aged 25 years and under**, with diverse locations, backgrounds, families, beliefs, and personalities like anyone else (beyond just being 'transgender')<br><br>• **Accept that transgender youth may have binary or non-binary identities, various or no gender affirmations, variable body part combinations** depending on many factors<br><br>• **Recognise the needs and challenges experienced by transgender youth can be distinct** from those of cisgender lesbian, gay, bisexual and intersex people |
| Treat transgender youth respectfully | • **Respond to individuals' self-perception and self-declaration of their transgender status or gender identity and expression.** It is up to the individual (not to service providers) to determine<br><br>• **Collect gender identity and pronoun info on in-take forms** for transgender youth (and all clients) or simply ask the individual how they like to be treated in terms of gender if unsure<br><br>• **Use the preferred names, pronouns and language requested** by transgender youth<br><br>• **Use neutral language about body parts**, or ask for transgender youth own preferred terms when these are relevant to services<br><br>• **React professionally to transgender youth's disclosures or bodies**; do not show titillation or shock<br><br>• **Consider whether an issue is directly or indirectly related to the child's transgender status**, and to try to understand and discuss the relationship rather than rely on assumptions<br><br>• **Address complaints** about mistreatment of transgender youth in an appropriate and timely manner |
| Coordinate transgender youth care collaboratively | • **Engage in inter-sectoral collaborative networking and communication** to enhance support efforts<br><br>• **Compile cross-sector services support information, contacts and links** for transgender youth in the local area<br><br>• **Make appropriate referrals for transgender youth** when issues beyond an area of professional expertise arise<br><br>• **Engage with local transgender services** where these can collaborate or offer feedback<br><br>• **Support the funding efforts of transgender services** where relevant with letters of support |

| Provide transgender youth specific information | • Provide easily accessible service-related information and support for transgender youth on multiple platforms including face-to-face, by phone, online and/or via mobile apps with due consideration for the socio-cultural context<br>• Provide easily accessible service-related information and support for parents, families and guardians<br>• Review information provisions regularly to update content and remove outdated details |
|---|---|
| Facilitate sector reform | • Engage in service-specific advocacy and reform<br>• Engage in sector-related policy advocacy for transgender youth rights or issues where relevant<br>• Engage in education of the sector on issues of gender and transgender youth where possible<br>• Support whole group advocacy for transgender youth broadly in non-exposing ways, whilst working to support the privacy and choices of individual transgender youth<br>• Offer opportunities for transgender youth to contribute in visible or discreet ways to education and activism work |

## Future research on services for transgender youth

Several areas for further investigation in research have emerged in this book, based on a lack of current data. Future studies should address:

- transgender youth in younger age brackets – including needs assessments, service trials and evaluations, and finally best-practice service models

- comparisons of different international service provision to transgender youth

- theoretical and clinical development of the 'Informed Consent Model' of transgender medical affirmation

- comparisons of benefits and deficits in the 'Informed Consent Model' compared to the 'Diagnostic Model' of transgender medical affirmation

- transgender youth's and professionals' evaluations of different service delivery modes (in-person, online, mobile phone, individual and peer-support)

- methods for keeping homeless transgender youth safe in shelters; helping transgender youth break cycles of homelessness and poverty; and address transphobic bullying and violence in schools, etc.

- the service needs of diverse transgender youth including those who live with a disability
- the benefits and deficits of transgender-specific services vs. inclusion of transgender people in general services
- the service areas or themes most benefiting from transgender staff input, vs. the areas for which cisgender or transgender staff are equally suitable.

## Conclusion

This book is dedicated to all the service providers, practitioners and professionals who have worked or are working to help transgender youth around the world and across many different service provision areas. Ideally, this book will encourage you to understand the urgent need for your service, the value of inclusive and affirming approaches to transgender youth, and the deep appreciation transgender youth feel for efforts at supporting them. I hope it has helped you to understand transgender youth more, your service area's role in providing for their needs and how this can relate to other service areas, and some solutions for key problems impeding service provision. Too many transgender youth have experienced difficulties in receiving services or felt they had to drop out of them or avoid them altogether. With such vulnerabilities in play, it is vital to ensure these young people know that we support them.

Transgender youth were shown in this book to be much more than victims; examples were given of youth promoting non-discrimination and inclusion online or in-person, alone or in groups. They could be deep thinkers about gender binaries, offering perspectives on social roles and bodies that challenge old-school thinking. They could be strategists with wonderful techniques for resilience potentially useful to other groups. They could withstand rejection or hardship and nonetheless harbour colourful dreams of bright altruistic futures. Transgender youth also showed themselves as agents of change within various service sectors. Service providers, practitioners and professionals should respond to their ideas for positive, lasting change.

# References

Ainsworth, C. (2015) 'Sex redefined.' *Nature 518*, 1, 288–291.
Alsop, Z. (2009) 'Uganda's Anti-Gay Bill: Inspired by the U.S.' *Time.* Retrieved from http://content.time.com/time/world/article/0,8599,1946645,00.html on 04 March 2018.
Altman, D. (1997) 'Global Gaze/Global Gays.' *GLQ: A Journal of Lesbian and Gay Studies 3*, 4, 417–436.
Altman, D. (2013) 'Sexuality and globalization.' *Sexuality Research & Social Policy 1*, 1, 63–68.
Alvarez, Z., Iranipour, A., Trolli, C. & Weston, J. (2013) *Supporting LGBTQ Students in Schools: A Three-tiered Approach.* Paper presented at the National Association of School Psychologists, Seattle, WA.
APA Task Force on Appropriate Therapeutic Responses to Sexual Orientation (2009) *Report of the Task Force on Appropriate Therapeutic Responses to Sexual Orientation.* Washington, DC: American Psychological Assocation.
Australian Bureau of Statistics (2012) *1301.0 – Year Book Australia: Educational Attainment.* Retrieved from www.abs.gov.au/ausstats/abs@.nsf/Lookup/by%20Subject/1301.0~2012~Main%20Features~Educational%20attainment~110 on 04 March 2018.
Badgett, M.V., Nezhad, S., Waaldijk, K. & van der Meulen Rodgers, Y. (2014) *The Relationship between LGBT Inclusion and Economic Development: An Analysis of Emerging Economies.* Los Angeles, CA: The Williams Institute.
Bannerman, M. (2014) 'Family Court Chief Justice calls for rethink on how High Court handles cases involving transgender children.' *ABC News.* Retrieved from www.abc.net.au/news/2014-11-17/chief-justice-calls-for-rethink-on-transgender-childrens-cases/5894698 on 04 March 2018.
Baraitser, P., Syred, J., Spencer-Hughes, V., Howroyd, C., Free, C. & Holdsworth, G. (2015) 'How online sexual health services could work; generating theory to support development.' *BMC Health Services Research 15*, 1, 540.
Bartholomaeus, C. & Riggs, D. (2017) 'Whole-of-school approaches to supporting transgender students, staff, and parents.' *International Journal of Transgenderism 18*, 4, 361–366.
Barton, L. (1997) 'Inclusive education: Romantic, subversive or realistic?' *International Journal of Inclusive Education 1*, 3, 231–242.
Bauer, G., Braimoh, J., Scheim, A. & Dharma, C. (2017) 'Transgender-inclusive measures of sex/gender for population surveys: Mixed-methods evaluation and recommendations.' *PLoS One 12*, 5, e0178043.
Baum, F. (2007) 'Cracking the nut of health equity: Top down and bottom up pressure for action on the social determinants of health.' *International Journal of Health Promotion and Education 1* 24, 90–95.
Bazzul, J. & Sykes, H. (2011) 'The secret identity of a biology textbook: Straight and naturally sexed.' *Cultural Studies of Science Education 6*, 2, 265–286.
Bessant, J. & Webber, R. (2009) 'Youth workers, professional identities and narratives of workplace change.' *Journal of Australian Studies 27*, 78, 25–38.
Binnie, J. (2004) *The Globalization of Sexuality.* London: SAGE Publications Ltd.

Bockting, W., Benner, A. & Coleman, E. (2009) 'Gay and bisexual identity development among female-to-male transsexuals in North America: Emergence of a transgender sexuality.' *Archives of Sexual Behavior 38*, 5, 688–701.

Bockting, W.O., Robinson, B.E. & Rosser, B.R.S. (1998) 'Transgender HIV prevention: A qualitative needs assessment.' *AIDS Care 10*, 4, 505–526.

Brill, S. & Pepper, R. (2008) *The Transgender Child.* San Francisco, CA: Cleis Press.

Brown, M. (2015) 'Top 15 famous transgender athletes.' *The Sportster.* Retrieved from www.thesportster.com/entertainment/top-15-famous-transgender-athletes on 04 March 2018.

Brown, M. & Rownsley, C.A. (1996) *True Selves: Understanding Transsexualism for Family, Friends, Co-workers and Helping Professionals.* San Francisco, CA: Jossey-Bass.

Brown, T., Herman, J. & Park, A. (2017) *Exploring International Priorities and Best Practices for the Collection of Data about Gender Minorities, Report of Meeting.* Los Angeles, CA: The Williams Institute.

Bungener, S., Steensma, T., Cohen-Kettenis, P.T. & De Vries, A. (2017) 'Sexual and romantic experiences of transgender youth before gender-affirmative treatment.' *Pediatrics 139*, 3, 1.

Butler, J. (1990) *Gender Trouble: Feminism and the Subversion of Identity.* London: Routledge.

Byron, P. & Hunt, J. (2016) '"That happened to me too": Young people's informal knowledge of diverse genders and sexualities.' *Sex Education 17*, 3, 319–332.

Cancer Australia (2016) *All Cancers in Australia.* Canberra, ACT: Australian Government. Retrieved from https://canceraustralia.gov.au/affected-cancer/what-cancer/cancer-australia-statistics on 04 March 2018.

Cancer Council (2017) *Early Detection.* Retrieved from www.cancer.org.au/about-cancer/early-detection on 04 March 2018.

Capous-Desyllas, M. & Barron, C. (2017) 'Identifying and navigating social and institutional challenges of transgender children and families.' *Child & Adolescent Social Work Journal 34*, 6, 527–542.

Carman, M., Mitchell, A., Schlichthorst, M. & Smith, A. (2011) 'Teacher training in sexuality education in Australia: How well are teachers prepared for the job?' *Sexual Health 8*, 3, 269–271.

Carrera, M., DePalma, R. & Lameiras, M. (2012) 'Sex/gender identity: Moving beyond fixed and "natural" categories.' *Journal of Sexualities 15*, 8, 995–1016.

Carroll, L. (2005a) 'Gender Identity.' In J.T. Sears (ed.), *Youth, Education and Sexualities: An International Encyclopedia (Vol. One: A–J).* Westport, CT: Greenwood Press.

Carroll, L. (2005b) 'Intersex.' In J.T. Sears (ed.), *Youth, Education and Sexualities: An International Encyclopedia (Vol. One: A–J).* Westport, CT: Greenwood Press.

Carver, P.R., Yunger, J.L. & Perry, D.G. (2003) 'Gender identity and adjustment in middle childhood.' *Sex Roles 49*, 3/4, 95–109.

Chauncey, G. (1989) 'Christian Brotherhood or Sexual Perversion? Homosexual Identities and the Construction of Sexual Boundaries in the World War 1 Era.' In M. Duberman, M. Vicinus & G. Chauncey (eds), *Hidden from History: Reclaiming Gay and Lesbian Past.* New York: Meridian.

Clark, B., Veale, J., Greyson, D. & Saewyc, E. (2018) 'Primary care access and foregone care: A survey of transgender adolescents and young adults.' *Family Practice 35*, 3, 203–306.

Clark, T.C., Lucassen, M., Bullen, P. & Denny, S. (2014) 'The health and well-being of transgender high school students: Results from the New Zealand adolescent health survey.' *Journal of Adolescent Health 55*, 1, 93–99.

Cloud, J. (2005) 'The battle over gay teens.' *Time Magazine,* October 02.

Condon, J. (2012) 'Clarification regarding interview comments on homosexuality.' *The Salvation Army Website.* Retrieved from https://salvos.org.au/about-us/latest-news/media-newsroom/20120623-clarification-sexuality-joyfm on 04 March 2018.

Corliss, H., Belzer, M., Forbes, C. & Wilson, E. (2007) 'An evaluation of service utilization among male to female transgender youth: Qualitative study of a clinic-based sample.' *Journal of LGBT Health Research 3*, 1, 49–61.

Couch, M., Pitts, M., Mulcare, H., Croy, S., Mitchell, A. & Patel, S. (2007) *Tranznation: A report on the health and wellbeing of transgendered people in Australia and New Zealand.* Melbourne: ARCSHS.

Davies, A., Bouman, W.P., Richards, C., Barrett, J. *et al.* (2013) 'Patient satisfaction with gender identity clinic services in the United Kingdom.' *Sexual and Relationship Therapy 28*, 4, 400–418.

## References

del Pozo de Bolger, A., Jones, T., Dunstan, D. & Lykins, A. (2014) 'Australian trans men: Development, sexuality, and mental health.' *Australian Psychologist 49*, 6, 395–402.

Devor, A. (2013) *Reed Erickson and the Erickson Educational Foundation*. Victoria: University of Victoria Sociology Department.

Dibben, K. (2013) 'School in backflip over transgender child's use of girls' toilet.' *The Courier Mail*, June 15. Retrieved from www.couriermail.com.au/news/queensland/school-in-backflip-over-transgender-childs-use-of-girls-toilet/story-fnihsrf2-1226664333520 on 04 March 2018.

DiMaggio, P. & Powell, W. (1983) 'The iron cage revisited: Institutional isomorphism and collective rationality in organizational fields.' *American Sociological Review 48*, 2, 147–160.

Donatone, B. & Rachlin, K. (2013) 'An intake template for transgender, transsexual, genderqueer, gender nonconforming, and gender variant college students seeking mental health services.' *Journal of College Student Psychotherapy 27*, 3, 200–211.

Drescher, J. (2013) 'Controversies in gender diagnoses.' *LGBT Health 1*, 1, 9–13.

Drescher, J. & Byne, W. (2012) 'Gender dysphoric/gender variant (GD/GV) children and adolescents: Summarizing what we know and what we have yet to learn.' *Journal of Homosexuality 59*, 3, 501–510.

Dugin, A. (1997) *Foundations of Geopolitics: The Geopolitical Future of Russia*. Moscow: Arktogeya.

Edwards, D. & Tencer, D. (2009) 'US conservatives flee Uganda "kill gays" controversy.' *Raw Story*, 11 December. Retrieved from www.rawstory.com/2009/12/conservatives-flee-uganda-gay-law on 05 March 2018.

Edwards, J.W., Fisher, D.G. & Reynolds, G.L. (2007) 'Male-to-female transgender and transsexual clients of HIV service programmes in Los Angeles County, California.' *American Journal of Public Health 97*, 6, 1030–1033.

Egan, R.D. & Hawkes, G. (2010) *Theorizing the Sexual Child in Modernity*. New York: Palgrave Macmillan.

Elia, J.P. (2005) 'Sexuality Education.' In J.T. Sears (ed.), *Youth, Education and Sexualities: An International Encyclopedia (Vol. One: A–J)*. Westport, CT: Greenwood Press.

Elischberger, H., Glazier, J., Hill, E. & Verduzco-Baker, L. (2018) 'Attitudes toward and beliefs about transgender youth: A cross-cultural comparison between the United States and India.' *Sex Roles 78*, 1–2, 142–160.

Esteva de Antonio, I. & Gómez-Gil, E. (2013) 'Coordination of healthcare for transsexual persons.' *Current Opinion in Endocrinology & Diabetes and Obesity 20*, 6, 585–591.

Fausto-Sterling, A. (1993) 'The five sexes: Why male and female are not enough.' *The Sciences*, March/April, pp.20–24.

Ferreyra, M. (2010) 'Gender Identity and Extreme Poverty.' In I. Dubel & A. Hielkema (eds), *Urgency Required: Gay and Lesbian Rights are Human Rights*. Hivos: Humanist Institute for Cooperation with Developing Countries.

Fisher, E.S. (2014) 'Best Practices in Supporting Students who are Lesbian, Gay, Bisexual, Transgender, and Questioning.' In P. Harrison & A. Thomas (eds), *Best Practices in School Psychology*. Bethesda, MD: NASP.

Foucault, M. (1980) *Power/Knowledge*. New York: Pantheon.

Freedom Centre (2013) About Freedom Centre. Retrieved from www.freedom.org.au/index.php?option=com_content&view=category&layout=blog&id=36&Itemid=55 on 05 March 2018.

Freud, S. (1905) *Three Essays on the Theory of Sexuality* (J. Strachey, Trans. 1961 ed.). London: Penguin.

Freud, S. (1910) *The Psychology of Love* (S. Whiteside, Trans. 2006 ed.). London: Penguin.

Gahan, L. & Jones, T. (2013) *Heaven Bent: Australian Lesbian, Gay, Bisexual, Transgender and Intersex Experiences of Faith, Religion and Spirituality*. Melbourne: Clouds of Magellan.

Gahan, L., Jones, T. & Hillier, L. (2014) 'An unresolved journey: Religious discourse and same-sex attracted and gender questioning young people.' *The Social Scientific Study of Religion 25*, 1, 202–229.

Garber, M. (1992) *Vested Interests: Cross-dressing and Cultural Anxiety*. New York and London: Routledge.

Gardner, I. & Safer, J. (2013) 'Progress on the road to better medical care for transgender patients.' *Current Opinion in Endocrinology Diabetes and Obesity 20*, 6, 553–558.

Garofalo, R., Deleon, J., Osmer, E., Doll, M. & Harper, G.W. (2006) 'Overlooked, misunderstood and at risk: Exploring the lives and HIV risk of ethnic minority male-to-female transgender youth.' *Journal of Adolescent Health 38*, 1, 230–236.

Global Impact (2017) *Unitarian Universalist Service Committee: LGBTQI Rights In Africa.* Retrieved from https://charity.org/resource-center/success-stories/unitarian-universalist-service-committee-lgbtqi-rights-africa on 05 March 2018.
GLSEN (2012) *Ready, Set, Respect! GLSEN's Elementary School Toolkit.* New York: Gay, Lesbian and Straight Education Network.
Gooren, L. & Lips, P. (2014) 'Conjectures concerning cross-sex hormone treatment of aging transsexual persons.' *The Journal of Sexual Medicine 11*, 8, 2012–2019.
Gooren, L., Sungkaew, T. & Giltay, E. (2013) 'Exploration of functional health, mental well-being and cross-sex hormone use in a sample of Thai male-to-female transgendered persons (kathoeys).' *Asian Journal of Andrology 15*, 2, 280–285.
Gooren, L., Sungkaew, T., Giltay, E. & Guadamuz, T. (2015) 'Cross-sex hormone use, functional health and mental well-being among transgender men (Toms) and Transgender Women (Kathoeys) in Thailand.' *Culture, Health & Sexuality 17*, 1, 92–103.
Grant, J.M., Mottet, L.A., Tanis, J., Harrison, J., Herman, J.L. & Keislung, M., K. (2011) *Injustice at Every Turn.* Retrieved from www.thetaskforce.org/static_html/downloads/reports/reports/ntds_full.pdf on 05 June 2018.
Gray, E., Harris, A. & Jones, T. (2016) 'Australian LGBTQ teachers, exclusionary spaces and points of interruption.' *Sexualities 19*, 3, 286–303.
Grimes, K.M. (2016) 'Theology of whose body?: Sexual complementarity, intersex conditions, and La Virgen de Guadalupe.' *Journal of Feminist Studies in Religion 32*, 1, 75–93.
Grossman, A.H. & D'Augelli, A.R. (2006) 'Transgender youth: Invisible and vulnerable.' *Journal of Homosexuality 51*, 1, 111–128.
Grossman, A.H., D'Augelli, A.R., Howell, T.J. & Hubbard, S. (2005) 'Parents' reactions to transgender youth' gender nonconforming expression and identity.' *Journal of Gay & Lesbian Social Services 18*, 1, 3–16.
Grossman, A.H. & D'Augelli, A.R. (2007) 'Transgender youth and life threatening behaviour.' *Suicide and Life-Threatening Behaviour 37*, 1, 527–537.
H, M. (2017) 'Why transgender people are being sterilised in some European countries.' *The Economist*, September 01. Retrieved from https://www.economist.com/blogs/economist-explains/2017/09/economist-explains on 05 March 2018.
Haas, A.P., Eliason, M., Mays, V.M., Mathy, R.M. *et al.* (2011) 'Suicide and suicide risk in lesbian, gay, bisexual, and transgender populations: Review and recommendations.' *Journal of Homosexuality 58*, 1, 10–51.
Hakak, Y. (2016) 'Battling against interfaith relations in Israel: Religion, therapy, and social services.' *Journal of Marital and Family Therapy 42*, 1, 45–57.
Halberstam, J. (2012) 'Boys will be… Bois? Or, Transgender Feminism and Forgetful Fish.' In D. Richardson, J. McLaughlin & M.E. Casey (eds), *Intersections Between Feminist and Queer Theory.* New York: Palgrave MacMillan.
Hardisty, J. (1999) *Mobilizing Resentment.* Boston, MA: Beacon Press.
Hare, L., Bernard, P., Sánchez, F., Baird, P. *et al.* (2009) 'Androgen receptor repeat length polymorphism associated with male-to-female transsexualism.' *Biological Psychiatry 65*, 1, 93–96.
Harris, A. & Jones, T. (2014) 'Trans Teacher Experiences and the Failure of Visibility.' In A. Harris & E. Gray (eds), *Queer Teachers, Identity and Performativity.* London: Palgrave Macmillan.
Herdt, G. & McClintock, M. (2000) 'The magical age of 10.' *Archives of Sexual Behavior 29*, 6, 586–606.
Hillier, L., Jones, T., Monagle, M., Overton, N. *et al.* (2010) *Writing Themselves In 3: The Third National Study on the Sexual Health and Wellbeing of Same-sex Attracted and Gender Questioning Young People.* Retrieved from www.acon.org.au/wp-content/uploads/2015/04/Writing-Themselves-In-3-2010.pdf on 05 June 2018.
Hines, S. (2007) *Transforming Gender: Transgender Practices of Identity, Intimacy and Care.* Bristol: Policy Press.
Hirschfeld, M. (1908) *Zeitschrift für Sexualwissenschaft.* Frankfurt: Sauerländer's Verlag.
Holt, V., Skagerberg, E. & Dunsford, M. (2016) 'Young people with features of gender dysphoria: Demographics and associated difficulties.' *Clinical Child Psychology and Psychiatry 21*, 1, 108–118.

## References

Human Rights Watch (2016) *The Nail That Sticks Out Gets Hammered Down*. Tokyo: Human Rights Watch.

Human Rights Watch (2018) 'No Choice but to Deny Who I Am: Violence and Discrimination against LGBT People in Ghana.' Retrieved from www.hrw.org/report/2018/01/08/no-choice-deny-who-i-am/violence-and-discrimination-against-lgbt-people-ghana on 05 March 2018.

Iantaffi, A. & Bockting, W.O. (2011) 'Views from both sides of the bridge? Gender, sexual legitimacy and transgender people's experiences of relationships.' *Culture Health & Sexuality 13*, 3, 355–370.

ILGA Europe (2009) *Marriage and partnership rights for same-sex partners: country-by-country*. Retrieved from www.ilga-europe.org/rainboweurope on 05 June 2018.

International School Psychology Association (2011) Code of Ethics. Retrieved from http://www.ispaweb.org/wp-content/uploads/2013/01/The_ISPA_Code_of_Ethics_2011.pdf on 05 March 2018.

Irvine, J. (2002) *Talk about Sex: The Battles over Sex Education in the United States*. Berkeley, CA & London: University of California Press.

Isaac, M. & Shane, S. (2017) 'Facebook's Russia-linked ads came in many disguises.' *New York Times*, October 02. Retrieved from www.nytimes.com/2017/10/02/technology/facebook-russia-ads-.html on 05 March 2018.

James, S., Herman, J., Rankin, S., Keisling, M., Mottet, L. & Anafi, M. (2016) *The Report of the 2015 U.S. Transgender Survey*. Washington, DC: National Center for Transgender Equality.

Jones, T. (2009) 'The Queer joys of sexless marriage: Coupled citizenship's hot bed!' *Sextures 1*, 1, 1–25.

Jones, T. (2011a) 'Saving rhetorical children: Sexuality education discourses from conservative to post-modern.' *Sex Education 11*, 4, 369–387.

Jones, T. (2011b) 'A sexuality education discourses framework: Conservative, liberal, critical and post-modern.' *American Journal of Sexuality Education 6*, 2, 133–175.

Jones, T. (2013) 'Damned If You Do? LGBTI Students and Religious Sexuality Education.' In L. Gahan & T. Jones (eds), *Heaven Bent: Australian Lesbian, Gay, Bisexual, Transgender and Intersex Experiences of Faith, Religion and Spirituality*. Melbourne: Clouds of Magellan.

Jones, T. (2015a) 'Comparing rural and urban educational contexts for GLBTIQ students.' *Australian and International Journal of Rural Education 25*, 2, 44–55.

Jones, T. (2015b) *Policy and Gay, Lesbian, Bisexual, Transgender and Intersex Students*. Cham, Heidelberg, New York, Dordrecht and London: Springer.

Jones, T. (2016a) 'Female-to-Male (FtM) Transgender Employees in Australia.' In T. Kollen (ed.), *Sexual Orientation and Transgender Issues in Organizations – Global Perspectives on LGBT Workforce Diversity*. Vienna: Springer.

Jones, T. (2016b) 'Researching and working for transgender youth: Contexts, problems and solutions.' *Social Sciences 5*, 3, 1–15.

Jones, T. (2017a) 'Evidence affirming school supports for Australian transgender and gender diverse students.' *Sexual Health 14*, 6, 412–416.

Jones, T. (2017b) 'LGBTI youth shamelessness and safety called "bullying": Beyond Valentine Road.' *LGBT Youth 14*, 2, 228–232.

Jones, T. (2018) 'Trump, trans students and transnational progress.' *Sex Education 18*, 4, 479–494.

Jones, T., del Pozo de Bolger, A., Dunne, T., Lykins, A. & Hawkes, G. (2015) *Female-to-Male (FtM) Transgender People's Experiences in Australia*. Cham, Heidelberg, New York, Dordrecht and London: Springer.

Jones, T., Gray, E. & Harris, A. (2014) 'GLBTIQ teachers in Australian education policy: Protections, suspicions, and restrictions.' *Sex Education: Sexuality, Society and Learning 14*, 3, 338–353.

Jones, T., Hart, B., Carpenter, M., Ansara, G., Leonard, W. & Lucke, J. (2016) *Intersex: Stories and Statistics from Australia*. London: Open Book Publisher.

Jones, T. & Hillier, L. (2012) 'Sexuality education school policy for GLBTIQ students.' *Sex Education 12*, 4, 437–454.

Jones, T. & Hillier, L. (2013) 'Comparing trans-spectrum and same sex attracted youth in Australia: Increased risks, increased activisms.' *Journal of LGBT Youth 10*, 4, 287–307.

Jones, T. & Lasser, J. (2017) 'School Psychology with Gay, Lesbian, Bisexual, Transgender, Intersex, and Questioning (GLBTIQ) Youth.' In M. Thielking & M. Terjesen (eds), *Handbook On Australian School Psychology: Bridging the Gaps in International Research, Practice, and Policy.* Dordrecht: Springer.

Jones, T., Smith, E., Ward, R., Dixon, J., Hillier, L. & Mitchell, A. (2016) 'School experiences of transgender and gender diverse students in Australia.' *Sex Education 16,* 2, 156–171.

Kerr, L. & Jones, T. (2017) 'Cancer Screening for Trans and Gender Diverse People.' In T. Jones (ed.), *Bent Street.* Melbourne: Clouds of Magellan.

Kingsley, J. (1944) *Representative Bureaucracy: An Interpretation of the British Civil Service.* Yellow Springs, OH: Antioch Press.

Kinsey, A.C., Pomeroy, W.R. & Martin, C.E. (1948) *Sexual Behaviour in the Human Male.* Philadelphia, PA: W.B. Saunders.

Kondou, A. (2016) 'Improving health care for young transgender people: Working for a service that provides inclusive health care and social support for gender diverse people is rewarding, says one new graduate nurse.' *Kai Tiaki: Nursing New Zealand,* April, 25.

Kosciw, J., Greytak, E.A., Palmer, N. & Boesen, M. (2014) *The 2013 National School Climate Survey: The experiences of Lesbian, Gay, Bisexual and Transgender Youth in Our Nation's Schools.* New York: GLSEN.

Kosciw, J. & Pizmony-Levy, O. (2013) *Fostering a Global Dialogue about LGBT Youth and Schools.* Proceedings from a meeting of the Global Network Combating Homophobic and Transphobic Prejudice and Violence in Schools. New York: GLSEN and UNESCO.

Kumar, V., Abbas, A. & Aster, J. (eds) (2015) *Robbins and Cotran Pathologic Basis of Disease* (9th ed). Canada: Saunders, Elsevier Inc.

Kuper, L., Nussbaum, R. & Mustanski, B. (2012) 'Exploring the diversity of gender and sexual orientation identities in an online sample of transgender individuals.' *Journal of Sex Research 49,* 2–3, 244–254.

Kussin-Shoptaw, A., Fletcher, J. & Reback, C. (2017) 'Physical and/or sexual abuse is associated with increased psychological and emotional distress among transgender women.' *LGBT Health 4,* 4, 268–274.

Lasser, J. & Tharinger, D. (2003) 'Visibility management in school and beyond: A qualitative study of gay, lesbian, and bisexual youth.' *Journal of Adolescence 26,* 1, 234–244.

Lefkowitz, A. & Mannell, J. (2017) 'Sexual health service providers' perceptions of transgender youth in England.' *Health & Social Care in the Community 25,* 3, 1237–1246.

Lenning, E. & Buist, C.L. (2013) 'Social, psychological and economic challenges faced by transgender individuals and their significant others: Gaining insight through personal narratives.' *Cult Health Sex 15,* 1, 44–57.

Leonnig, C., Hamburger, T. & Helderman, R. (2017) 'Russian firm tied to pro-Kremlin propaganda advertised on Facebook during election.' *The Washington Post,* September 06. Retrieved from www.washingtonpost.com/politics/facebook-says-it-sold-political-ads-to-russian-company-during-2016-election/2017/09/06/32f01fd2-931e-11e7-89fa-bb822a46da5b_story.html?utm_term=.d157381408df on 05 March 2018.

Leroux-Nega, E. (2014) 'Uganda shrugs off aid cuts over anti-gay law.' *Sydney Morning Herald,* February 27. Retrieved from www.smh.com.au/world/uganda-shrugs-off-aid-cuts-over-antigay-law-20140227-hvdz8.html on 05 March 2018.

Levitt, H.M. & Ippolito, M.R. (2014) 'Being transgender: Navigating minority stressors and developing authentic self-presentation.' *Psychology of Women Quarterly 38,* 1, 46–64.

Lindner, A. (2014) 'Familial support and celebration of gender nonconforming children.' *Sex Roles,* 1, 1–3.

Lurie, S. (2005) 'Identifying training needs of health-care providers related to treatment and care of transgendered patients: A qualitative needs assessment conducted in New England.' *The International Journal of Transgenderism 8,* 1, 2–3.

Macgillivray, I.K. & Jennings, T. (2008) 'A content analysis exploring lesbian, gay, bisexual, and transgender topics in foundations of education textbooks.' *Journal of Teacher Education 59,* 2, 170–188.

Malkin, B. (2014) 'Vladimir Putin signs anti-gay propaganda bill.' *The Telegraph*. Retrieved from www.telegraph.co.uk/news/worldnews/europe/russia/10151790/Vladimir-Putin-signs-anti-gay-propaganda-bill.html on 05 June 2018.

Mallon, G.P. & DeCrescenzo, T. (2006) 'Transgender children and youth: A child welfare practice perspective.' *Child Welfare League of America 85*, 2, 215–241.

Martin, C. & Ruble, D. (2013) 'Patterns of gender development.' *Annual Review of Psychology 61*, 1, 353–381.

McCredie, J. (2008) 'Gender troubles.' *Australian Doctor*, October 31, 23.

McGuire, J., Anderson, C., Toomey, R. & Russell, S.T. (2010) 'School climate for transgender youth: A mixed method investigation of student experiences and school responses.' *Journal of Youth and Adolescence 39*, 10, 1175–1188.

McHardie, D. (2016) 'New Brunswick will now cover gender-confirming surgeries.' *CBS News*, June 03. Retrieved from www.cbc.ca/news/canada/new-brunswick/gender-confirming-surgeries-1.3614766 on 05 March 2018.

McKay, S., Moro, D., Teasdale, S. & Clifford, D. (2015) 'The marketization of charities in England and Wales.' *Voluntas 26*, 1, 336–354.

McLean, A. (2011) 'A "Gender Centre" for Melbourne? Assessing the need for a transgender specific service provider.' *Gay & Lesbian Issues and Psychology Review 7*, 1, 33–42.

McNeil, J., Bailey, L., Ellis, J., Morton, J. & Regan, M. (2012) *Trans Mental Health Study 2012*. Retrieved from www.scottishtrans.org/our-work/research on 05 March 2018.

Meier, S., Sharp, C., Michonski, J., Babcock, J. & Fitzgerald, K. (2013) 'Romantic relationships of female-to-male trans men: A descriptive study.' *International Journal of Transgenderism 14*, 2, 75–85.

Menvielle, E. (2012) 'A comprehensive programme for children with gender variant behaviours and gender identity disorders.' *Journal of Homosexuality 59*, 3, 357–368.

Mohler, R. (2017) 'The transgender challenge: An evangelical response.' *Decision Magazine*, January 03. Retrieved from Billy Graham Evangelistic Association Website https://billygraham.org/decision-magazine/january-2017/transgender-challenge-evangelical-response on 05 March 2018.

Moran, J.P. (2000) *Teaching Sex: The Shaping of Adolescence in the 20th Century*. London: Harvard University Press.

Muller, A., Rohrs, S., Hoffman-Wanderer, Y. & Moult, K. (2016) 'You have to make a judgement call – Morals, judgements and the provision of quality sexual and reproductive health services for adolescents in South Africa.' *Social Science & Medicine 148*, 1, 71–78.

National LGBTI Health Alliance (2016) *Making the Count: Addressing data integrity gaps in Australian standards for collecting sex and gender information*. Sydney: National LGBTI Health Alliance.

New York Times Editorial Staff (2016) 'Obama cuts all funding for Christian-based "Abstinence Only" sex-ed programs.' *New York Times*, February 18. Retrieved from www.nytlive.nytimes.com/womenintheworld/2016/02/18/president-obama-cuts-funding-for-all-abstinence-only-sex-education on 05 March 2018.

Newfield, E., Hart, S., Dibble, S. & Kohler, L. (2006) 'Female-to-male transgender quality of life.' *Quality of Life Research 15*, 9, 1447–1457.

OECD (2003) *Diversity, Inclusion and Equity: Insights from Special Needs Provision*. Paris: Organisation for Economic Co-operation and Development.

OII Australia (2012) *Intersex for allies*. Retrieved from: www.oii.org.au/21336/intersex-for-allies on 05 March 2018.

Olson, K., Key, A. & Eaton, N. (2015) 'Gender cognition in transgender children.' *Psychological Science 26*, 4, 467–474.

Onuah, F. (2014) 'Nigeria criminalises same-sex relationships.' *The Sydney Morning Herald*. Retrieved from www.smh.com.au/world/nigeria-criminalises-samesex-relationships-20140114-30raz.html on 05 June 2018.

Outright Action International (2016) *Human Rights Report: Being Transgender in Iran*. New York: Outright Action International.

Parke, C. (2016) 'The Christian Right on the gender frontier: The growing anti-trans offensive.' *Political Research Quarterly*, October 05. Retrieved from www.politicalresearch.org/2016/10/05/the-christian-right-on-the-gender-frontier-the-growing-anti-trans-offensive/#sthash.urlW9p9k.dpuf on 05 March 2018.

Pazos, S. (2000) 'Practice with female-to-male transgendered youth.' *Journal of Gay & Lesbian Social Services 10*, 3–4, 65–82.

Pease, B. & Pease, A. (2003) *Why Men Don't Listen and Women Can't Read Maps*. London: Orion Publishing Group.

Phillips, J., Fein-Zachary, V., Mehta, T., Littlehale, N., Venkataraman, S. & Slanetz, P. (2014) 'Breast imaging in the transgender patient.' *American Journal of Roentgenology 202*, 1, 1149–1156.

Pinheiro, P.S. (2006) *UN World Report on Violence Against Children*. Geneva: United Nations Secretary General's Study on Violence Against Children.

Pivo, S., Montes, J., Schwartz, S., Chun, J. *et al.* (2016) 'Breast cancer risk assessment and screening in transgender patients.' *Clinical Breast Cancer 17*, 5, e225–e227.

Plan International Thailand & International Center for Research on Women (2015) *Are Schools Safe and Equal Places for Girls and Boys in Asia? Research Findings on School-Related Gender-Based Violence*. Bangkok: Plan International.

Potter, J., Peitzmeier, S.M., Bernstein, I., Reisner, S.L. *et al.* (2015) 'Cervical cancer screening for patients on the female-to-male spectrum: A narrative review and guide for clinicians.' *Journal of General Internal Medicine 30*, 12, 1857–1864.

Raymond, J. (1994) *The Transsexual Empire: The Making of the She-Male*. New York: Teacher's College Press.

Riggs, D. (2011) 'Queering evidence-based practice.' *Psychology & Sexuality 2*, 1, 87–98.

Riggs, D. (2018) 'An Examination of "Just in Case" Arguments as They Are Applied to Fertility Preservation for Transgender People.' In V. Mackie, S. Ferber & N. Marks (eds), *The Body and the Globe: From IVF to Global Reproductive Industry*. New York: Lexington Books.

Riggs, D., Ansara, G. & Treharne, G. (2015) 'An evidence-based model for understanding the mental health experiences of transgender Australians.' *Australian Psychologist 59*, 1, 32–39.

Riggs, D. & Bartholomaeus, C. (2017) 'Transgender young people's narratives of intimacy and sexual health: Implications for sexuality education.' *Sex Education 17*, 3, 1–15.

Riggs, D. & Due, C. (2013) *Gender Identity Australia: The healthcare experiences of people whose gender identity differs from that expected of their natally assigned sex*. Adelaide: Flinders University.

Riggs, D., von Doussa, H. & Power, J. (2015) 'The family and romantic relationships of trans and gender diverse Australians: An exploratory survey.' *Sexual and Relationship Therapy 30*, 2, 243–255.

Robinson, K.H. (2002) 'Making the invisible visible: Gay and lesbian issues in early childhood education.' *Contemporary Issues in Early Childhood 3*, 2, 415–434.

Roden, L. (2017) 'Swedish kids to learn computer coding and how to spot fake news in primary school.' *The Local*, March 13. Retrieved from www.thelocal.se/20170313/swedish-kids-to-learn-computer-coding-and-how-to-spot-fake-news-in-primary-school on 05 March 2018.

Rogers, K. (2014) 'Uganda's anti-gay law: A silver lining for LGBTI aid?' *DEVEX*, February 27. Retrieved from www.devex.com/news/ugandas-anti-gay-law-a-silver-lining-for-lgbti-aid-82935 on 05 March 2018.

Rowniak, S., Chesla, C., Rose, C.D. & Holzemer, W.L. (2011) 'Transmen: The HIV risk of gay identity.' *AIDS Education and Prevention 23*, 1, 508–520.

Russell, S.T., Ryan, C., Toomey, R., Diaz, R.M. & Sanchez, J. (2011) 'Lesbian, gay, bisexual, and transgender adolescent school victimization: Implications for young adult health and adjustment.' *Journal of School Health 81*, 5, 223–230.

Safer, J. & Pearce, E. (2013) 'A simple curriculum content change increased medical student comfort with transgender medicine.' *Endocrine Practice 19*, 4, 633–637.

Salvation Army Media Newsroom (2014) *Response to Guardian Australia Report on Gay Asylum Seekers*. Sydney: The Salvation Army.

Sanchez, A., Southgate, E., Rogers, G. & Duvivier, R. (2017) 'Inclusion of lesbian, gay, bisexual, transgender, queer, and intersex health in Australian and New Zealand medical education.' *LGBT Health 4*, 4, 295–303.

Savin-Williams, R.C. (1996) 'Dating and Romantic Relationships among Gay, Lesbian, and Bisexual Youths.' In R.C. Savin-Williams & K.M. Cohen (eds), *The Lives of Lesbians, Gays, and Bisexuals: Children to Adults*. Fort Worth, TX: Harcourt Brace.

Schaefer, A.G., Iyengar, R., Kadiyala, S., Kavanagh, J. et al. (2016) *Assessing the Implications of Allowing Transgender Personnel to Serve Openly*. Retrieved from www.rand.org/pubs/research_reports/RR1530.html on 05 March 2018.

Schleifer, D. (2006) 'Make me feel mighty real: Gay female-to-male transgenderists negotiating sex, gender, and sexuality.' *Sexualities 9*, 1, 57–75.

Schulz, S. (2018) 'The informed consent model of transgender care: An alternative to the diagnosis of gender dysphoria.' *Journal of Humanistic Psychology 58*, 1, 72–92.

Sears, J.T. (2005) *Youth, Education And Sexualities: An International Encyclopedia* (Vol. One: A–J). Westport, CT: Greenwood Press.

Seu, I., Flanagan, F. & Orgad, S. (2015) 'The good Samaritan and the marketer: Public perceptions of humanitarian and international development NGOs.' *International Journal of Nonprofit and Voluntary Sector Marketing 20*, 1, 211–225.

Shane, S. & Goel, V. (2017) 'Fake Russian Facebook accounts bought $100,000 in political ads.' *The New York Times*, September 06. Retrieved from www.nytimes.com/2017/09/06/technology/facebook-russian-political-ads.html on 05 March 2018.

Singh, A.A., Meng, S.E. & Hansen, A.W. (2014) '"I am my own gender": Resilience strategies of trans youth.' *Journal of Counseling & Development 92*, 2, 208–218.

Smith, E., Jones, T., Ward, R., Dixon, J., Mitchell, A. & Hillier, L. (2014) *From Blues to Rainbows: The Mental Health and Well-being of Gender Diverse and Transgender Young People in Australia*. Melbourne: Australian Research Centre in Sex Health and Society.

South Australia Department for Education and Child Development (2017) *Transgender and Intersex Student Support*. Adelaide: South Australia Department for Education and Child Development.

Sperber, J., Landers, S. & Lawrence, S. (2005) 'Access to health care for transgendered persons: Results of a needs assessment in Boston.' *International Journal of Transgenderism 8*, 1, 75–91.

Spies-Butcher, B. (2014) 'Marketisation and the dual welfare state: Neoliberalism and inequality in Australia.' *Economic and Labour Relations Review 25*, 2, 185–201.

Sprigg, P. (2016) 'Uniting nations for a family-friendly world.' *Washington Update*. Washington, DC: Family Rights Council.

Starnes, T. (2013) Calif. Governor Signs Transgender Bathroom Bill. Retrieved from www.factsoffaith.org/library/general/3801-calif/download.html on 05 June 2018.

Stephens, S.C., Bernstein, K.T. & Philip, S.S. (2011) 'Male to female and female to male transgender persons have different sexual risk behaviours yet similar rates of STDs and HIV.' *AIDS and Behaviour 15*, 1, 683–686.

Stieglitz, K. (2010) 'Development, risk and resilience of transgender youth.' *Journal of the Association of Nurses in AIDS Care 21*, 3, 192–206.

Stone, S. (1991) 'The Empire Strikes Back: A Posttranssexual Manifesto.' In J. Epstein & K. Straub (eds), *Body Guards: The Cultural Politics of Gender Ambiguity*. New York: Routledge.

Tait, G. (2012) *Making Sense of Education*. New York: Cambridge University Press.

Taylor, C. & Peter, T. (2011) *Every Class in Every School: Final Report on the First National Climate Survey on Homophobia, Biphobia and Transphobia in Canadian Schools*. Toronto: EGALE and Canada Human Rights Trust.

Taylor, E. & Bryson, M. (2016) 'Cancer's margins: Trans* and gender nonconforming people's access to knowledge, experiences of cancer health, and decision-making.' *LGBT Health 3*, 1, 79–89.

TGEU (2018) *Legal Situation*. Berlin: Transgender Europe.

The GenIUSS Group (2014) *Best Practices for Asking Questions to Identify Transgender and Other Gender Minority Respondents on Population-Based Surveys*. California: Williams Institute.

Tishelman, A.C., Kaufman, R., Edwards-Leeper, L., Mandel, F.H., Shumer, D.E. & Spack, N.P. (2015) 'Serving transgender youth: Challenges, dilemmas, and clinical examples.' *Professional Psychology: Research and Practice 46*, 1, 37–45.

Trotta, D. (2017) 'Trump revokes Obama guidelines on transgender bathrooms.' *Reuters*, February 22. Retrieved from www.reuters.com/article/us-usa-trump-lgbt-idUSKBN161243 on 05 March 2018.

Tuttle, L. (1986) *Encyclopedia of Feminism*. London: Arrow Books.

Ullman, J. (2016) 'Teacher positivity towards gender diversity: Exploring relationships and school outcomes for transgender and gender-diverse students.' *Sex Education 17*, 3, 276–289.

UN Human Rights Office of the High Commissioner, UNDP, UNESCO, UNFPA *et al.* (2015) *Ending Violence and Discrimination Against Lesbian, Gay, Bisexual, Transgender and Intersex People*. Paris: United Nations.

UN Secretary-General (2011) 'Message to event on ending violence and discrimination based on sexual orientation and gender identity.' *Office of the High Commissioner for Human Rights*. Retrieved from www.ohchr.org/en/NewsEvents/Pages/DisplayNews.aspx?NewsID=11717&LangID=E on 05 March 2018.

UNESCO (2009) *International Technical Guidance on Sexuality Education: An evidence-informed approach for schools, teachers and health educators* (Vol. 1 The rationale for sexuality education). Paris: UNESCO Section on HIV and AIDS, Division for the Coordination of UN Priorities in Education, Education Sector.

UNESCO (2011) *Rio Statement on Homophobic Bullying and Education for All*. Rio de Janiero, Brazil: UNESCO.

UNESCO (2012a) *Education Sector Responses to Homophobic Bullying*. Paris: UNESCO.

UNESCO (2012b) *Review of Homophobic Bullying in Educational Institutions*. Paris: UNESCO.

UNESCO (2015) *Insult to Inclusion: Asia-Pacific report on school bullying, violence and discrimination on the basis of sexual orientation and gender identity*. Bangkok: UNESCO.

UNESCO (2016a) *Call for Action by Ministers: Inclusive and equitable education for all learners in an environment free from discrimination and violence*. Paris: UNESCO.

UNESCO (2016b) *Out in the Open: Education sector responses to violence based on sexual orientation and gender identity/expression*. Paris: UNESCO.

UNESCO (2016c) *Reaching Out Vol 1: Preventing and Addressing School-related Gender-based Violence in Viet Nam*. Paris Ha Noi and Bangkok: UNESCO.

UNESCO (2016d) *Reaching Out Vol 2: Preventing and Addressing SOGIE-related School Violence in Viet Nam*. Paris Ha Noi and Bangkok: UNESCO.

United Nations (2012) *Born Free and Equal: Sexual orientation and gender identity in international human rights law*. New York and Geneva: United Nations Human Rights Office of the High Commissioner.

US Department of Justice & US Department of Education (2016) *Dear Colleague Letter on Transgender Students*. Washington: US Department of Justice Civil Rights Division and US Department of Education Office for Civil Rights.

US Department of Justice & US Department of Education (2017) *Dear Colleague Letter*. Washington: US Department of Justice and US Department of Education.

US Government (2016) *Examples of Policies and Emerging Practices for Supporting Transgender Students*. Washington: U.S. Department of Education Office of Elementary and Secondary Education and Office of Safe and Healthy Students.

Valentine, S., Peitzmeier, S., King, D., O'Cleirigh, C. *et al.* (2017) 'Disparities in exposure to intimate partner violence among transgender/gender nonconforming and sexual minority primary care patients.' *LGBT Health 4*, 4, 260–267.

van Schalkwyk, G., Klingensmith, K. & Volkmarb, F. (2015) 'Gender identity and autism spectrum disorders.' *Yale Journal of Biology and Medicine 88*, 1, 81–83.

Vance, K. (2011) *UN Human Rights Council: A Stunning Development Against Violence. Unprecedented Support for Statement on Sexual Orientation and Gender Identity*. Geneva: ARC International.

Varjas, K., Dew, B., Marshall, M., Graybill, E. *et al.* (2008) 'Bullying in schools towards sexual minority youth.' *Journal of School Violence 7*, 1, 59–86.

Veale, J., Watson, R., Peter, T. & Saewyc, E. (2017) 'The mental health of Canadian transgender youth compared with the Canadian population.' *Journal of Adolescent Health 60*, 1, 44–49.

Weeks, J. (1999) 'The Sexual Citizen.' In M. Featherstone (ed.), *Love and Eroticism*. London, Thousand Oaks, New Delhi: Theory, Culture & Society/Sage.

Weyers, S., Decaestecker, K., Verstraelen, H., Monstrey, S. *et al.* (2009) 'Clinical and transvaginal sonographic evaluation of the prostate in transsexual women.' *Urology 74*, 1, 191–196.

William, P. & Kellan, B. (2017) 'Coverage for gender-affirming care: Making health insurance work for transgender Americans.' *LGBT Health 4*, 4, 244–247.

Wilson, D., Marais, A., de Villiers, A., Addinall, R. & Campbell, M. (2014) 'Transgender issues in South Africa, with particular reference to the Groote Schuur Hospital Transgender Unit.' *South African Medical Journal 104*, 6, 448–449.

Winter, S., Diamond, M., Green, J., Karasic, D. *et al.* (2016) 'Transgender people: Health at the margins of society.' *The Lancet 388*, 10042, 390–400.

World Health Organisation (2006) *Defining Sexual Health: Report of a technical consultation on sexual health 28–31 January 2002, Geneva.* Geneva: World Health Organisation.

World Professional Association for Transgender Health (2011) *Standards of Care for the Health of Transsexual, Transgender, and Gender Nonconforming People.* Brussels: World Professional Association for Transgender Health.

Young, A.J. & Middleton, M.J. (2002) 'The Gay Ghetto in the Geography of Education.' In R. Kissen (ed.), *Getting Ready for Benjamin: Preparing Teachers for Sexual Diversity in the Classroom.* Lanham, MD: Rowman & Littlefield.

Yule, M. A., Brotto, L.A. & Gorzalka, B.B. (2013) 'Mental health and interpersonal functioning in self-identified asexual men and women.' *Psychology & Sexuality 4*, 2, 136–151.

# Subject Index

abuse
  presumption of 66
  sexual 125–6
activism 61–2
affirmation *see* gender affirmation
age (of transgender youth) 25–8
alcohol/drug use 87–9
androgynous (definition) 7
anxiety 47–51
apps (for sexual health service
    delivery) 109–10
'asexual' identity 120
assignment at birth 29–30
athletes, transgender 86–7
autism 29
awareness/realisation (of
    transgender status) 33–5

bathrooms 150–1
Billy Graham Evangelistic
    Association 162–3
binding 7
birth, sex assigned at 29–30
bisexual (definition) 7
body dysmorphic disorder 47
borderline personality disorder 47
*Born Free and Equal* (2012) 41
bottom surgery 7
'brain sex' 43
bullying, in educational settings 147–50

cancer risk/screening 89–91
chest surgery 7
cisgender (definition) 7
cisnormativity/cissexism
  definitions 8
  in education/school 155–6
  in mental health services 67–9
  in physical health services 97–9
  in sexual health services 129–31
  in social services 182–3
clinics, access to 63
conversion therapies 40, 107
coping mechanisms 34
criminalised work 177
culturally specific gender roles 24

depo-provera 8
depression 47–51
*Diagnostic and Statistical Manual of*
    *Mental Disorders (DSM)*
  changes in 43
  historic diagnoses in 40
disability/disorder framing 29
disclosure statistics 171–2
drug sales 177
drug/alcohol use 87–9

eating disorder 47
education/school
  anti-discriminatory policy in 151–2
  attainment/attendance levels 142–3

education/school *cont.*
  attitudes towards transgender
    youth in 146–7
  bathrooms in 150–1
  bullying/violence in 147–50
  cisnormativity/cissexism in 155–6
  contemporary services 139–42
  contributing role of 189
  deficiencies in 152–3
  early dropout 28
  ethics 157
  good experiences 153–5
  historic approaches 137–8
  key points 136
  mental health services in 69–71
  political influence on 140–2
  recommendations 157–9
  sex education in 110–1, 127–31
  shift to an inclusive approach 139
  structural supports in 143–5
  textbooks 152–3
  training and 157
  uniforms 145–6
Elbe, Lile 78
Erickson Educational Foundation
  (EEF) 138
ethics
  education/school 157
  mental health services 71–2
  physical health services 100
  sexual health services 131–2
  social services 183–4
eugenics programme (Sweden) 78
evangelist education 107
Exodus International 107

family *see* parents
fashion models 87
feminism, post-structural 42
fertility/reproduction 84–5
financing treatment 79–80
First UNESCO International
  Consultation (2011) 41

gay (definition) 8
gender, as cultural construction 42

gender affirmation
  definition 10
  expressing self via 59–60
  legal 82
  satisfaction with 86
  social 81
  *see also* medical treatment
gender clinics, access to 63
gender dysphoria
  definition 8
  DSM diagnosis of 43
  self-reporting of 44
gender expression incongruence
  (definition) 26–7
gender identity (definition) 8
'Gender Identity Disorder (GID)' 40
gender identity expression 30–2
gender identity incongruence
  (definition) 26–7
genderqueer (definition) 8

health *see* physical health;
  physical health services
HIV/AIDS
  diagnosis and medical transition 84
  sexual health services 108
  statistics for transgender people 123
homelessness 175–7
hormone therapy 9, 83–4, 91–2
human rights position 41, 108, 168

identity
  gender identity (definition) 8
  gender identity expression 30–2
  gender identity incongruence
    (definition) 26–7
  sexual identity labels 118–21
informed consent model 80
international perspective 24, 168
Internet
  online communities 58
  online delivery of sexual health
    services 109–10
  sexual health information on 108–10
  social media 57
  as source of information 57–8

## Subject Index

intersex status 8–9
inversion, historic concept of 39–40

knowledge, mental health
    professional's 65–6

labels, sexual identity 118–21
language *see* pronouns; terminology
legal gender affirmation 82
life satisfaction 45–7

marital options 111–3
medical treatment
    access to clinics 63
    diagnosis required for 43–4, 80
    financing 79–80
    hormone therapy 83–4, 91–2
    overview 82–3
    responsibility for decision 84
    surgery 7, 84–6
mental health
    anxiety 47–51
    contemporary research 42–5
    depression 47–51
mental health *cont.*
    key points 38
    positive life satisfaction 45–7
    protective factors 55–61
    self-harm 51–5
    statistics 47
    stress 47–51
    suicidality 51–5
mental health services
    access to 62–5
    cisnormativity/cissexism in 67–9
    contemporary 45
    contributing role of 188
    ethics 71–2
    helpful attributes of 65–7
    historic 39–41
    missing/avoiding 62–5
    motivations for using 64
    negative experiences with 63
    recommendations for 72–4
    satisfaction levels 64–5
    in schools 69–71
    shift in emphasis within 42
    training 71–2
models, fashion 87

networks *see* support
norms *see* cisnormativity/cissexism

Obama Administration 140–1
obsessive compulsive disorder 47
omnisexual (definition) 9

packing/padding 9
pansexual (definition) 9
parents
    abusive behaviour from 54, 63
    attitude of 53–4, 171
    'fault' of 40–1
    rejection by 173–4
    support from 55–7
partner violence 125–6
paying for treatment 79–80
phone apps (for sexual health
    service delivery) 109–10
physical health
    alcohol/drug use 87–9
    black market hormones 91–2
    cancer risk/screening 89–91
    future reproductive possibilities 84–5
    transgender people's 86–7
physical health services
    cisnormativity/cissexism in 97–9
    contemporary (overview) 79–80
    contributing role of 188
    displaying supportive symbols 95
    ethics 100
    good experiences with 95–7
    historic 77–8
    key points 76
    mixed/bad experiences 92–5
    recommendations 100–2
    training 100
physical hygiene approaches
    (historic) 106–7
police mistreatment 177
political influences 140–2
positive life satisfaction 45–7

post-structural feminism 42
post-traumatic stress disorder 47
poverty 175–7
pregnancy 123–5
prison 177
privacy concerns 178–80
pronouns 33, 66–7, 154
puberty blockers 9

queer (definition) 9
queer theory 42

realisation/awareness (of transgender status) 33–5
rejection, social 172–5
relationship status
  marital options 111–3
  romantic attraction 115–8
  statistics 113–4
religious organisations
  Billy Graham Evangelistic Association 162–3
  rejection by 178
  sex education within 107
  social services provided by 162–3, 164–5
  Unitarian Universalist Service Committee 164–5
reproduction/fertility 84–5
Richter, Dora 78
*Rio Statement* (2011) 41
romantic attraction 115–8

Salvation Army 162
schizophrenia 47
school *see* education/school
self-comfort/support 58–9
self-harm 51–5
self-identified transgender 26–7
sex (definition) 9–10
sex education 106, 107, 110–1, 126–31
sex work 177
sexual abuse 125–6
sexual attraction 115–8
sexual health services

cisnormativity/cissexism in 129–31
contemporary 108–11
contributing role of 188
deficiencies in 126–7
ethics 131–2
good experiences in 128–9
historic 105–7
holistic approach 110
home testing 109
key points 104–5
phone/online delivery of 109–10
physical hygiene approaches (historic) 106–7
recommendations 132–4
STI protection information 125
training 131–2
UNAIDS 106
sexual identity labels 118–21
sexual life, impacts on 121–3
sexual morality messages 106–7
sexual protection 123–5
social attitudes 167–70
social gender affirmation 81
social media 57
social rejection 172–5
social services
  cisnormativity/cissexism in 182–3
  contemporary 164–7
  contributing role of 189
  deficiencies in 180
  ethics 183–4
  good experiences in 181–2
  government-provided 165–7
  historic 162–4
  key points 160–1
  privacy and 178–80
  recommendations 184–6
  religious organisations' provision 162–3, 164–5
  Salvation Army 162
  social workers 164
  training 183–4
social support 172–5
social workers 164
sterilisation policy 78

Subject Index 209

STI risk 123–5
  *see also* sexual health services
stress 47–51
suicidality 51–5
support
  displaying symbols 95
  networks 57–8
  online communities 58
  parental 55–7
  self-comforting 58–9
  social 172–5
surgical treatment 7, 84–6

terminology 23–4
textbooks, school 152–3
toilets 150–1
training
  education/school 157
  mental health services 71–2
  physical health services 100
  sexual health services 131–2
  social services 183–4
transgender, status dimensions of 26–7
transgender FtM 10

transgender MtF 10
transgender youth
  age of 25–8
  background 28
  defining 23–5
  key points 22
  location 28
  social attitudes to 167–70
  statistics 25
Trump Administration 80, 107, 140–1

UNAIDS 106
underground economy 177
unemployment 175–7
uniform, school 145–6
Unitarian Universalist Service
  Committee 164–5

violence
  in education/school settings 147–50
  partner 125–6

World Professional Association for
  Transgender Health 138

# Author Index

Abbas, A. 89
Ainsworth, C. 97
Alsop, Z. 141
Altman, D. 105, 106
Alvarez, Z. 70
Ansara, G. 88, 93
APA Task Force on Appropriate
    Therapeutic Responses to
    Sexual Orientation 40, 107
Aster, J. 89
Australian Bureau of Statistics 142

Badgett, M.V. 175
Bannerman, M. 44
Baraitser, P. 109, 110
Barron, C. 169
Bartholomaeus, C. 108, 130, 156
Barton, L. 111
Bauer, G. 26
Baum, F. 67
Bazzul, J. 152
Benner, A. 125
Bernstein, K.T. 123
Bessant, J. 163, 164
Binnie, J. 105, 106
Bockting, W. 108, 125, 127, 153
Brill, S. 25, 41, 56, 77, 98,
    153, 171, 183
Brotto, L.A. 120
Brown, M. 34, 87
Brown, T. 27

Bryson, M. 89
Buist, C.L. 47
Bungener, S. 113, 121
Butler, J. 42, 68
Byne, W. 40, 43, 68, 70
Byron, P. 108

Cancer Australia 89
Cancer Council 90, 91
Capous-Desyllas, M. 169
Carman, M. 157
Carrera, M. 42
Carroll, L. 25, 30
Carver, P.R. 25, 170
Chauncey, G. 39
Clark, B. 62
Clark, T.C. 47, 49, 51, 93, 115
Cloud, J. 107
Coleman, E. 125
Condon, J. 162
Corliss, H. 92, 93
Couch, M. 29, 42, 47, 85, 87, 88, 142

D'Augelli, A.R. 25, 68, 170, 173
Davies, A. 79
DeCrescenzo, T. 170
del Pozo de Bolger, A. 47, 51, 120
DePalma, R. 42
Devor, A. 138
Dibben, K. 150
DiMaggio, P. 163

Donatone, B. 42
Drescher, J. 29, 40, 43, 68, 70
Due, C. 88, 93
Dugin, A. 140
Dunsford, M. 51

Eaton, N. 25
Edwards, D. 141
Edwards, J.W. 29
Egan, R.D. 137
Elia, J.P. 106
Elischberger, H. 167, 169
Esteva de Antonio, I. 79

Fausto-Sterling, A. 30
Ferreyra, M. 142, 176
Fisher, D.G. 29
Fisher, E.S. 70, 71
Flanagan, F. 162
Fletcher, J. 125
Foucault, M. 39
Freedom Centre 191
Freud, S. 39, 40

Gahan, L. 178
Garber, M. 39
Gardner, I. 92
Garofalo, R. 29, 108, 127, 153
GenIUSS Group 27
Giltay, E. 29
Global Impact 165
GLSEN 139
Goel, V. 140
Gómez-Gil, E. 79
Gooren, L. 29, 79, 89
Gorzalka, B.B. 120
Grant, J.M. 51
Gray, E. 42, 157
Grimes, K.M. 178
Grossman, A.H. 25, 56, 68, 170, 173

H, M. 78, 112
Haas, A.P. 20, 27, 67, 149
Hakak, Y. 182
Halberstam, J. 40
Hamburger, T. 140

Hansen, A.W. 30
Hardisty, J. 107
Hare, L. 29
Harris, A. 42, 157, 175
Hart, B. 97
Hawkes, G. 137
Helderman, R. 140
Herdt, G. 25, 27, 28
Herman, J. 26
Hillier, L. 13, 25, 28, 47, 61, 67, 72,
    89, 97, 108, 118, 127, 128,
    131, 139, 142, 146, 148, 171,
    172, 173, 175, 178, 181, 182
Hines, S. 125
Hirschfield, M. 78
Holt, V. 51
Human Rights Watch 139,
    146, 149, 152, 180
Hunt, J. 108

Iantaffi, A. 125
ILGA Europe 112
International Center for Research
    on Women 149
International School Psychology
    Association 71
Ippolito, M.R. 49
Irvine, J. 106, 107
Isaac, M. 140

James, S. 23, 25, 26, 30, 82, 123,
    126, 145, 148, 150, 171,
    175, 176, 177, 178, 180
Jennings, T. 152
Jones, T. 7, 13, 23, 24, 25, 28, 29, 30,
    31, 33, 42, 45, 47, 49, 51, 52, 58,
    60, 61, 62, 64, 65, 67, 68, 70, 71,
    79, 80, 81, 82, 85, 86, 87, 88, 89,
    90, 91, 93, 95, 97, 98, 106, 107,
    108, 110, 111, 112, 114, 115, 116,
    118, 119, 120, 121, 122, 124, 125,
    127, 128, 129, 130, 131, 137, 138,
    139, 140, 143, 145, 146, 148, 150,
    151, 152, 153, 154, 155, 156, 157,
    158, 165, 166, 167, 170, 171, 172,
    173, 175, 178, 179, 181, 182, 183

Kellan, B. 79, 80
Kerr, L. 89, 90, 91, 97, 98
Key, A. 25
Kingsley, J. 182
Kinsey, A.C. 40
Klingensmith, K. 29
Kondou, A. 80, 166, 183
Kosciw, J. 139, 141, 153
Kumar, V. 89
Kuper, L. 30
Kussin-Shoptaw, A. 125, 126

Lameiras, M. 42
Landers, S. 92
Lasser, J. 42, 67, 68, 70, 71
Lawrence, S. 92
Lefkowitz, A. 126, 127, 129
Lenning, E. 47
Leonnig, C. 140
Leroux-Nega, E. 141
Levitt, H.M. 49
Lindner, A. 55
Lips, P. 89
Lurie, S. 92

McClintock, M. 25, 27, 28
McCredie, J. 153
Macgillivray, I.K. 152
McGuire, J. 108
McHardie, D. 79
McKay, S. 162, 163
McLean, A. 93
McNeil, J. 47, 59, 62, 93
Malkin, B. 140
Mallon, G.P. 170
Mannell, J. 126, 127, 129
Martin, C. 25, 40, 131, 147
Meier, S. 125
Meng, S.E. 30
Menvielle, E. 42
Middleton, M.J. 152
Mohler, R. 163
Moran, J.P. 138
Muller, A. 126
Mustanski, B. 30

National LGBTI Health Alliance 26
New York Times Editorial Staff 141
Newfield, E. 30
Nussbaum, R. 30

OECD 111
OII Australia 30
Olson, K. 25, 131, 147
Onuah, F. 140
Orgad, S. 162
Outright Action International 112

Park, A. 26
Parke, C. 141
Pazos, S. 34
Pearce, E. 92
Pease, A. 43
Pease, B. 43
Pepper, R. 25, 41, 56, 77, 98, 153, 171, 183
Perry, D.G. 25
Peter, T. 147
Philip, S.S. 123
Phillips, J. 90
Pinheiro, P.S. 147
Pivo, S. 90
Pizmony-Levy, O. 139, 141
Plan International Thailand 149
Pomeroy, W.R. 40
Potter, J. 90, 98
Powell, W. 163
Power, J. 113

Rachlin, K. 42
Raymond, J. 138
Reback, C. 125
Reynolds, G.L. 29
Riggs, D. 67, 68, 69, 84, 85, 88, 93, 108, 113, 125, 130, 156
Robinson, B.E. 108
Robinson, K.H. 111
Roden, L. 142
Rogers, K. 140
Rosser, B.R.S. 108
Rowniak, S. 123

Rownsley, C.A. 34
Ruble, D. 25, 131, 147
Russell, S.T. 139

Safer, J. 92
Salvation Army Media Newsroom 162
Sanchez, A. 100
Savin-Williams, R.C. 25, 170
Schaefer, A.G. 80
Schleifer, D. 125
Schulz, S. 80, 92
Sears, J.T. 40
Seu, I. 162, 163
Shane, S. 140
Singh, A.A. 30
Skagerberg, E. 51
Smith, E. 13, 23, 25, 26, 27, 28, 29, 31, 33, 42, 44, 49, 52, 56, 57, 58, 60, 61, 62, 63, 64, 66, 67, 70, 79, 81, 82, 85, 88, 89, 94, 110, 113, 115, 117, 118, 119, 120, 121, 127, 129, 139, 143, 153, 154, 155, 156, 175, 178, 179, 181
South Australia Department for Education and Child Development 152
Sperber, J. 92
Spies-Butcher, B. 163
Sprigg, P. 141
Starnes, T. 150
Stephens, S.C. 123
Stieglitz, K. 25, 108, 127, 153, 170
Stone, S. 42, 138
Sungkaew, T. 29
Sykes, H. 152

Tait, G. 137
Taylor, C. 147
Taylor, E. 89
Tencer, D. 141
TGEU 168

Tharinger, D. 70, 71
Tishelman, A.C. 77
Treharne, G. 88
Trotta, D. 141
Tuttle, L. 137

Ullman, J. 128
UN Human Rights Office of the High Commissioner 139
UN Secretary-General 139
UNESCO 13, 24, 28, 30, 41, 44, 107, 108, 110, 111, 127, 131, 139, 142, 146, 147, 148, 149, 151, 153, 157, 165, 167, 175
United Nations 41, 78, 139
US Department of Education 140, 141
US Department of Justice 140, 141
US Government 141

Valentine, S. 125
van Schalkwyk, G. 29
Vance, K. 139
Varjas, K. 149
Veale, J. 51, 124
Volkmarb, F. 29
von Doussa, H. 113, 125

Webber, R. 163, 164
Weeks, J. 111
Weyers, S. 91
William, P. 79, 80
Wilson, D. 79
Winter, S. 93
World Health Organisation 108
World Professional Association for Transgender Health 81, 82, 84, 100, 131

Young, A.J. 152
Yule, M. A. 120
Yunger, J.L. 25